D1391803

Also available at all good book stores

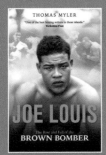

THOMAS MYLER

"One of the best boxing writers in these islands."
Yorkshire Post

JOE LOUIS

The Rise and Fall of the
BROWN BOMBER

9781785315367

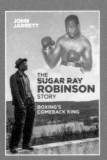

JOHN JARRETT

THE
**SUGAR RAY
ROBINSON**
STORY

BOXING'S
COMEBACK KING

9781785315350

TALES FROM
The Top Table

How boxing's superstars took over a town

CRAIG BIRCH

9781785315374

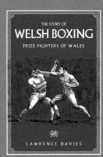

THE STORY OF
WELSH BOXING

PRIZE FIGHTERS OF WALES

LAWRENCE DAVIES

9781785315039

JAMES COOK MBE
MY STORY

GUARDIAN
OF THE STREETS

WITH MELANIE LLOYD

9781785314919

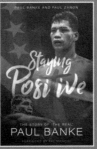

PAUL BANKE AND PAUL ZANON

*Staying
Positive*

THE STORY OF 'THE REAL'
PAUL BANKE

FOREWORD BY RAY MANCINI

9781785315404

SUPER

THE AUTOBIOGRAPHY OF
SCOTT DIXON

9781785315190

THE FINAL ROUND
WITH ABI SMITH

THE AUTOBIOGRAPHY OF
JANE
COUCH
MBE

9781785315626

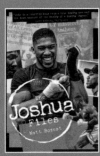

The
Joshua
Files

Matt Bozeat

9781785313912

ALEX DALEY

**BOXING
NOSTALGIA**

★★★ THE GOOD, THE BAD ★★★
AND THE WEIRD

9781785314551

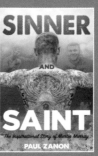

SINNER
AND
SAINT

The Inspirational Story of Martin Murray
PAUL ZANON

9781785313851

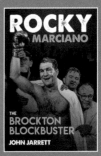

ROCKY
MARCIANO

THE
**BROCKTON
BLOCKBUSTER**

JOHN JARRETT

9781785313813

amazon.co.uk W Waterstones WHSmith

FIGHTING BACK

FIGHTING BACK

THE **TYSON FURY** STORY

MATT BOZEAT

First published by Pitch Publishing, 2019

Pitch Publishing
A2 Yeoman Gate
Yeoman Way
Worthing
Sussex
BN13 3QZ
www.pitchpublishing.co.uk
info@pitchpublishing.co.uk

© 2019, Matt Bozeat

Every effort has been made to trace the copyright.
Any oversight will be rectified in future editions at the
earliest opportunity by the publisher.

All rights reserved. No part of this book may be reproduced,
sold or utilised in any form or transmitted in any form or by
any means, electronic or mechanical, including photocopying,
recording or by any information storage and retrieval system,
without prior permission in writing from the Publisher.

A CIP catalogue record is available for this book
from the British Library.

ISBN 978-1-78531-552-7

Typesetting and origination by Pitch Publishing
Printed and bound in the UK by TJ International Ltd

Contents

DEDICATION

For Mum, Dad and my perfect little
girl Carla Diana

Forever in my thoughts Mum

This book is dedicated to the memory of
Hughie Fury because without his friendship,
it would have not been possible. I miss talking
boxing with you, my friend

CHAPTER 1

Born to Fight

IT WAS the sort of name you don't forget, the sort of name that demands an exclamation mark.

Tyson Fury was coming to box in Hinckley, just a few miles up the road from my flat in Leicester.

Whoever he was.

'I went in the corner with a boxer called Phill Fury when he boxed on a club show in Birmingham, he liked what I did and started boxing for us,' remembered Nick Griffin, head coach at Heart of England Amateur Boxing Club.

'He made the trip down from Preston and every now and then he would bring his cousin with him and he had a few training session with us.

'When he was ready to box, I got him matched on our show.'

That was in May 2005 in a function suite at Hinckley United Football Club's ground, the Marston's Stadium.

'I remember waiting to see the doctor before I had my medical and this huge shadow appeared behind me,' recalled Kieran Pitman, who also boxed on the show.

'I turned round and was looking at someone's chest. I thought, "I hope I'm not fighting him."'

He wasn't.

Jamie Waddell was fighting Fury.

'I wasn't really keen on taking the fight,' admitted Ray Revell, Waddell's coach at Wellingborough Amateur Boxing Club. But I was struggling to get Jamie matched and he was always fearless.'

Pitman was in no rush to swap places with him.

'Everyone in the changing room was talking about Tyson, saying, "Have you seen the size of him?"' he remembered.

'It was a big changing room and he was dominating it. He was a monster. Everyone was talking about him before he even put his kit on.'

Fury also left an impression on Kyle Haywood, another future professional who fought that night.

'He was wearing odd boots, one was red, the other blue,' said Haywood, 'and his shorts didn't fit him either.

'He looked a real character.

'Everything about him was unorthodox. He was a big unit and you just thought, "Who is this guy?"

'I asked someone and they said: "That's Tyson Fury." I thought they were joking. It sounded like a made-up name, a stage name or something. I mean, who ever heard of anyone called Tyson Fury?'

Yet there he was, all 6ft 9ins of him.

'Some fighters you remember,' said Ash Lane, beaten on points by Haywood that night.

'I remember Tyson Fury!

'It wasn't just his size, he had a real swagger about him as well. Nobody knew who he was, but watching him in the changing room, you could tell he thought he was the kiddy.'

Fury eased himself into the ring and, spotting my notebook on the ringside table in front of me, raised his eyebrows in a friendly gesture.

'If nobody talked about boxing or wrote about it, Tyson would find something else to do with his time,' his late uncle Hughie once told me.

Elsewhere in the room, Pitman was making mental notes.

'The lad [Waddell] was tough,' he said, 'but Tyson boxed his head off, gave him a boxing lesson. Tyson wasn't a massive puncher, but he jabbed, moved and made him miss. I remember thinking, "That's how to use your range. He will do all right, he's not bad."'

Revell wasn't a fan.

'He was talking to Jamie all the way through the fight,' he said, 'trying to wind him up.

' He was saying, "You can't beat me, you can't even get near me."

'I shouted at the referee about it – and I got a telling off!

'I remember Jamie saying to me after the first round, "I can't get close to him and when I do, he holds."

'Tyson did box well, he was skilful. But I didn't like him. I thought he was arrogant and a spoiler.'

Fury handed Waddell a standing count in the last round, but couldn't force the stoppage – and chaos followed the announcement of his unanimous points win.

'I heard they were betting on Tyson getting a stoppage in the crowd,' said Haywood, 'and when the fight went the distance, a big row broke out.'

'Someone got in the ring and tried to give a speech I think and then it went crazy for a few minutes,' remembered Sam 'Bullet' Bowen, who went on to win the British super featherweight title as a professional.

'Tyson's opponent was trying to push his way through to the changing room and I thought, "He's massive, I had better get out of his way!"'

Order was restored after a few minutes, but the official in charge, Bill Evans, decided to cancel the rest of the show.

'I was warming up my lads in the changing room,' remembered Griffin, 'and then I had to tell them they weren't boxing after all.'

Waddell boxed only twice more, but he did toy with the idea of making a comeback more than a decade later.

'Jamie came back to the gym for a few weeks,' said Revell, 'but he didn't stick at it.

'I gave him his amateur card because of the name he's got on it. He seemed very matter of fact about it. I said, "Not many people can say they boxed a future world champion and you've got the proof."

'Jamie didn't seem very bothered. I think he was still upset that he lost.'

SO, who was Tyson Fury?

He was a member of the travelling community that was estimated to number around 60,000 across the United Kingdom and Ireland.

They lived in tight-knit communities on caravan sites, working mainly in gardening and construction and maintaining devout religious beliefs.

To Travellers, family pride and honour are everything and traditionally their passions were hunting and fighting.

'Every travelling man, born from his mother, wants a fight, simple,' said Fury.

'If you're not a fighter, you're no good, you're useless.

11

'A Traveller's highest ranking, here's how it goes: a fighting man is number one, if you're not a good fighting man, you have to be a good man who can earn a living. So it comes to money.

'Then it comes to horses, I think. I've never been involved with horses because I can't stand them.'

Most Traveller boys box as amateurs and at schoolboy, junior and youth level. They tend to dominate but few go on to have successful professional boxing careers.

'If you go to any schoolboy championship or ABA finals in the last ten years, 80 per cent of the boxers will be Traveller kids in finals and boxing each other,' said Isaac Lowe, who has gone on to have a good professional career, winning the Commonwealth featherweight title.

'Sadly, they get to the age of 16 or 17 and go to work or worry about different sides of life.

'They get the urge to go to work. Traveller kids fend for themselves. We go to work as soon as we can. We then get money and we're introduced to the nightclub life.'

Travellers also tend to marry young and the roles of man and wife are clearly defined, as Fury explained once.

'People have got to understand that our lifestyle is totally, totally different,' he said.

'We may be the same colour, and we may speak the same language, but deep inside we are nothing alike. We are aliens. In our culture, it is all about the men. The men can do everything, and women just clean and cook and have children and look after that man.'

Women in the travelling community, Fury explained once, had to be 'pure and respectful'.

He said, 'There are these girls who want to open their legs for every Tom, Dick and Harry. But they are looked upon as rubbish in our community. We don't do stuff like that. If I had a sister who did that, I'd hang her. She would bring disgrace to the family. It is a very, very bad thing to do, that. Women have to be pure and respectful.'

Tyson's parents were Amber Burton and John Fury.

Tyson's mother grew up in Newry, Northern Ireland, and was a Romany gypsy.

The Furys explained to me that Romany gypsies have their roots in India and Afghanistan and were always fighters, making their own weapons and battling Genghis Khan before fleeing and settling in Yugoslavia, Ireland and elsewhere. Amber wanted to call her second son Luke Fury but on the insistence of John, he was named after the youngest, and in his opinion greatest, world heavyweight champion of them all.

Mike Tyson proved himself to be, at the very least, the best heavyweight of his generation on 27 June 1988, when in a fight billed as *Once and For All* he took just 91 seconds to punch Michael Spinks into semi-consciousness.

Spinks, a former world light-heavyweight champion who was unbeaten in 31 fights, had a claim to the heavyweight championship having twice controversially outpointed Larry Holmes for the IBF belt and then vacated to take a lucrative match with Gerry Cooney.

Faced with Tyson, Spinks froze and was dropped twice.

Seven weeks after Tyson's defining night, on 12 August 1988, Tyson Luke Fury was born seven weeks premature in Manchester. At birth, he weighed only one pound and his heart stopped beating three times while he was in an incubator.

'Tyson was an unexpected pregnancy, given we had lost several children between him and his eldest brother,' remembered John.

'We were just hoping we could bring life and keep it in the world.

'He had came [sic] into the world, had breathing difficulties – no one was optimistic.

'I could put him in the palm of my hand and looking at him I thought, "This is a strange encounter with life." I had this tremendous feeling.

'I sat with him day and night, kept playing with him, working his little legs and arms, talking to him. There was something special about him. I thought, "You're a special human being."'

Tyson survived, but his early years were tough.

'He used to imagine the curtains on fire or lions chewing his feet,' remembered John.

'He'd have a high temperature and we'd have to ice him down or often take him to hospital.'

Tyson believed he was born to fight.

'If two fighting families come together, they are going to breed fighters,' he explained.

Both his parents came from fighting families.

Amber's uncle was Uriah 'Big Just' Burton and he was 'The King of the Gypsies', the title awarded to the best man in the bare-knuckle fighting that is a tradition among Travellers. When Burton relinquished his crown, his nephew, Bartley Gorman, took it on and for two decades he reigned, often ironing out opponents with his 'bull hammer' punch, a right hand delivered with tremendous force between the eyes.

Gorman wrote in his autobiography, *King of the Gypsies*, 'Travelling men fight. Not all of them and all the time, but many of them and often.

'They would rather settle a row with knuckles than resort to the courts or call the police. Their contests may be held at fairs like Appleby in Cumbria, Musselburgh in Scotland or Ballinasloe in Ireland; at race meetings like Doncaster or Epsom; in a field or at an encampment; on the spur of the moment in a pub or club, at a wedding or a funeral.

'The fighters may have trained for months or be drunk as lords. Sometimes there are rules: no biting, no butting, no gouging, no kicking, no hitting a man when he is down.

'Often there are not. When a fight is "all in", anything goes.'

John Fury described Gorman as 'one of the hardest men who has ever lived' – and he was a hard man himself.

'I WAS born in Ireland, my father's side are Roscommon people, but I came over to Leiston [Suffolk] when I was a week old and we travelled all over,' John Fury told *Boxing Monthly* in 2009.

'Growing up, I used to wake up every morning and think, "I'm John Fury, me. I'm taking no backward steps, no shit."

'Our family might be the only ones at a school of pits lads' [miners] sons and I'd have at least three fights every day.

'I was always big for my age and was fighting grown men from the age of about 12. As I got older, men would challenge me in the pubs and I'd say, "I can beat you, but I'm drunk." So we'd meet the next morning at six o'clock, shirts off.

'Most times, money never changed hands, just pride. If a copper caught two willing lads having a fight, nine times out of ten, it was scratched out.

'I never got more than a few stitches, a black eye, a couple of teeth missing. It was enjoyable fun.

'Then, in the late 1980s, no one would give me a job [Fury worked on the roads] and I didn't have a pot to piss in. I weren't an educated man and Travellers classed you as a bit of an idiot without pride if you took social security. I didn't want to commit crime, so I had to use what tools I had and fight my way out.

'I soon learned you could earn a good few quid on the knuckle jobs [bareknuckle boxing], winner take all.

'It was no rules – head butts, elbows, teeth, gouging the eyes. In a proper bareknuckle fight, you should be able to keep winging until one falls.

'Within the travelling community, you win a few, get a reputation, and, if you're "The Man", you will get opposition. Everywhere you went, someone wanted to fight you: Scots, Irish, Welsh, Romany.

'It'd happen anywhere: a Travellers' site, a barn, usually outside. The big tournaments were held in secret. They didn't want the police involved because it can be very brutal. Sometimes, they can fight for an hour at a time without any referee.'

Tommy Miller, a boxing manager from Halifax with one of the biggest stables of fighters in the country, watched Fury fight and convinced him to try professional boxing. Fury didn't take the sport as seriously as he might. He took fights at short notice and wasn't a regular at the gym. Brendan Ingle was in his corner once and told his son Dominic, 'Look at this man with the crazy mop of black hair. He doesn't bother training, he just fights.'

Nonetheless, Fury fought his way into contention for the British heavyweight title. He was paired with the North East's Manny Burgo in an eliminator, but as Fury remembered it, Burgo pulled out three days before the fight, to be replaced by Henry Akinwande, an entirely different proposition.

Akinwande was a gangly Londoner who, at 6ft 7ins, towered over Fury by four inches and would go on to win the WBO heavyweight championship.

Fury said Akinwande 'ripped me head off with a double left hook' in the third round and 'after that, it was back to Plan B – the knuckle.

'You needed at least ten grand to make an entry, so I sold my lorry and my van,' he said. 'My 5k [£5,000] caravan. Gambled the lot. I probably had about 20 knuckle fights with a stake involved.

'There's a lot of physical contact, so I'd pay five of the biggest, strongest lads I could find to wrestle me. I'd also chop trees in the forest, run in army boots with a van tyre around my waist and hit a big bag bare-fisted.

'As a young fighting lad, I was just raw and powerful. I didn't have a particularly heavy punch, but I had plenty of spirit, could outgame them. But, after I turned pro and learned how to box properly, it was a completely different ball game. They'd come in square on, trying to take it all. Against a trained boxer, you just can't do that.

'The reason I never lost weren't because of how great I was, it was the fellas I fought were fucking useless. Game, strong lads, but no skill or ability, could give it, but they couldn't take the pain.

'It was like taking candy off a baby.

'The fights I had outside were usually over within seconds. I weren't an especially big puncher but once I got going, I'd not stop swinging until they were out cold. I'd not come up for air. I just wanted to kill.

'I had a completely different level of fitness, so I'd be able to apply pressure until they couldn't breathe. I'd hit them with fists, elbows, head, teeth and feet until they dropped and give best [surrendered].

'If they didn't, I'd kick their face off, it was up to them. Afterwards, shake hands and on to the next one. In my twenties, I was a really formidable force.

'In 1992, I fought the so-called champion at the time, an Irishman whose name I can't even remember, over in Ireland. With stakes and everything, I came up over a hundred grand.

'As a young kid, Tyson and his brothers would watch me set upon people who tried to rip me off or take liberties. They've seen me use the baseball bat and, trust me, the more damage I inflicted, the more they liked it. So Tyson's got that [affinity with] violence himself.'

Tyson has always said he only fought outside the boxing ring once.

'My brother set me up to fight my next-door neighbour,' he remembered.

'I was nine years old and he was 11. They just wanted to know who would win, so we had a fight. My trousers kept falling down and every time I moved to pull them up, he punched me in the face.'

Fury described that fight as 'a draw'.

John remembered other occasions when Tyson used his fists outside the ring.

He said, 'Though he has this shy, cheerful side, trust me, he's had his share of scuffles down the town and at weddings. When he clicks into fighting mode, trust me, he's an evil, nasty bastard who wants to hurt you badly.

'He'd have made a great knuckle fighter. What idle chance would an outside man stand against him? None. But Tyson's never known the gypsy life. I didn't want my kids brought up in the tough environment that I was raised. Since three years old, he was bred on a farm. Unlike myself, I always ensured Tyson had the money to train proper.'

'I WAS brought up in Wilmslow, a little village in Cheshire,' said Tyson.

'When my dad was 18, he bought a piece of land, nothing on it, a piece of green grass.

'Then, with his boxing money, he bought a bungalow and every fight he had, that money was for some roof tiles or some bricks, so it got built over a period of three years.

'Then we moved in.

'Later, he sold it and bought a small holding in a little village called Styal in Wilmslow.

'So, all the caravan stuff. The only time I have ever lived in a caravan was when the whole lane, Moss Lane, got flooded because of the little stream that ran behind it. So then we lived in a caravan for about a year until it was all fully refurbished.'

Fury described Styal as 'lots of wildlife, no crime'.

'I had a great childhood. We just went out on our quad bikes.'

Even though he didn't live the traditional Traveller's life, he still lived by their code, reading the Bible daily and working.

Tyson was taken out of the village school when he was 11, a former governor remembering, 'The scariest thing about them [the Furys] was their huge dog.'

John explained, 'They learn different things when they are not at school – more streetwise. He helped me build the house.'

Teachers at Tyson's primary school had been impressed by his English and arithmetic, and those skills proved useful to his father.

'My reading wasn't so good,' said John. 'I'd get letters and ask him, "What does that mean?" He'd tell me. He'd add up the money.'

The young Tyson also developed an obsession with boxing.

'The boxing used to fascinate me,' said Tyson. 'Other kids watched cartoons, but me and me brothers only watched boxing DVDs.'

They sparred as well.

'There was only one pair of gloves in the house,' he remembered. 'I don't know why – they were my dad's old gloves from when he used to train – and they were all stinky and sweaty. So we used to put one glove on each and have tea towels wrapped around our other hand. We used to spar full on in the kitchen, plates going everywhere.

'We used to have this rug in the kitchen. It wasn't very big and whoever went off the mat first was out. We'd trade punches. Even before I had an amateur fight, me and my dad would spar in the garden.'

John said, 'I was on the grass one Sunday, it was a lovely sunny afternoon, and him and [younger brother] Shane asked me to spar with them.

'Tyson hit me with a left hook and I felt a searing pain in my side.

'I thought, "What, from a 14-year-old lad?" I thought to myself, "I'll have a sit down." But when I moved to get off the wall, I couldn't move. I had three cracked ribs.

'He was a big 14, around 6ft 5ins, 16 stone. He was a fat kid. He was not tall and lean. He loved McDonald's and burgers. A friend of mine said that although he had layers of fat on him, he had never seen anyone move like him and that he could be a champion.'

Nonetheless, Tyson said his father 'didn't want us involved' in boxing.

Tyson ignored him.

'I REMEMBER the local hooligan telling me there was a gym a couple of miles away and I didn't believe him,' said Tyson. 'I thought I would have heard about it.'

The gym was the home of Ringway Amateur Boxing Club and at the gym was a giant, unbeaten amateur heavyweight known as 'Big Lewis'. 'I was made to spar him and he punched the shit out of me,' remembered Fury. 'My nose was bloodied and my face a right mess.'

Tyson would get his revenge.

His uncle, Hughie, was training a professional heavyweight, Dave Ingleby, a big, tough novice from Morecambe, and Tyson said, 'Every Saturday, I would go over there for sparring. I was naturally fit and I remember thinking, "I can do this."

'I went back to see "Big Lewis". He had been the kingpin at the gym for a long time, but I had got better and he hadn't. He never went back to the gym after we sparred again.'

FOLLOWING his amateur debut in Hinckley, Fury kept winning and picked up a nickname – not that anyone called Tyson Fury needs one.

He was known as 'The Facebreaker' after breaking an opponent's jaw and eye socket, and such performances aroused suspicion.

'When I was 16, the ABA [Amateur Boxing Association] suspended the junior super heavyweight division for that year only because they reckoned I looked about 25!' said Fury.

'At 17, I had nowhere to go except the senior novices, fighting fully fledged men. I got roughed up in there, but showed good grit and determination and ultimately proved too skilful.'

The novices was a championship for fighters with fewer than 20 bouts and Fury reached the final after a bizarre incident during the semi-finals in Nottingham.

He was gloved up and ready to box, only to be handed a bye after both fighters in the preceding semi-final were disqualified following a filthy tussle.

Fury won the final and suffered his first defeat at the World Junior Championships in Morocco in 2006, a 36-31 points reverse to Sardor Abdullayev from Uzbekistan.

Fury's confidence wasn't dented. He had a T-shirt printed that read, 'Tyson Fury 2008 Beijing Olympic champion.'

To get to China, he would have to beat David Price, the towering Liverpudlian who was by some distance Britain's leading super heavyweight. Price was a seasoned international who earlier that year had won Commonwealth Games gold in India.

By comparison, Fury was a teenage novice.

Had the match between Price and Fury been mooted for an amateur club show, it surely would not have been allowed to take place.

It would have been considered a mismatch. Fury would surely have had no chance.

Tyson himself never thought there was an opponent he couldn't beat and at 18 he entered the ABA Championships, putting himself on course for a fight with Price.

There was huge interest when they met in the North West final in November 2006 and hundreds of Travellers were locked out.

'I was 18 years old and had 12 amateur fights,' said Fury. 'He was Commonwealth Games gold medallist.'

The 22-8 decision went Price's way, but Fury had his moments.

'I had him over in the second round,' remembered Tyson, 'but there was no count.

'I was trying to hurt him with big shots and he went into his shell after I connected.

'I sparred him at an England training camp after that and did better.'

Tyson also suffered a points loss to Ivan Bezverhiy of the Ukraine in a multi-nations tournament, which was reversed when they fought again in the semi-finals of the European Junior Championships in Hungary.

In the final, Fury faced Russia's Maxim Babanin.

'I must have hit him with 20 jabs in the first,' he said, 'and at the end of the round, the score was 2-2.

'My dad shouted that I should give it to him, so I did and ended up being 10-6 down!

'I was outpunching him three to one in the third and the score was 22-11.'

Price remained the target and Fury called for a box-off with him after outpointing American number one Michael Hunter in an international match.

Fury was told there would be no box-off against Price and decided to take another route.

Fury's maternal grandfather was born in Wales and he explored the possibility of representing them at the 2007 World Championships in Chicago, a qualifier for the following year's Olympics.

'They told me I didn't have enough amateur experience to go and said they wanted me to be Olympic champion in 2012,' said Fury.

'I told them to take 2012 and stick it up their arse. I just wanted to box.'

Fury was convinced that should he get to the Olympics, he would do well.

But he had to get there.

Next, he tried to qualify through the Irish amateur system. Both his parents were born in Ireland.

'I got through to the semi-finals [of the Irish championships],' said Tyson, 'and the day before I was supposed to box in Dublin, they wanted to see my documents to prove I was Irish. We didn't have the time.'

NEXT time I saw Fury, he started punching my friend in the face.

Nick Griffin had rung to say Tyson was in Hinckley looking for sparring and wondered if Paul Butlin was available.

Butlin would tell Sky Sports ahead of a *Prizefighter* tournament that he was the good-looking heavyweight hope Britain was waiting for, but a brief spell in the domestic top ten aside, he spent most of his career fighting for money.

'I just asked what the money is,' he said, 'and as long as they didn't take the mickey, I said, "Yes."'

That attitude took him around Europe. The heavily tattooed Butlin never could turn down a fight or a tough spar. Of course he would go to Hinckley to spar Fury. Butlin was also a boxing fan and if there was a new heavyweight around, he wanted to know how good he was and how far he might go.

Butlin was soon convinced of Fury's capabilities. The plan was for Fury and Butlin to spar six rounds but after a couple, Griffin decided Butlin should take no more punishment.

'Butlin was a tough, hard pro,' remembered Griffin, 'but after a couple of rounds he was crumbling. I thought the best thing to do was to get Paul out of there.'

Butlin didn't complain about his judgement and told me on the drive home, 'He's as good as anyone out there already. You can't get near him. You can't wade into him because he will poke his left out and push you back. He's quick for a big man and goes to the body well.'

Butlin reckoned Fury compared well to the professional champions and contenders he had fought and sparred, but Fury was still an amateur at the time and his target was the Amateur Boxing Association Championships.

In the semi-finals, he met Nottingham's hard Shane McPhilbin for the third time.

'The first time we boxed,' said McPhilbin, 'I walked into the changing room, saw this huge lad standing there and said, "You must be Tyson."

'He shook his head, pointed at someone even bigger and said, "No, that's Tyson." I thought, "Fuck, I'm in trouble here."'

McPhilbin, who never let his boxing get in the way of his social life, lost that fight on points and when they boxed again, the result was the same.

Their third meeting was for a place in the ABA final and Fury forced the stoppage, a sign of his improvement.

'Tyson is hard to get into and hit,' said McPhilbin, who grew up with a father who told him and his brothers, 'If you don't fight, you don't eat.'

'But before I boxed him the last time, I thought I knew how to get round his jab.

'Even when I did, I ended up taking uppercuts and hooks.

'He was a clever fighter even then. He knows what you're thinking and is a step ahead.'

The ABA final was against Damien Campbell, from the successful Repton gym in London, and he couldn't figure out Fury, either.

According to the judges at ringside, Campbell landed only one punch to Fury's 19.

Nineteen-year-old Fury was the ABA super heavyweight champion.

'Then I went on holiday and thought about turning professional,' he said.

CHAPTER 2

Turning Professional

GIVEN THE chance to create their own boxer, every manager and promoter would create Tyson Fury.

Firstly, there was a name that even a Hollywood script writer would struggle to match.

That instantly created interest and Fury's sheer size made him a curiosity to an audience beyond boxing fans.

Hughie once made his nephew stand against the kitchen wall and measured him at 6ft 8¾ins tall.

'Someone told me that with my size I should be in Los Angeles playing basketball,' said Tyson.

'He reckoned I could go over there and get $1 million a year playing in the NBA. I told him I was born to be a boxer. You don't get many basketball players called Tyson.'

The first time Fury watched Mike Tyson he was 11 years old and, to the disappointment of the former world heavyweight champion, the fight only lasted 38 seconds.

Tyson mauled Lou Savarese at Glasgow's Hampden Park – and also dropped the referee.

'A left hook landed bang on the button, Savarese's body sagged and his hands dropped,' remembered John Coyle. 'I didn't want Tyson to have any free shots, so I called, "Stop boxing" and physically stood between them. I was about to say, "Sorry, kid" to Savarese to console him and then wallop! I felt a crunch on my shoulder and I was down.'

Tyson was so intent on smashing Savarese into oblivion that he ignored Coyle's demand to stop boxing and carried on his attack until he spotted his cornermen entering the ring. 'I must have stopped hundreds of fights,' said Coyle, 'and it was the only fight when it was the winner who wanted to carry on! Usually the loser says, "Come on, ref, I can carry on" and the winner walks away happy enough with his money. Tyson had another agenda. He really wanted to put the guy away. I had to stop him doing what he wanted to do – and he took some convincing!'

Tyson Fury also had the looks to do 'a few bits and bobs' of modelling, which he wasn't keen to talk about, and he was charming.

The threats he would make to opponents were softened by a slight lisp and a boyish twinkle in his eye.

Fury was well mannered and quick to put people at their ease. More than once, he was referred to by reporters as a 'Big Friendly Giant', a character created by children's author Roald Dahl, and he was chatty.

'Talking's my favourite hobby,' said Tyson 'to anybody about anything and if it's about boxing, you can kiss goodbye to a couple of weeks because I can talk a glass eye to sleep about boxing.'

HUGHIE asked me to write a profile of Tyson to show to potential promoters and this is how it read.

'Introducing the future of heavyweight boxing. The name will grab your attention – and wait until you see Tyson Fury!

'He stands 6ft 8¾ins tall, tips the scales at more than 18 stones and has the looks that had modelling agencies drooling.

'Tyson chose the boxing ring rather than the catwalk and has been grabbing the headlines in trade paper *Boxing News* since his first amateur fight.

'Tyson was a world-class amateur. He won bronze at the World Junior Championships, gold at the European Union juniors, was unbeaten when representing Ireland and stormed to the ABA super heavyweight title in 2008.

'His outstanding credentials weren't enough to secure a plane ticket to Beijing for the Olympics and now Tyson wants to put the sparkle back into professional heavyweight boxing with the help of his family.

'Father "Gypsy" John Fury was a contender for the British heavyweight title and he is part of the team behind Tyson's bid to conquer the world and become a global star.

'They are planning to revolutionise boxing, with plans for Tyson to meet three opponents in the same night and offer massive financial rewards to anyone who thinks they can beat him.

'Tyson is utterly fearless and has vowed to "destroy" every heavyweight who stands in his path.

'It's going to be great fun watching him do it.'

Every major promoter in Britain was interested in signing Fury.

The Furys stormed out of a meeting with Frank Maloney after being made what they thought was a derisory offer, but in former WBA featherweight champion Barry McGuigan and Mick Hennessy, they found promoters whose valuation of Tyson matched their own.

They chose Hennessy on a three-year deal, primarily because he had a television contract with ITV.

Hennessy was an East Londoner – 'I was born off the Old Kent Road,' he told *Boxing News* in 2010 – who would spend his school lunch breaks watching sparring at the Thomas A'Becket gym.

In his teens, Hennessy boxed as an amateur before a shoulder injury prevented him competing and he started working as an agent and business manager for Panos Eliades, the head of Panix Promotions.

Eliades promoted Lennox Lewis from 1992 until a bitter fall-out around a decade later.

Lewis won a court case and Eliades subsequently had his licence suspended by the British Boxing Board of Control for financial irregularities, leading him to walk away from the sport.

Hennessy stuck with boxing and put together 'The Class of 2002', a group of fighters that included Carl Froch, Matthew Thirlwall, Lee Meager and David Walker, which the BBC agreed to screen.

Hennessy went on to get a contract with Sky Sports and though reluctant to reveal too much of himself in interviews, he was more than happy to talk about how good his fighters were, the way a good boxing promoter should.

Hennessy was a salesman – he sold himself to his fighters and his fighters to television bosses and the public – and hugely ambitious.

He booked big venues for his shows and while Froch, Darren Barker and John Murray proved to be good bill-toppers, Walker, Thirlwall and John O'Donnell didn't live up to Hennessy's lofty estimations of them.

Sky Sports became infuriated with the chaotic nature of his shows – the bills were forever changing and Hennessy could be hard to contact –

but ITV found a home for them. The channel had been showing Frank Warren's stable of fighters, including Joe Calzaghe and Amir Khan, but the deal was lost after ITV cut its sports budget.

Hennessy promised ITV bosses his shows would be cheaper – and of the highest quality.

'I've got two fighters who will be world champions,' he told Mark Sharman, ITV's director of news and sport.

'Carl Froch and this new heavyweight called Tyson Fury.'

Sharman was impressed enough to hand Hennessy a contract that included smaller shows on ITV4 and major shows on the station's main channel.

HENNESSY gave Fury a hefty signing-on fee of £100,000, a third to be paid at the start of each year of the contract. It was a huge outlay for a fighter without an Olympic medal and only 35 amateur bouts behind him.

Hennessy took risks. There were stories of him running up debts to land big fights and fighters, and he felt Fury was worth a sizeable investment after watching him spar former top Cuban amateur Mike Perez in Dublin.

Fury hadn't spent much time in the gym in the five months since he won the ABA championship, but still, Hennessy reckoned he had the upper hand in what he described as 'a complete war'.

The following day, they sparred again and according to Hennessy, Perez didn't complete the scheduled eight rounds, getting out after six.

'Tyson looked a million dollars,' said Hennessy. 'I thought, "I've got to work something out for this kid because if he stays focused and applies himself, he can become heavyweight champion of the world."'

To the Furys, television exposure was arguably more important than money and Hennessy offered Tyson the chance to make his professional debut on the undercard of a world title fight, if he could sort out the paperwork and get back from honeymoon in time.

FURY had first met Paris Mulroy at the wedding of a mutual family friend when she was 15 years old.

'Even though Tyson was a similar age to me, he looked about 25 as he was so big,' remembered Paris, who hailed from a travelling family in Doncaster.

'He had all his facial hair and a beard and these big sideburns.

'I remember seeing Tyson as soon as my friend and I got out of the car to go to the wedding and I have to admit I did refer to him as "Farmer Giles" and have a laugh at his expense.

'Then his aunt, who I had known all my life as she was my mum's friend, told me she wanted to introduce me to her nephew.

'I was wearing a hat for the wedding and I remember hardly being able to see Tyson from under my hat as he was so tall.

'We only saw each other for a split second and I really didn't give him another thought.'

That was until they bumped into each other at Paris's 16th birthday party in her home town, Doncaster.

They started going to the cinema and ice skating at weekends and then Tyson decided they were getting married.

'Tyson never actually proposed to me,' said Paris. 'He just told me we were getting married!

'We were having a picnic and chatting about his future as a boxer and he turned to me and said, "First, I am going to turn professional, then win the English title, then the British title, then I'm going to marry you." I was a bit shocked, but also very happy.'

They were married in Doncaster on 21 November 2008.

'We didn't sleep together until after we got married,' said Paris. 'That is the Travellers' way and the gypsy way of life.'

The newlyweds headed to the Algarve for their honeymoon and while they were there, Fury decided to turn professional and, if possible, make his debut on the undercard of Carl Froch fighting Jean Pascal for the vacant WBC super middleweight title at Nottingham Arena.

'Mick faxed me a contract to the hotel, so I signed it and sent it back,' said Fury.

'I cut my honeymoon short, did all my medicals and boxed the next day. I just wanted to get started.'

THE Furys asked for a match with Lee Swaby, a bold move.

Swaby was a southpaw from Lincoln who had settled into the role of tough opponent after twice missing out on British cruiserweight honours.

Hennessy decided that he was too tough for a 20-year-old debutant who had spent the last two weeks eating and drinking as much as he wanted.

'The holiday was all inclusive in the Algarve,' said Fury. 'You could eat and drink as much as you wanted – and I did.'

Hennessy asked matchmaker John Ingle to find someone and he rang Mickey Helliet, a West London workaholic who managed and promoted fighters, and also worked as an agent.

'We need to find someone who has zero chance of winning,' Ingle told him.

'If Fury loses, it will be a disaster.'

Helliet knew his job, made a few phone calls and came up with Bela Gyongyosi, a Hungarian cruiserweight who had a record of three wins, nine defeats and two draws.

Ahead of the opening bell, Gyongyosi oozed all the confidence of a naughty schoolboy waiting outside the headmaster's office – and no wonder.

As well as being several inches shorter, he weighed just 13st 9lbs 4ozs to Fury's blubbery 18st 9lbs.

'We saw Fury,' said Sharman, 'and thought, "Is this fat kid really going to be world heavyweight champion?"'

Fury didn't give Gyongyosi the chance to build any confidence, sticking hard jabs into his face from the opening seconds before finding the finishing punch towards the end of the first round.

Fury let go a flurry of punches to Gyongyosi's head and when the Hungarian brought his gloves up to protect himself, Fury banged in a hard left hook to the ribs that dropped him.

Gyongyosi beat the count, rising at 'nine', but his face was still screwed up in pain and the referee decided he didn't need to take any more.

'Tyson had spent two weeks eating chocolates on his honeymoon, so he wasn't ready for a real test,' explained Hughie.

Tyson said he was keen for tougher challenges.

'I don't want to be like Audley Harrison and fight people half my size who won't hit me back,' said Tyson ahead of his second fight. 'I don't want to fight nobodies who don't stand a chance.

'I want to take on big men who come to fight. They will be too big to run away and that means they get knocked out quicker!'

Harrison had won Olympic gold in Sydney in 2000 but then undone much of the goodwill the British public showed him by fighting a succession of soft opponents at the start of his professional career.

The BBC had paid Harrison £1 million to screen his first ten fights and a general public who were unaware how the boxing business works warmed to the butchers and private investigators thrown to the big southpaw if they were able to weather the early storm and show signs of rallying.

Fury was very different.

'HAVE you ever heard of anyone fighting someone with a record like that in only his second fight?' asked Hughie.

No, I hadn't.

The opponent Hughie was talking about was Marcel Zeller, a 35-year-old German who had 21 wins from 24 fights – 20 by knockout.

As is often the way in professional boxing, statistics don't tell the full story. Zeller had been inactive and was stopped in his previous fight, but still, he would come with ambition, could punch and also did his best to get sections of the crowd at the Robin Park Centre in Wigan on his side.

Lee McAllister had brought big support with him from Aberdeen for his clash with British lightweight champion John Murray and they warmed to Zeller after he walked to the ring wearing a kilt and a T-shirt that read 'Highlander'.

There were cheers when Zeller came out tossing right hands at Fury, but they fell short and within a minute or so, he was pinned in a corner as he tried to dodge Fury's punches.

Zeller stayed under fire until the final minute of the third when, after seeing Fury slam a clean left hook off Zeller's jaw, referee Howard Foster decided the fight was over.

'I don't think anyone else in this country would fight an opponent with a record like that in their second professional fight,' said Fury afterwards.

'I know some people looked at his record and thought I was crazy to take the fight, but I want to take on opponents that will make people sit up and take notice.'

There was further disappointment for the travelling Scottish fans later that night when, in the top-of-the-bill fight, Murray broke down McAllister in eight rounds to keep his British title.

CHAPTER 3

Climbing the Rankings

THE GYM where the future heavyweight champion of the world trained was a gym like no other.

It was in a corrugated tin shed at the back of his uncle Hughie's six-bedroom house in Lancaster.

'The coldest gym in England,' reckoned Tyson, his breath visible under the lights to prove his point.

It was wet as well. Rain had dripped through a hole in the roof and on to the stereo, ruining the CD player. Only the cassette player worked and the only cassette Hughie had in his collection appeared to be *Roy Orbison's Greatest Hits*. Hughie would call for 'non-stop punching' from Tyson, while Roy sang his heart out.

The ring had been brought over from Ireland by John Fury. 'It was in a shed in Dundalk,' he remembered. 'We took our van, caught the ferry from Heysham to Belfast and drove to the border. We found some rusty weights in the same shed and brought them back, too.'

Hughie got Tyson sparring his son, Phill, a super welterweight who looked on course for a better professional career than his father had.

Hughie had ten fights between 1988 and 1992, winning three, drawing one and losing the rest. 'I didn't really give a fuck if I won or lost most of the time,' he admitted. 'I just wanted the money.'

But Hughie could fight when his pride was pricked.

'I opened *Boxing News* one week and there was a piece saying I didn't turn up to fight Barry Downes,' he said. 'But I didn't know anything about it.

'Back then, there were no mobile phones and my brother John had forgotten to pass on the message from my manager that I had a fight. I was angry. I used to get two words in *Boxing News* when I boxed and when I didn't box, I got the headlines. I got offered the fight two weeks later and took it.'

Hughie took 25 seconds to prove his point. 'I threw more right hands in those 25 seconds than I did in the rest of my fights put together,' he smiled.

Hughie took the career of his nephew rather more seriously and there were regular visits to Brendan Ingle's gym in Sheffield for sparring.

The Ingle way was to hit and not get hit, and Brendan told Tyson, 'Nobody can touch you. They won't be able to cope with your style. You will beat everybody.'

NEXT for Tyson to beat was Daniel Peret, a cheery soul who was used to losing and didn't mind too much.

Born in Russia and based in Norway, he had turned professional at 31 with the intention of becoming a journeyman on the European circuit – and he was a good one.

'If any of these prospects want to be anything, they must test themselves against me,' he said.

'I am a good journeyman, not one of these Romanians or Latvians who just fall down in round one.'

Peret was known to British fans for being durable. Four weeks before he faced Fury in Norwich, Peret had extended unbeaten Dereck Chisora the full eight rounds and Hughie said ahead of the fight, 'People have been saying Tyson can't punch, so hopefully we will put that to bed.'

As he was in Norwich, Fury took the chance to goad the city's heavyweight, Sam Sexton, the Southern Area champion.

'I looked him straight in the eye [at the press conference],' said Fury, 'and I could see that he didn't want to know.

'But I'm ready, willing and able whenever he wants to get it on.

'Probably the whole of Norwich is asking him when is he going to shut this Tyson Fury lad up, but Sexton's just like the rest of the British heavyweights out there, they don't want anything to do with me.

'If I've got such a big mouth, you'd imagine that there would be a queue of people outside my door looking to shut me up, but no one's stepped forward.

'In the meantime, I'll just look to keep knocking over whoever Mick Hennessy puts in front of me and look to build towards a British title fight.'

The victory over Peret was straightforward enough.

'Everyone says he has a good defence,' said Fury, 'but every punch I threw hit him flush in the face.'

By the end of the first, Peret had a bloodied nose and was grazed around the left eye.

The second round was similarly one-sided and at the end of the session, Peret's corner pulled him out.

'Are you crazy?' he fumed, but it looked a compassionate decision.

FURY had to wait until his fourth fight to have his chin tested – but not by his opponent.

Hughie had fancied Lee Swaby for Tyson's debut opponent, only for Hennessy to talk him out of it, but they finally met in Birmingham in March 2009.

Swaby was having his 48th fight – 23 wins, 22 losses and two draws – and though he had been fighting on the right-hand side of the bill for a while, he still fought to win and took the fight to Fury.

He struggled to pin him down and when Tyson fired back, Swaby was forced on to the back foot.

He stayed there until his corner retired him at the end of the fourth.

During that fourth round, Fury aimed a right uppercut at Swaby but instead hit himself flush in the face.

'It stunned me for a bit, more out of surprise than anything else,' said Tyson. 'The punch would have knocked out a lot of boxers.'

Fury seemed pleased enough with his night's work. 'The plan was to soften him up and then get him out of there,' he said.

Following the Swaby fight, Hughie made an interesting revelation. He claimed Tyson was ambidextrous and was thinking of turning him southpaw.

FOUR weeks later, Fury was back in the ring to face a fighter who once said he would be 'the best heavyweight to ever come out of Britain'.

Mathew Ellis fell way short of that because although he had quick hands and could fight, he was small at 5ft 11ins tall and loved the bright lights of home town Blackpool rather too much.

His bubble had been burst way before he met Fury at the York Hall in Bethnal Green in April 2009, but Ellis still had his pride and there was always the chance he might be able to get his head on Fury's chest and put him under pressure.

It took Fury all of 48 seconds to dispose of him.

Tyson, who winked at his opponent during the referee's pre-fight instructions, twice clubbed Ellis to his knees with right hands.

Ellis was counted out in the act of rising after the second knockdown.

'Ellis is the only heavyweight who dared to get in there with me,' said Tyson afterwards. 'I will do a job on anyone who is game enough to get in there with me.'

Hennessy shared his confidence. 'He could win the British title tomorrow,' he said of Fury. 'He is the most exciting heavyweight since Mike Tyson.'

THESE were exciting times for the heavyweight division in Britain.

David Price, Fury's former amateur rival, had launched his pro career with a stoppage, Dereck Chisora was unbeaten and promoter Frank Maloney had muscular Londoner Larry Olubamiwo and Tom Dallas, a roofer from Chatham who stood a lofty 6ft 6ins tall and had a solid amateur pedigree behind him, in his stable.

The stock of Scott Belshaw, a former rugby player from Belfast, had fallen after Peret outhustled him over six rounds to snap the winning start to his pro career.

Belshaw won the rematch and went on to face Fury in Watford in May 2009. Unlike most of his opponents, Belshaw didn't need the help of a stepladder to look Fury in the eye.

Not that being 6ft 7¼ins tall had done Belshaw any good when he sparred Tyson a year or so earlier. He got out of the ring sighing, 'I can't hit you,' but talked rather more positively ahead of their fight, promising to put Fury under pressure.

Fury was in Germany ahead of the fight, sparring the 7ft, 23-stone Finnish hope Robert Helenius.

A Finnish television crew was there and Hughie laughed later, 'I said to the cameraman afterwards, "You haven't got much footage from that, have you?" and he shook his head.

'I was shouting to Tyson "Gypsy style" because I wanted the gypsies in Finland to get behind him – if they understood what I was saying!'

The fight with Belshaw was all Fury as well.

His jab soon brought blood from Belshaw's nose and Fury stiffened his legs with a right hand to the chin.

Belshaw stayed upright from that punch, but when Tyson dug a left hook into the pit of his stomach, he took a step back and then dropped to his knee.

After the completion of the 'eight' count, Fury targeted the same spot and a similar punch put Belshaw on the floor, clearly in a lot of pain. Again, he pulled himself upright at the count of 'eight' and the bell rang before any more punches could be thrown.

At the start of the second, Belshaw tossed over a few desperate rights that Fury dodged with ease and he answered with another left hook to the body that left Scott doubled over, paralysed by the pain. Fury drew his right fist back to deliver the knockout blow, but recognising his opponent was defenceless, chose not to throw it and the referee stepped in after 42 seconds of the round.

'I could have let that last punch go and put his lights out,' said Fury. 'I know it's a brutal sport, but I didn't need to do that.'

FURY had to wait for his seventh fight.

The plan had been for him to fight in Wigan the following month and the Furys hoped to have a big name coming out of the opposite corner.

An approach was made to Oliver McCall, the 44-year-old former WBC champion.

He turned the fight down but suggested a match with his 21-year-old son, Elijah, who was unbeaten in four fights (one draw).

The Furys accepted and the fight was on, until Tyson suffered a trapped nerve and internal bleeding in his back during a spar with Richard Towers, a new professional from the Ingles' gym who stood 6ft 7ins tall.

That slowed Fury's progress – he had been fighting every month since turning professional – but at least growing interest in a fight with Chisora kept him in the thoughts of the boxing public.

Born in Zimbabwe and based in north London, Chisora had a curled-lipped contempt for many of his opponents – and even the rules.

He was handed a four-month ban for biting Midlands journeyman Paul Butlin, a decision that ruled him out of challenging British champion Danny Williams, and with no fight to train for, Chisora kept himself busy writing a letter to *Boxing News*.

In it, Chisora admitted he had turned down an offer to fight Fury, but added it could go ahead if he was offered 'the right money'.

Hughie made an improved offer. 'Tyson will give Chisora his purse if Dereck wins,' he said. 'If Tyson wins, Chisora will still get paid. We can't say fairer than that.

'Chisora is confident he can beat Tyson and we are confident he can't, so we are willing to back our man.

'We will also have a side bet with his team if they are interested.'

The more immediate problem facing the Furys was a familiar one. Who would Tyson fight next?

THERE was talk of a match with Coleman Barrett or Ian Tims for the vacant Irish title and when neither materialised, the fight was offered to a fighter who was even bigger than Fury at 6ft 9ins tall and around 20 stones.

Evgeny Orlov, known as 'The Molecule From Hell', agreed to the fight but, according to Fury, then had a rethink after recalling a sparring session.

In the end, Fury faced Aleksandrs Selezens, a 29-year-old Latvian who had never been stopped during a nine-fight (three wins, six losses) career and bore some resemblance to English champion John McDermott.

The British Boxing Board of Control had made Fury his mandatory challenger and the whisper was the fight would go ahead in September – provided Fury didn't suffer any mishaps against Selezens, that is.

Selezens had turned professional just before his 28th birthday with the intention of fighting for money.

He knew there would always be work for a heavyweight who could give prospects rounds and he discovered the best way to get through fights was to smother, hold and throw punches in occasional bursts.

Against Fury, the tactics didn't work. Badly hurt by a body punch in the third, Selezens was pounded to his knees and his corner threw in the towel. Selezens left the ring holding his ribs.

'I'm going to be in 100 per cent better condition for John McMuffin,' said Fury, mocking McDermott's blubbery physique by renaming him after a popular fast food.

'They are a similar size and I'm sure McMuffin will have watched that and got confident. I'm going to destroy him. He will never want to fight again.'

CHAPTER 4

Champion

TYSON AND Hughie Fury were forever falling out.

Hughie was exasperated by his nephew's diet.

'I'm in bed some nights and see lights come on and I know it's Tyson off to an all-night garage for some chocolate,' he said.

'He read somewhere that athletes eat Jaffa Cakes to give them energy, so he started eating two packets a day and wondered why he was fat!'

Tyson had grievances of his own and let off some steam about his uncle after the Selezens fight.

'I was staying up there for six months and I had had enough,' he said. 'I didn't like the atmosphere around there. It was like Alcatraz. You drive for five minutes before you get to the motorway, then you have to go 60–70 miles before you find anything else.'

It was agreed Hughie would be paid expenses to travel to Manchester to train Tyson, but still there was a clash.

Hughie was a disciplinarian, Tyson a free spirit.

Hughie wasn't in a good mood when I rang him for a progress report ahead of the Selezens fight. He couldn't find his nephew. 'I imagine,' said Hughie tetchily, 'a new cake shop has opened in his neighbourhood and that's where he will be.'

For the McDermott fight, Tyson said he was going to team up with Tony Sims in Essex and bring in quality sparring from abroad, but instead he went back to his amateur coach, Steve Egan.

Egan, head coach at a club named after his late father, Jimmy, did have hopes of training Fury when he turned professional, but in gypsy culture family comes first. As well as training with Egan, Tyson also spent time with his uncle Peter at a gym he had built on a holiday camp he owned just outside Lymm, near Warrington.

There was also an offer to train with Emanuel Steward at the Kronk gym in Detroit, but with wife Paris pregnant, Tyson declined.

The split from Hughie seemed poorly timed. Tyson had the toughest fight of his career coming up, for the English heavyweight championship.

'It's time to find out if I'm as good as I think I am,' said Fury ahead of his challenge for McDermott's title.

McDERMOTT represented a significant step up from Fury's previous seven opponents and promoter Frank Maloney was convinced the 29-year-old from Essex was the fighter to shut Fury's mouth.

McDermott, a sculptor and artist who once raised £1,000 for charity with a copy of a Van Gogh painting, was considered a solid domestic heavyweight who had three times missed out on the British title.

He folded inside a round against Matt Skelton when he went into the ring concerned over his daughter's health, but two battles with Danny Williams had provided a better guide to McDermott's capabilities.

There was controversy after the south Londoner outpointed him on a majority vote in July 2008. Williams was docked three points in the last two rounds, yet still scraped home on two of the cards. Afterwards, Maloney called for the two judges concerned to be 'shot'.

The rematch also went Williams' way, this time on a split decision, and though the defeat hurt McDermott, he seemed to take confidence from the performance.

He referred to Williams as 'one of the biggest-punching heavyweights out there' and he had been able to take his shots.

Fury fancied he would punch too hard for McDermott.

'He won't last four rounds,' Tyson told me ahead of the fight.

'McDermott is one-dimensional. He has got nothing to beat me with. He's not going to be quicker, stronger or hit harder. Unless I stick my chin out and let him hit me four times, there's no way he can beat me – and that's not in the game plan!

'I'm going to be in the best shape of my career. I haven't really shown what I can do yet.

'All I've shown is that I have a good jab and left hook to the body, and you're going to see a lot more from me against McDermott. I know he's tough, but he has never faced anyone of my calibre yet. Danny Williams was washed up when he boxed him.

'I don't think any of the heavyweights out there can throw as many punches as me. Anyone can box for ten rounds if you only throw three punches every round.

'I really want to prove to people I've got stamina and can take a punch because I know it's there.'

Tyson told me that after reuniting with Egan, he shed seven kilograms and weighed 17st 9lbs, the lightest of his career.

McDermott said Fury calling him 'McMuffin' had driven him to 'train like a maniac'.

Trainer CJ Hussein said, 'John is a bit soft. He would say to me, "I'm a nice guy, why's he saying that about me?"

'To beat Tyson, you need a good jab and John had a good jab.

'The way to beat Tyson was to throw the double jab at his chest and body to straighten him up and then let the right hand go over the top.'

McDermott looked blubbery at 18st 1lb, but Hussein said, 'John worked hard in the gym and I knew he could put combinations together from round one to round 12.'

In contrast, Fury had yet to go beyond four.

Tyson had a height advantage of around six inches and was eight years younger, but had fought only 26 rounds in his professional career to McDermott's 135 and had been desperately short of sparring.

So desperate did Fury become, he took to social media to appeal for sparring partners. The offer was '£10,000 if you can knock me out'.

Milton Keynes hard man Matt Legg liked the sound of that, but asked, 'What if I don't knock you out?'

Fury offered him £350 for a day's sparring.

'I hadn't been training so I was in no sort of shape,' said Legg, 'but I was a bit short of money at the time, so the next day I got on a train to Manchester.'

Tyson and younger brother Shane met him at the station and took him to the gym. 'I did a round, then Shane did a round,' is how Legg remembered the sparring. 'I did about six rounds – and landed one punch!

'Tyson paid me and took me back to the station.'

His lack of experience or sparring wasn't on Fury's mind as he made his way to the ring to fight McDermott. He happily danced away to his music.

'Confidence is the key to winning all fights because a confident man is a winner,' Tyson explained once. 'If you're negative and down in the ring, your opponent can see that. But if you're confident, and you're ready, then he's not going to be so brave.'

There were times in the early rounds when Fury's confidence appeared misplaced.

The 6ft 3ins McDermott chugged forward, slipping jabs and countering with right hands.

It seemed McDermott couldn't miss with the punch, but whenever he landed, Fury took it well and pumped punches straight back at him.

At the end of the first, Fury rubbed his forehead against McDermott's cheek, McDermott lunged back and both sets of corner men flew into the ring to separate them.

Referee Terry O'Connor spoke to both fighters before the second round got under way.

The action in the first two rounds was back and forth, but by the third, it appeared that Fury had settled and that his jab may give him control.

The fourth was closer, Fury landing jabs and body shots, while McDermott slammed back with eye-catching hooks.

This was a hard, close fight in hot conditions and according to Sky Sports, McDermott landed enough punches to be ahead after four rounds.

Never beyond four before, Fury still had six to go – and McDermott looked fresh and motivated.

McDermott didn't do a lot in the sixth, allowing Fury to win the round behind his jab, but the champion wasn't fading, just taking a breather.

He rallied in the seventh to bounce heavy clumps off Fury's chin. Fury was unmoved and flung his fists straight back at him, but still, this was turning out to be rather more of a struggle than Tyson had anticipated.

During the eighth, Hennessy was on his feet at ringside. 'Let's go Tyson,' he screamed, willing his fighter to drag more out of his tired and aching body.

Fury threw more punches in a gruelling ninth, but still, ahead of the tenth and final round, his corner told him to go for the knockout.

Across the ring, CJ Hussein told McDermott he was four rounds up, an opinion that was shared by Sky Sports and most journalists at ringside.

Fury thought the right uppercut was the punch to knock out McDermott. He tried it several times throughout the final three minutes and though he didn't land it cleanly, he looked to have done enough to win a scruffy round.

There were still puzzled looks among ringsiders when, at the final bell, O'Connor reached over to Fury's hand to raise it in victory.

Sky commentator Jim Watt, the former WBC lightweight champion, had McDermott ahead 96-94 and said, 'I can't explain that.'

There was further surprise when it was revealed O'Connor had scored it 98-92, meaning Fury had won eight of the ten rounds.

Maloney described the scoring as 'a disgrace'. The feeling was that even if Fury had won, it was surely only by a couple of rounds.

'I worked harder than him,' was Fury's assessment of the fight.

'He caught me with a few rights over the top, but he was mauling and I was working.'

Tyson looked close to tears as he admitted, 'I had to dig so deep. It was a lot harder than I thought it would be. I thought I worked harder throughout the fight and deserved the verdict. I showed enough to beat a veteran of 30 fights. I showed grit and determination.'

McDermott was fuming. 'What have I done to people ?' he said. 'I'm a nice guy. I beat Danny Williams and now this.'

Fury and McDermott were agreed on one thing. There had to be a rematch.

CHAPTER 5

Redemption

PROMOTER FRANK Maloney suffered a mild heart attack after Fury had his hand raised, fans rioted and the British Boxing Board of Control launched an inquiry into the scoring of the fight.

Tyson Fury didn't know what all the fuss was about.

'I've watched the fight ten times and I think I won it,' he said. 'I had us level after eight rounds and I won the last two rounds clearly enough.'

Tyson told me he thought the reaction to the fight was 'over the top' and added, 'It was too much. But any publicity is good publicity. It kept people talking about me.'

He did admit he had underestimated McDermott, however.

'Maybe I wasn't prepared for a war as much as I should have been,' he said. 'McDermott gained my respect that night for being one hell of a tough fighter.

'John showed that night he is one of the best heavyweights in Britain apart from me and David Haye. John would beat the likes of Chisora or [Audley] Harrison if he had the opportunity.'

The Board ordered a rematch, but before that happened, Fury was able to squeeze in two more fights – with two different trainers.

Fifteen days after the McDermott fight, Fury fought Tomas Mrazek in Dublin and he had Robert McCracken, the former world-class middleweight who trained most of Hennessy's fighters, in his corner.

Mrazek was a southpaw from the Czech Republic who came to survive. He managed it after Fury injured his right hand during the second of their scheduled six-round fight.

Fury won the first five rounds with his jab and then went for Mrazek in the last, turning southpaw and heaving left hands at him.

Mrazek was bundled over in the last 30 seconds, but picked himself up and made it through to the final bell.

Ahead of his next fight, Fury turned to a trainer he described as 'the Cus D'Amato of British boxing'.

D'AMATO produced world champions Floyd Patterson, Jose Torres and Mike Tyson during half a century of training and managing fighters, and Brian Hughes had his success stories as well.

Hughes set up the Collyhurst and Moston Lads' Club in Manchester in the 1960s and it was Pat 'Black Flash' Barrett who brought the wider boxing public's attention to the gym two decades later.

Barrett was a devastating puncher who twice lost world title challenges and behind him came Michael Gomez, Michael Jennings and Robin Reid, who won the WBC super middleweight championship.

Barrett suggested Fury should train under Hughes, whose assistants included Mike Jackson.

Jackson remembered Fury as 'fit and hard working', but when he got into the ring to face Germany's Hans-Joerg Blasko at Huddersfield Leisure Centre in March 2010, things didn't go according to plan.

'We did so much work on teaching Tyson how to block the right hand,' said Jackson, 'and within 20 seconds of the fight starting he almost had his head taken off by a right hand.'

Fury wasn't bothered and went on to win inside a round, but Jackson said, 'It felt like a defeat. That was how it felt in the changing room afterwards.

'I was working nights at the time [as a chemical process officer] and had booked the day off work, but after the fight, I rang my gaffer and asked to go in. I just wanted to forget about the fight.'

Fury said afterwards, presumably with tongue in cheek, that he was toying with the idea of having a different trainer for every fight, but for the rematch with McDermott, he went back to Hughie.

THE McDermott rematch almost didn't happen.

'My cousin was working in Holland and I was skint, so I packed my bags and was going to see him,' said Tyson.

'I drove to Hull and missed the boat by five minutes. I was thinking about going to London and catching the plane, but decided not to bother. The next day, Hughie rang me and said we had a date for the McDermott rematch, but I didn't have long to prepare.'

It was only five weeks away and Hughie was going to spend those five weeks 'getting Tyson to hit properly'.

He explained, 'I had to have him punching with his knuckles down. I wanted him to hit McDermott hard,' emphasising his point by slamming fist into open palm.

'I was going to retire if I lost the rematch and just forget about boxing,' said Tyson.

'I knew if I was going anywhere, I had to beat him. I didn't want to carry on boxing if I was just going to be a journeyman and knew it would take me three years to get back to where I was. I knew I couldn't walk down the street again if I let him beat me. I've got a big name – and a lot to live up to. Nobody would care if I was called John Smith.'

The fight wouldn't just be won in the gym and ring, however.

'Gypsies have been persecuted for hundreds of years,' explained Hughie. 'We've learned you have to be crafty sometimes to survive. I've sold door to door and sold cars. I can read people.'

Hughie fancied he could read McDermott.

On the Facebook social networking site, the Furys posted a message saying Tyson was weighing more than 20 stones. 'John is the type of person who will think about things and burn himself out,' said Hughie. 'We wanted him to think Tyson was going to be heavy – and hitting hard.

'We knew John is an intelligent man and that we could push him under. We would say nice things about him, then say he was a big pudding who was going to get knocked out. We knew he would burn mental energy wrapping it around his mind, winding himself up and getting confused. If he was stupid, none of that would have bothered him.'

The scales showed that between the first and second McDermott fights, Tyson had piled on 23 pounds – or had he?

'I drank a bottle of water before I went on the scales and stuffed my pockets with my wallet, mobile phone, keys and anything else I could find,' he said. 'I didn't say anything nasty about him. All I said was that I was going to hit him properly this time because I didn't the first time we boxed.'

McDermott had a new trainer for the fight, Jim McDonnell, who in his own ring career had lost challenges for separate versions of the world super featherweight title to African greats Azumah Nelson and Brian Mitchell, as well as ended the career of Irish idol Barry McGuigan.

McDonnell was a fitness fanatic who ran the London Marathon in under three hours and pushed his fighters hard in the gym.

The whisper was that McDermott would be in the best shape of his career for the rematch.

Maloney also asked McDonnell to work on McDermott's confidence. Maloney regarded McDermott as 'the biggest worrier I've ever known'.

THE controversy over Terry O'Connor's scoring of the first fight led to a change in the rules.

The Board decided three judges would score English title fights and there was more than Fury's St George's belt at stake when he faced McDermott again, nine months after their first fight.

The rematch was also a final eliminator for the British title, held by Dereck Chisora, and because of that status, the fight would be over 12 rounds rather than ten.

Tyson did less talking before the bout but at ringside at a sweltering and highly charged Brentwood Leisure Centre on the night of the fight, there was plenty of talking and most of it was about gloves.

Fury had chosen to wear gloves made by Cleto Reyes, which were smaller, harder and the choice of knockout punchers. That, along with Tyson's extra weight, made ringsiders expect an early bombardment from Fury. The truth was rather more straightforward.

'It was hard to close those BBE gloves we used in the first fight,' said Tyson. '[Promoter] Frank [Maloney] had a deal with BBE to use their gloves in top-of-the-bill fights on his shows, but the contract said I could choose different gloves, but it would cost me. I paid £3,000 out of my purse to wear different gloves. Cleto Reyes gloves fit me better.'

Believing the Furys were trying to gain an advantage, McDermott's trainers threatened to pull him out of the fight and away from the Board officials and television cameras, the two camps headed outside.

Hughie remembered: 'I told them we had gone there for a fight and we would fight them without gloves or even there and then in the car park. We said that if McDermott pulled out, Tyson would get in the ring to show he was there and ready to fight.'

McDermott decided to fight and almost found himself fighting John Fury, rather than Tyson. After entering the ring, a fired-up McDermott would lean over the top of each set of ropes, beat his chest and roar into the crowd. He did it again in the rematch – until he bumped into John. 'Fuck off or I will knock you out,' John told him. 'McDermott shrunk,' said Hughie. 'We wanted him to think there was no way he could win.'

Hughie had also worked out the tactics to win the fight – and it cost him £500. 'McDermott showed in the first fight that he could time his right hand and I didn't want Tyson running on to it,' said Hughie, 'so I told him to keep moving to his right. He was above me in the corner and I could see him shaping to move to his left, so I reached into the ring, slapped him on the ankle and shouted, "That way!" at him.'

Board officials fined Hughie £500. 'I think the Board saw the funny side,' he smiled, 'but they had to act.'

Fury came out jabbing and moving, his face etched in concentration. He didn't stand still long enough for McDermott to land a punch of note until the final minute of the second, when he was able to manoeuvre Fury into a neutral corner and crash a right hand on to his chin.

Tyson was untroubled. He spun his way out of the corner and unloaded with both fists, driving McDermott into the ropes.

Fury looked much sharper, the jab was accurate and whenever McDermott came bustling in and tried to let his hands go, Fury would lean back and fire a fast right-hand counter.

McDermott started to look frustrated and when he tried to up the pace in the fourth, Fury slowed him down with hard whacks to the body.

Fury was winning the rounds, but throwing a lot of punches to win them, and after the fifth there were signs he was feeling the pace.

He slumped on his stool and told Hughie, 'I'm fucked.' There was urgency in Tyson's voice when he asked for water.

Early in the sixth, Fury was taking deep gulps of breath and Maloney urged McDermott, 'Jump on him! Punch! Punch!'

The crowd roared as McDermott stepped up his attacks and a clash of heads left Fury bleeding from a cut on his right eyebrow.

This was a crisis for Fury.

The mood in McDermott's camp at the end of the sixth was buoyant. 'A million per cent I thought he would go on and win,' said McDonnell later.

Never cut before, Fury held his boxing together and had a better seventh, but had a point taken off him for holding as McDermott kept the pressure on.

'I was moving around a lot and it was so hot in there,' said Fury. 'I was so tired, but I knew I couldn't lose.

'I just thought, "I'm not losing" and remembered a line from the film *Pearl Harbor*.

'The pilots are thinking about the lives they left behind back home and say, "It's back to the farm, boys." They thought about going back home to work on the farm and feed the pigs rather than being a pilot. I thought about that. I didn't want to have to go out and get a job. I kept thinking, "Back to the farm, boys."'

Hughie told his nephew before the eighth, 'He's more tired than you are, now go out there and hit him as hard as you can!'

The fight's decisive moment came in the last 30 seconds of the round.

Fury put together a two-fisted flurry on the inside and McDermott crumpled to the canvas.

The bell came before Fury could throw another punch and the minute's break was enough for McDermott to gather himself for one final, all-or-nothing attack.

He waded into Tyson at the start of the ninth.

They launched right hands simultaneously, both connected and McDermott hit the deck.

He beat the count and went for broke. There was an exciting exchange as both put everything into every punch. McDermott landed a thumping left hook that Fury ignored and he answered by slamming a chopping right hand on to McDermott's chin. McDermott flopped to the floor, looking like a beaten man.

Somehow, he dragged himself up at the count of 'nine', but he was unsteady on his legs and referee Dave Parris waved the fight off.

'I love boxing,' said Fury later. 'I just love to be in there fighting. That helped me pull it out of the bag.'

CHAPTER 6

Del Boy and Drama

THE WIN over McDermott made Fury the mandatory challenger for the British heavyweight title, held by Dereck Chisora.

Chisora was aiming higher.

Twice he was set to challenge Wladimir Klitschko, the holder of the WBO and IBF belts and the division's number one, and twice the fight fell through.

Fury had troubles of his own – or rather his promoter did.

Hennessy saw his contract with ITV cancelled towards the end of 2009 – despite his shows bringing in good ratings.

'I lost the ITV contract through no fault of my own because they were cutting back and had finished with Formula One and we were left in no man's land, with no TV,' he said.

The likelihood was, his fighters would leave him.

'A lot of people [promoters] wanted Tyson at the time because he'd had a good build-up on ITV and was looking really good,' said Hennessy.

Hennessy explained the situation to Fury and told him that without television, the next year or so could be tough. He no longer had the financial backing needed to get Fury the big fights he wanted.

Fury told him, 'If there's no money on the table, I will fight for nothing.'

He explained later, 'I'm not the sort of person to leave someone at their lowest point.

'It's like someone dying in your family and then your wife leaves you. It's not a good time. It's wrong.

'I'm not a disloyal person. I signed up with Mick Hennessy in the beginning. He had belief in me and I believed in him. My dad always told me, "You don't get any luck from abandoning a sinking ship," so I stayed with Mick.'

Fury drew a comparison with the film *Jerry Maguire*, in which Tom Cruise's sports agent stays afloat thanks to the loyalty of one client, played by Cuba Gooding Jr.

'You know that film *Jerry Maguire*?' Fury said to Hennessy. 'That's me and you.'

Hennessy wanted to keep Fury fighting while the back-and-forth between Chisora and Klitschko went on, and found a spot for him on the Irish-backed channel Premier Sports.

According to Shane Fury, their viewers were entitled to think his elder brother was 'useless'.

The eight-round fight was against an opponent who also had a name plucked from a Hollywood script.

Tyson Fury against Rich Power looked good on the fight posters and what's more, both were unbeaten.

Hailing from Michigan, Power had won all 11 fights, but the punches that had been too much for the mediocre opponents he had been facing on club shows in the Detroit suburbs never troubled Fury.

Tyson boxed his way to a comfortable victory, winning all eight rounds on the referee's scorecard.

'I could beat you myself,' Shane told Tyson afterwards. 'You're useless.'

Tyson sought out a second opinion from the best boxing trainer in the world.

EMANUEL Steward knew of Fury through one of his fighters.

Steward had Irish middleweight, Andy Lee, in the gym. He was a cousin of Fury's and set up the chance for Tyson to work with a trainer whose knowledge and communication skills were proved by a CV that showed 40 world champions, including Thomas Hearns, Lennox Lewis and Wladimir Klitschko.

Steward reinvented Klitschko, who came to him as a vulnerable ex-champion and went on to become the virtually untouchable, dominant heavyweight of his era.

Steward always had an eye on the future and was therefore keen to have a look at Fury.

'It was an overnight decision,' said Fury, 'because the more I think about stuff, the more I don't want to do it.

'I got over there not knowing what to expect. I was left stranded at Detroit Airport because Emanuel had his phone switched off and didn't know I was coming so soon.

'I had no address, so I got in a taxi and asked to be taken to the Kronk gym. So he [the taxi driver] took me to the one that's not there any more.

'He phoned a radio station and asked where the gym was and took me there.

'I walked in there with my bag and luckily Emanuel's nephew – who I'd met last year – was there.'

Steward was impressed by Fury during their four weeks together and after training, Tyson showed a completely carefree confidence in himself. The only white man in most of the bars he visited with Steward, Tyson danced freely with the locals.

'Tyson Fury will be the next boxing superstar,' said Steward later. 'He can be the complete package. He's got talent, he's good looking and has charisma.'

The link-up with Steward led to Fury being invited to train with his leading heavyweight, Wladimir Klitschko, who was in camp in Austria preparing for the proposed fight with Chisora.

Fury didn't spar Klitschko, but still believed he scored a moral victory over the world champion.

'During the camp, he had a bit of an attitude because Emanuel kept saying, "Tyson is the next heavyweight king,"' said Fury.

'Wladimir is known as the sauna king, I can't stand them, but I'm competitive at everything I do.

'This sauna was the hottest thing I had been in in my life. Everyone was naked and one by one people started leaving, then Wlad stands up and starts waving a towel around.

'I felt like I was going to pass out, but I thought, "I'm not going to quit because if he beats me here he was got a mental win over me."

'So I leant back and thought, "Fuck it, if I pass out, they won't let me die in here."

'So I am staring at him and he is staring at me and finally, he stands up at about 35 minutes, grunts and walks out and goes straight to his room.

'I got up and almost fainted in the shower. But he knows he won't beat me at anything.'

Fury also squeezed in a training camp in Canada and secured a spot on the Bernard Hopkins–Jean Pascal undercard in Quebec City.

Tyson called for a fight with a fringe contender like Hasim Rahman or Fres Oquendo, but instead went in with Zack Page, a cagey 37-year-old who gave everyone rounds.

Fury won all eight rounds on all three scorecards for his 13th straight win.

TYSON'S next fight would be his first without his father, John.

John Fury was a proud and hard man. In my company, he's only ever been polite and genial, but he had a temper and when he felt he had been wronged or challenged, or that family honour was at stake, Fury liked a bareknuckle fight to resolve matters.

Fury was a formidable opponent. He stood 6ft 3ins tall and was around the same width, a huge bear of a man who fought to win at all costs.

'I'm not a feather duster man,' he once said.

On seeing Oathie Sykes at a car auction in Belle Vue, Manchester, Fury decided a decade-long feud should be settled there and then.

Once good friends, Fury and Sykes had apparently fallen out over a bottle of beer while on a trip to Cyprus in 1999 and in Fury's mind, the issue was unresolved.

John described what followed as 'a fair fight between travelling people... a hard contest'.

Tyson would later say his father had to fight three rivals.

After the 'contest', Sykes's right eye became infected and had to be removed.

Fury accepted responsibility when arrested a month later, saying he was 'a man of honour', and was charged with grievous bodily harm.

In court, Fury said his intention wasn't to blind his rival, just win the fight and settle the feud, but he was sentenced to 11 years in prison, just days before his son's next fight, against an unbeaten knockout specialist.

BOXING managers follow the mantra that their fighters should only fight a puncher when they have to, but right from the start Tyson set out to be different from everyone else.

With the Chisora fight on the horizon, he took a fight with an opponent whose 13-0 record showed eight first-round knockouts.

Brazil isn't known for the quality of its boxers but with a record like his, Marcelo Nascimento got in the ring at Wembley Arena to face Fury believing he had a puncher's chance against anyone.

First impressions of Nascimento were that he had long limbs and swung every punch hard, but there was a jerky, disjointed look about his boxing.

He hurled big, arcing punches at Fury and the punches Tyson fired back were straight. Nascimento's swings missed, while Fury's kept finding the target.

Midway through the opening round, Fury let go a right hand that connected flush on the Brazilian's chin and put him on the seat of his trunks.

Nascimento was up quickly and tightened his defence. He lifted his hands high and, spotting Nascimento's ribs were unprotected, Fury made them his target. When Fury stopped punching, Nascimento swung back – and missed.

'You have to be relaxed to see the punches coming,' explained Hughie. 'Tyson goes in loose and without any fear. If you go in there stiff and worried, you're going to get beaten.'

As the fight went on, there were fewer swings for Tyson to avoid. Fury was able to keep Nascimento quiet trying to avoid his jab and by the end of the fourth, the signs were that all the swinging and missing had tired the Brazilian out.

Fury opened up in the fifth, driving Nascimento back with left-rights until a final right hand landed on his temple and sent him crashing heavily.

'I knew it was a good one,' said Fury afterwards, 'because I felt the shiver right up my arm.'

The way Nascimento landed, face first, everyone knew the fight was over and his cornermen were quick to jump into the ring to tend to him.

'That's what the public wants to see,' said Fury, 'a big guy flattening another big guy.'

Once Nascimento had recovered, Fury turned his attention to his domestic rivals, calling Chisora 'scared', Price 'chinny' and likening Dallas to a 'piece of wood'.

As for himself, Fury said, 'I may be fat and white as a ghost, but I can fight.' He also said that in 2012, he planned to become world heavyweight champion. 'I'd like to take it off David Haye,' he said, 'because I really believe that when he gets pegged properly, he'll go over like a rag.'

HIS father's imprisonment hit Fury hard.

Boxing News found him in a dark, contemplative mood when they visited him for a feature published after the Nascimento fight.

'I always thought life was so good growing up,' he said, 'but basically, I've got this, like, depression mode always on me and I think it's all worthless, pointless, because no matter what you do in life or where you go, you can only do the same things in every country in the world.

'You can go to the pub, get drunk, go to the movies, go play bowling, shoot some pool, take drugs, whatever. It's quite boring. There's nothing there.

'I've been searching for something that's not there. What can you do? You get rich and successful, but you're only gonna go and buy a better car or a better house, but you'll still associate with the same people. Life's pointless, life's shit and if God could take me now, I'd go, like that. But I'm very religious. I read the Bible a lot and someone who takes their own life ain't going to go to heaven. And I'd rather live in this country, this world, than go to hell.'

This was a bizarre, if brutally honest, admission of vulnerability from Fury.

He was clearly plagued by inner conflicts that his happy-go-lucky prizefighter persona had given no hint of.

No doubt his father's imprisonment had deepened Tyson's sense of melancholy, but fortunately he found another focus for his thoughts. The Chisora fight.

HENNESSY took another gamble.

Though he was without a deal with a television broadcaster, he still outbid Frank Warren for the right to promote the Chisora–Fury fight.

Hennessy then had to find a broadcaster to help cover the cost of the promotion.

Channel Five fancied a grudge fight between unbeaten heavyweights would pull in a sizeable audience and Hennessy booked Wembley Arena for 23 July 2011.

Fury had tried to get his hands on Chisora five months earlier.

Ringsiders turned their backs on Frankie Gavin's points win over Young Mutley at London's O2 Arena when they saw Fury approach Chisora.

Fury, incensed by comments Chisora had made in the national press, peeled his shirt off and stabbed a finger at the Londoner.

'Chisora went in the paper saying Mick Hennessy was trying to steal the titles without fighting for them by getting him stripped,' Tyson told me. 'I saw him walk past and said, "When I fight you, I will knock you out." He said, "There's not enough money in the fight," so I ripped my shirt off and said, "I don't fight for money, I fight for honour. Let's have a fight now, the old-fashioned, street-fighting way," and he bottled it.'

It took more than 20 security men to get Fury out of the exits. 'They asked me nicely to leave and I left nicely,' said Tyson. 'It's a good job they didn't try to push me out of the door.

'I paid £100 for the ticket and asked for a refund, but I didn't get it.'

Tyson took his own security along to the press conference to announce the fight with Chisora – a pair of dwarves – and then training started.

'I've locked him in a caravan in my back garden, so I can keep an eye on him,' said Hughie. 'I've taken his phones off him, sent his wife away and told all the cake shops in the area not to let him in.'

The opponent they were training for had a crowding, hooking style, similar to Joe Frazier.

Paul Butlin fought Chisora twice and said, 'Chisora tries to goad you into throwing punches, lets you work and when he thinks you're tired and want a breather, he explodes and starts throwing bombs.'

To prepare, Fury sparred Didier Bence, an unbeaten Canadian with a similar style.

There was a public spar at The Mall shopping centre in Luton 11 days before the fight and in a ring placed between two jewellery shops, a good gathering watched Tyson jab and move. When Bence did get close, he threw him off.

As always, Tyson was chatty and courteous afterwards but at the same time, he seemed distracted and agitated, his soft voice hardened by the thought of the fight. 'I'm going to teach him how to dance,' Tyson told me, sweat gluing his 'Team Fury' T-shirt to his body. 'I'm going to teach him how to dance and teach him some manners.

'I just don't like him. He's a cocky, arrogant prick. I'm going to show him how to fight. Only fighting men should fight. And there's nothing wrong with my toe.'

Earlier that month, David Haye had blamed a broken small toe for his failure to beat Wladimir Klitschko in their heavyweight title unification fight, a claim that Fury appeared to take as an affront to his profession.

He was furious with Chisora as well, calling him 'a coward' and 'a bully' and a telephone press conference a few days before the fight had to be cut short after Tyson threatened to 'kill' him.

Chisora put the phone down. The following day, Tyson apologised but later said, 'He knew he couldn't intimidate me. I got under his skin and he was scared after I offered to fight him at that show. If you bully a bully, he will fold. He couldn't take it.'

Chisora scaled a career-heaviest 18st 9lbs, with Fury weighing 18st 3lbs 8ozs.

'Weighing that much, there was only one way Chisora was going to fight,' said Hughie. 'We knew he would be going for the knockout.'

Not that Tyson was bothered by that. He spent the hours before the fight singing to his wife, joking and, in quieter moments, thinking about his father. He arrived at Wembley Arena early to take a ringside seat for cousin Phill's fight, but his encouragement couldn't prevent a points loss to heavy-handed Peter Vaughan over eight punishing rounds.

A couple of hours later, Tyson was in the spotlight, enjoying every second of his ring walk, wearing a T-shirt that declared, 'I Found Jesus' and singing along to U2's 'I Still Haven't Found What I'm Looking For'.

Chisora, the favourite with the bookmakers and trade paper *Boxing News*, chose an Irish folk jig for his entrance music and after easing himself between the ropes and into the ring, he headed for Fury's corner. Tyson came to meet him and spelled out his intentions before security jumped between them.

Throughout the introductions, Chisora's promoter, Frank Warren, pinched the back of his fighter's gown to hold him back and as referee Victor Loughlin issued his final instructions, a member of Chisora's team looked up at Fury and told him, 'You're not that tall.'

Tyson was that tall, however. He was around eight inches taller than Chisora. 'They were trying to wind up Tyson, make him lose his cool,' said Hughie.

The bell rang and the 4,000 crowd were instantly absorbed. All the shouts seemed to be for Fury. 'Hands up, Tyson', 'Jab him, Tyson', and, less helpfully, 'Kick him in the nuts, Tyson.' Tyson knew what he was doing.

Hughie explained, 'The plan was to throw solid, stiff punches and keep winning the rounds. We knew Chisora would get desperate if, after seven rounds, he had only won a couple. There's always a gameplan, but you also have to weigh opponents up and find out what works when you're in there. Tyson's savvy. He can think while he's fighting.'

Tyson looked so relaxed with his left hand slung low and when Chisora edged his feet into range, he was met with stiff two- and three-punch combinations. The second round was tougher for Fury.

Chisora quickened his feet and waded into him slinging looping hooks. A big swing caught Fury off balance and flung him into a neutral corner. Chisora followed him there and unloaded with both fists. Fury looked disorganised for a moment or two after a right-hand wallop exploded flush in his face, but he soon responded with a thudding combination of punches that made Chisora call off his attack. Tyson escaped to the middle of the ring and grabbed. Hughie asked Tyson at the end of the round, 'What are his punches like?'

Tyson wasn't impressed. 'I knew he was just wasting energy,' said Fury later and by the end of the third, Chisora was spitting out blood from a mouth wound.

Before the fourth, trainer Don Charles told Chisora to jab his way into range – and he didn't. He tried to rush Fury, but his punches were blocked – and Fury went on to dominate the rest of the round. Tyson offered his glove to Chisora at the bell but Chisora pushed past him.

In the final minute of the fifth, Fury started stepping in behind his punches and by the bell, Chisora was looking beaten.

Fury hurt a knuckle on his left hand during that fifth round, but still smiled at Chisora and friends sitting at ringside as he went about his work in the sixth. This time, Chisora touched his glove when it was offered at the bell as the gap between them widened on the scorecards.

At the end of the seventh, Charles threatened to pull Chisora out of the fight and although he started the eighth with another big attack, Tyson didn't take any clean punches and soon had Chisora pinned in a corner. Chisora gestured that Fury's punches were hitting his gloves and spat through his gumshield, 'Come on, come on' at Tyson.

'He was conning me on,' said Fury. 'He wanted me to unload so he could come back with about 25 shots.'

Nothing Chisora was trying was working and before the bell for the tenth round, cut man Dean Powell told him, 'Your titles are going to Manchester.'

Chisora responded with an astonishing burst of non-stop punches.

The sheer volume of blows appeared to take Fury by surprise, but hardly any landed and the row of ringsiders who had leapt to their feet when the onslaught started were soon back in their seats as Tyson took charge of the centre of the ring.

Fury did most of the punching in the last two rounds and at the final bell, he raised his arms in triumph, while Chisora headed to his corner.

The judges were in agreement with Fury – and everyone else – and scored the fight 118-111 and 117-112 (twice).

'I knew nobody could beat me that night,' said Tyson. 'Whatever he did, I knew I would have the answer. I would adapt and beat him. I was ready to box him, lean on, work the body, go toe to toe, bully him like he has bullied opponents.

'I knew he couldn't beat me. That's why I was asking for the fight for two years.

'I was joking, laughing, playing to the crowd. I was as relaxed as I would be in the gym just playing around.

'I was too big for him. He can fight. He had shown he could block and slip shots and was a clever fighter. But a good big 'un always wins!'

Hennessy had a spring in his step afterwards. 'If we have about five or six outings on terrestrial television, he's going to be a household name for sure,' he said.

THE Chisora fight went as well as could have been hoped.

Fury had turned what looked like a 50/50 fight into an exhibition of his skills and playful personality in front of a peak TV viewing audience of around three million.

A couple of weeks afterwards, Hughie invited me up to Lancaster to tell me how he and Tyson did it.

Except Tyson wasn't there.

An increasingly agitated Hughie ran through a list of possible explanations for his absence. 'New cake shop opened' was among them.

Eventually, Tyson walked in – hair dyed blonde.

As ever, he was good company, happy to talk through the fight and boxing in general. He flicked through the internet looking for fights and fighters to talk about and then picked up the phone and started dialling.

Tyson enquired about a second-hand car he had found on a website and after failing to get the seller to reduce his price, he put the phone down shaking his head.

'Worth a try,' said Fury.

At that time, Fury had a date for his next fight, 17 September, at the Kings Hall in Belfast, but there was no opponent to talk about.

Taxi driver-turned-fan-favourite Martin Rogan reportedly rejected £55,000 to fight Fury and David Price also wasn't interested.

Price had a British title eliminator against John McDermott scheduled, with the winner to face Fury.

There were only about two weeks left before the show when Tyson's opponent was confirmed.

Nicolai Firtha was a 32-year-old from Akron, Ohio, who had won 20 of his 29 fights (one draw), but was best known for one of his eight losses.

Nine months previously, he had been the full ten rounds with Alexander Povetkin, the bustling, heavy-handed Russian who had gone on to claim the vacant WBA heavyweight championship by outpointing Russian southpaw Ruslan Chagaev.

Fury saw the fight with Firtha as an opportunity to measure himself against Povetkin.

The loss to Povetkin was Firtha's only defeat in his previous five fights and he saw the Fury fight as an opportunity, rather than a payday.

At 6ft 6ins and around 18 stones, Firtha had the size to give Fury problems and there was a chance he would have some support in Belfast as his mother was Irish.

Belfast is a boxing city. Every taxi driver seems to have boxed as an amateur, or at the very least has a boxing story, and the atmosphere at the Kings Hall was one of feverish anticipation when Fury and Firtha clashed.

The sell-out crowd and millions watching on Channel 5 saw an exciting fight.

THE opening two rounds were one-sided. Fury soon bloodied Firtha's nose with jabs and had him grabbing desperately several times.

Firtha tried a few rushing attacks but Fury simply shifted his feet and walked him on to punches.

Fury simply looked too good – until midway through the third round.

He made the mistake of dropping his hands and squaring himself up, and Firtha punished him for it, whipping over a right hand that caught Tyson flush in the face. Firtha kept throwing and his next two punches crashed on to Fury's jaw.

The force of the punches made Tyson step back and his knee dipped dramatically, signalling he was hurt.

This was Firtha's chance and he went for Fury, pushing him to the ropes and putting maximum power into every punch.

Fury grabbed hold of Firtha, took a right uppercut when they separated and grabbed again while the crowd screamed. 'Take a point,' implored Firtha's corner.

There were signs in the final 30 seconds of the round that Fury's head had cleared and just before the bell, he had his successes in an exciting exchange of punches.

Hughie stayed calm in Tyson's corner, telling him to box from the outside, but within seconds of the fight restarting Fury sensed Firtha was tired, having put so much into the previous round, and went on the attack.

Under fire, Firtha tried to grab on to Fury but slid to his knees and the referee started to count. Firtha dragged himself up and to his huge relief, the bell rang before another punch could be thrown.

Firtha recovered well enough during the minute's break to hurl a right hand early in the fifth that smacked Fury on the chin.

Tyson ignored it and when his own right hand landed moments later, Firtha started to come apart.

His legs shuddered and Fury didn't let him recover. For the next minute or so, every punch Fury threw found Firtha's chin until a final looping right hand convinced referee John Keane he had taken enough.

Afterwards, Fury was quick to compare his performance against Fitha with Povetkin's.

'Povetkin hit him with every shot in the book,' he told Channel 5 viewers. 'It shows little men are little men and big men are big men. Stay out of my way!

'Once I get my jab working, nobody in the world will be able to deal with it.'

CHAPTER 7

Turning Point

TYSON FURY was troubled.

'There is a name for what I have, where one minute I'm happy and the next minute I'm sad, like commit-suicide sad. And for no reason. Nothing's changed,' he told *The Guardian*.

'I think I need a psychiatrist because I do believe I am mentally disturbed in some way.

'Maybe it was the fact that when I was a kid, we didn't have a family life. My mother and father were always shouting and screaming and hitting each other. My dad had different women and different kids down the road. My mum had 14 pregnancies, but only four of us survived. We had a little sister born for a few days and then she died. That would affect you.

'I do sometimes think life is pointless. One minute I'm over the moon and the next minute I feel like getting in the car and running it into a wall at 100mph. I don't know what's wrong with me. I'm messed up.'

Fury was talking before he defended the Commonwealth title against Neven Pajkic in Manchester in November 2011.

'I know this is terrible and I shouldn't say it,' he confided, 'but I'm in the mode to do serious damage.

'When I go in there, I'm trying to put my fist through the back of his head. I'm trying to break his ribs and make them stick out the other side. This kid has said some terrible things.'

Tyson explained the root of the bad feeling.

He remembered going to see Pajkic fight in Canada and said, 'As he was leaving the ring, I shouted, "Let's get it on! You're useless, I can beat you with one hand." He started laughing and walked away. I said, "You had better walk away" and he turned round and threw a towel at me. We were going to get stuck in, but about 50 people pulled us apart.

'We've called each other out since then. It's a grudge fight.'

The feeling was mutual. Pajkic called Fury 'a classless piece of shit'.

Fury became a father again weeks before the fight. Paris gave birth to son Prince John James and there was another split from his uncle Hughie.

Tyson decided to bring in a strength and conditioning coach but Hughie objected and there was a parting.

Tyson told me there would be more work on rowing machines and less weight lifting and running. 'Running didn't do Sugar Ray Robinson any harm,' countered Hughie.

Chris Johnson, bronze medallist for Canada at the 1992 Olympics and beaten only at the highest level in his 30-fight professional career, took on the trainer's job.

Fury and Johnson had done some work together in Canada and gelled.

'He focuses a lot of his training work on combinations,' said Fury. 'He's also experienced in teaching that American-style slipping and sliding technique of avoiding punches. This will help with my defence.'

Fury said Johnson would only train him for the Pajkic fight but was hopeful that if all went well, they could keep working together.

Pajkic was the Canadian champion, had won all 16 fights and was, according to Fury, 'an all action, Rocky fighter with no defence'.

'He just walks in throwing punches,' said Fury. 'He's a pressure fighter with no power.

'He's coming for a war. He wants to engage in a toe-to-toe brawl but I'm bigger, stronger and faster, so how's he going to beat me?'

There were moments during the second round of their fight when it looked like Pajkic might beat Fury.

PAJKIC was around six inches shorter at 6ft 3ins and technically levels below Fury.

He either rushed in with his head down chucking punches without looking where he was throwing them or stood off looking to slip Fury's jab and hurl rights at his jaw.

The first round was messy and Johnson wasn't entirely happy with Fury. He wanted to see more jabs from him and also advised, 'Step back and time the right hand.'

Fury got his jab working in the second and felt in control enough to raise his arms after landing a volley.

Then Firtha slung a looping right hand – and Fury landed on the seat of his trunks.

Up quickly, Tyson looked more annoyed than hurt as the referee completed the 'eight' count, but still, Pajkic took huge encouragement from the knockdown and poured on punches after the fight resumed.

Fury grabbed hold of Pajkic and once his head cleared, he started punching with him.

Pajkic connected with another right hand that had Tyson holding at the bell.

Fury had got through the crisis and during the minute's break between rounds, he looked to be in better shape than Firtha.

Firtha had put a lot into trying to finish Fury and was gulping in air.

Fury came out for the third jabbing positively and then let go a right hand that steadied Firtha.

Firtha wrapped himself around Fury but Tyson wriggled his right arm free and smashed him to his knees with four clobbering blows.

Firtha picked himself up and tried to slug his way out of trouble. Fury stood his ground and kept finding Firtha's chin with clean punches until he dropped in a heap.

The fight wasn't over yet. Firtha, nicknamed 'No Surrender' for a reason, dragged himself off the canvas again, only for referee Phil Edwards to step in a few seconds later after Fury had him wobbling with a clean right uppercut that Tyson later said 'would have knocked a big-rig down'.

Pajkic was furious. He wanted to carry on fighting and Fury seemed happy enough to oblige him until the corners entered the ring.

'I watched the fight on tape,' said Fury a few weeks later, 'and there was no boxing. It was just a slugging match, a shoot-out. I enjoyed it.'

THE 17th straight win of Fury's career felt like a defeat.

In his changing room afterwards, he stretched out on a bench and put his hands on his head. 'I quit,' he said to nobody in particular. 'I'm finished with boxing. I'm never going to be heavyweight champion of the world.' He touched his chin. 'I can't take a punch.'

Chris Eubank jr heard every word. The son of two-weight world champion Chris, he shared a changing room with Fury ahead of his professional debut.

He asked what happened – and Fury told him.

'You got up and knocked him out ?' said Eubank. 'You're a fighter, you're a champion.'

The disappointment Fury felt wouldn't go away and he found himself at the crossroads.

The year 2011 was a breakthrough year for him. He won the British and Commonwealth titles to climb up to number seven in the WBC rankings, but the wobbles against Firtha and Pajkic had made him wonder if he really wanted to fight again.

He was weighing a blubbery 23 stones and was still unsure whether he had found the right trainer.

'I looked in the mirror one day and I thought, "It's not for me, this, I'm going to do something else or get in proper shape,"' he said.

'I spun a coin – heads or tails, box or not box – and boxing won, so I decided to get myself in proper shape.'

Fury had concerns other than boxing.

'I came home one night and he [son Prince] looked perfect to me,' said Tyson. 'But Paris said, "No, he's stopped breathing, he keeps stopping breathing." I thought, "Don't be daft." But when I looked at him again, he was holding his breath for something like 40 seconds at a time, going blue in the face.

'We phoned for the ambulance and thankfully, they got to the house quickly. They put a heart monitor on Prince and noticed his heart rate had gone really, really low. They put him on the breathing machine there and then.

'He was in Doncaster Hospital for a few days. But he looked fine, as if nothing was wrong with him.

'People said he would be OK in a couple of days, so I left to take care of a bit of business at home.

'I was at the house when the phone rang and it was my wife telling me to get back to the hospital immediately because Prince had taken a turn for the worse.

'I thought she was exaggerating. You know what women can be like.

'But he was being rushed to the special care unit for children in Sheffield.

'He was unconscious when I got there and I wasn't expecting that at all. He was in a pod with wires and tubes everywhere. I was expecting to see a snotty-nosed little baby. Then, when I saw him a matter of hours later, he was [still] unconscious. He had lost a lot of weight and had black rings around his eyes. It was horrible. I went into shock.

'I didn't leave the hospital for ten days. Like so many other parents in the same position, I slept there, I ate there and I prayed there.

'We nearly lost him three times.

'Three times his heart stopped and three times the brilliant staff at the hospital pulled him through. No one can put into words the sense of relief, the sheer joy. I felt like I had been in a training camp for two years.'

Fury's next training camp would be with a new trainer.

SHORTLY after the Pajkic fight, Tyson told *Boxing News* he was in good spirits and had put the gloom that had enveloped him during his previous interview with the publication down to a death in the family.

'An uncle of mine just passed away and he was only 60,' he explained, 'and you don't realise how lucky you are until someone goes.

'I've got nothing to be depressed about. I'm 17-0, I've a lovely family, a lovely wife and I'm young.

'You can't buy youth and happiness. I'm on top of the world right now.'

He also revealed he was looking for a new trainer after deciding Johnson wasn't right for him.

'I might have a crack at Freddie Roach, Emanuel Steward or Joe Gallagher,' he said.

Fury ended up with another uncle, Peter, after John Fury arranged a meeting at Rochdale's Buckley Hall prison, where he was being held.

Peter was no stranger to prisons.

'I was wild when I was younger,' he said. 'I'd see someone walking down the street with a nice pair of trainers on and want to have a fight with them.

'Then anyone who wanted protection would come to me because I was seen as a tough young fella. They'd say, "This one or that one's picking on me." So you get dragged into a world where you don't belong.

'One thing led to another.

'I went from looking after people to looking after areas to looking after cities.

'Then, bang! You're involved with something without even having the realisation of what you're getting into.

'I lost my way.'

Fury had two spells in prison totalling around nine years, firstly for possession of and conspiracy to supply amphetamines and then for drug-related money laundering.

Peter described his spells in prison as 'hell on earth'.

'That man sat next to you can easily put a knife through your neck because they're in for life and are in despair with nothing to lose.

'You're on a knife edge. They soon get to know if you can fight and stand up for yourself. If you are weak in prison, then you quickly get found out. People get molested in there, used for wives and all sorts.

'I was regarded as dangerous, so I was locked up with IRA members and lifers. It was like being in the dark for 24 hours a day.

'I did have a few fights because you're locked up with 1,800 to 2,000 inmates who are all doing weights and think they're it.

'But I found fighting a way of release.

'I remember one visit with the wife where my hands were smashed to pieces.

'You can get beaten up in prison. You can get stabbed. But you can get all that on the streets as well. I'd dealt with that growing up.

'You sweat blood and tears in those cells and all these people who stick their chests out and say jail is easy are lying because there is nothing worse than being away from your home and family.

'But I took no drugs inside and kept myself super fit. I was in the gym for four hours a day for eight or nine years.

'If I could've been in the same condition I was in in prison when I boxed pro, I'd have been an excellent fighter.'

As it is, the record books show Peter had one professional fight and lost it.

Boxing only four days after his 20th birthday, he retired after the second round of what he remembered as 'a real slugfest' with journeyman David Jules and blamed 'fitness issues' for the defeat.

'In the dressing room afterwards, the doc discovered my blood pressure had risen so high that he referred me to the hospital for checks,' said Peter.

'I exerted too much effort and quickly discovered that you can't box professionally when you're three or four stones overweight! Our family always put on weight. That was my downfall as a young man.'

Peter found he was better at training fighters. He said that with his help, big brother John, Tyson's father, was fit enough to throw 'around a million punches' at Cesare Di Benedetto during a ten-round fight.

Peter was an altogether less intense character than his elder brothers, John and Hughie, but had an air of quiet authority about him.

American President Theodore Roosevelt once said, 'Speak softly and carry a big stick, you will go far,' and that was Peter's way.

He got the best out of John and his own son, Hughie.

'From a little boy at the age of five or six, you could see he [Hughie] had a real gift for it, I remember telling the wife that,' said Peter. 'And he always loved to train. You had to stop him.

'I wear the trousers in my house and, even when I was sent away, I instructed my wife to get Hughie fighting [boxing] as soon as he was able.

'I wanted him to get as many amateur fights as he could so that he got used to stepping inside that ring.

'During his mid-teens, Hughie was unhappy at the lack of coaching he was receiving in England so, upon my release, I arranged for him to come over to me in France, then Spain. I took him on full time, got him on a diet and he just went from strength to strength.'

Hughie won national honours with his father in his corner and Peter then turned his attention to his nephew.

TYSON remembered his first days training with Peter as 'mental and physical torture'.

He said, 'When I went to Peter, I was 296lbs and he made me run every day with a sweat suit on and a 10kg vest. He'd start by putting me on a running machine and I was so tired after about ten or 15 minutes, it was unbelievable.

'He'd put it on inclines, up and down the hills, and I'd be crying on the machine. What am I doing? Do I want this?'

'Then I'd have to get off there and do 30 minutes of skipping and he'd be on me all the time, making me double up every minute or so.

'I struggled and battled and we were doing circuits and stuff. I just knuckled down and thought, "If I pass out, I pass out. I'm not too bothered. They can chuck some water on me until I come round."

'I never want to give up on myself. If I start a run, I'm going to finish it, no matter if I'm dying or my legs are broke. If I aim to do 50 of something, I'll do it.'

Peter was far from impressed by his nephew when he started working with him.

'For a start, he had no balance or footwork, no defence,' said Peter. 'What he did have was a fighter's mentality, the heart of a lion, natural toughness and a good punch.'

The fight Peter had to train his nephew for was a huge one, against David Price, his former amateur adversary.

Price had become his mandatory challenger for the British title with a 73-second stoppage of John McDermott, a result that compared well with Fury's performances against him.

The question wasn't just who would win the fight between Fury and Price, but who would promote it.

Price was promoted by Maloney and boxed on Sky Sports, while Fury fought on Hennessy's shows, which were screened on Channel 5.

Who promoted the show would be decided by who tabled the highest purse bid – unless a private deal could be reached.

Hennessy offered Price £100,000 to fight Fury on Channel 5. His previous best purse was around £30,000 for the McDermott fight, but still, Price turned it down.

Maloney ended up winning the purse bids, but Fury gave up the belts rather than box on Sky Sports.

Maloney branded Fury 'a chicken' but the truth was, Fury would have fought Price – and Price would have been handsomely paid – but Maloney didn't want the fight on a rival television channel.

Fury instead fought for the vacant Irish title, against 40-year-old Martin Rogan.

Until he was 28 years old, Rogan was a hurler, taxi driver and part-time actor but, motivated by the murder of a close friend during the Troubles, he ended up as an Irish version of Rocky Marciano. Rogan came from nowhere to claim a breakthrough win in the inaugural *Prizefighter* – an eight-man tournament where the winner of three, three-round fights claimed the top prize – and then willed himself on to a ten-round points victory over Audley Harrison.

Rogan took great satisfaction from the fact that when he watched Harrison win Olympic gold in Sydney in 2000, he had yet to even lace on a pair of gloves.

By the time he faced Fury, Rogan had been inactive for 17 months and was, in Tyson's opinion, a good opponent to 'experiment on'.

Fury was easing his way in with a new trainer and wanted to try new things against an opponent who would make him work, but lose.

In the build-up to the Rogan fight, the Furys visited several gyms, including Clifton Mitchell's in Derby and the Ingles' in Sheffield.

Fury didn't say too much about his preparations, but Rogan was talkative.

'I don't believe he's got a lot of heart,' he said. 'He's been hurt several times and is always looking outside the ring for people to help him. They'll just be me and him and, trust me, I'll not be helping.'

Rogan promised to 'dominate him physically and I'm going to dominate his thoughts'.

Fury did say at a press conference, 'I've locked myself away and won't have seen my family for 15 weeks by the time of the fight. I've never put myself through this much training. I've been to hell and back and I've done that because I want to be in fantastic shape, get to world title level and then stay there as long as I want.'

Fury added, 'If I can't beat Martin Rogan, I have no chance of winning the world title. I will have to go and shine Martin's shoes for a living!'

The final press conference was good-natured. Rogan did a Frank Carson impression and both ended up singing.

Boxing News predicted a give-and-take thriller. They were wrong.

THE Fury who fought Rogan was a very different fighter to the one David Price had described as 'an accident waiting to happen'.

This Fury didn't stand and trade. He boxed and moved.

'I couldn't get near him,' shrugged Rogan after being stopped in the fifth round.

Fury weighed a career-lightest 17st 7lbs 12ozs and to the surprise of everyone, he boxed almost the entire fight as a southpaw.

He had switched stances during fights before, but against Rogan, Tyson mostly fought out of the left-handed stance.

The thinking was that it was the right hand that kept catching Tyson, but if he fought as a southpaw and put his weight on his back foot rather than leaning in behind a left jab, the right hand would have further to travel.

Against Rogan, it worked. Fury was just about punch perfect.

He got on the back foot to make Rogan fall short with his shots and when Fury sensed the time was right, he started stepping in behind his punches.

He dropped Rogan in the third with a right-left and the finishing punch was a scything left hook to the ribs in the fifth that left Rogan on his knees, his face screwed up in agony.

He was able to shake off the pain well enough to beat the count, but in the referee's opinion there was no point letting the fight continue.

'I didn't see the final punch coming,' said Rogan afterwards. 'He set it up really well and who knew he was going to come out as a southpaw?

'Tyson will go far in this game.'

Fury, the fast-food munching, fun-loving Traveller who loved a good scrap, had got serious.

NEXT up was Vinny Maddalone, an Italian-American clubfighter from New York who was beaten whenever he went anywhere near world class, but always fought his heart out. *Boxing News* once said of Maddalone that he would top any poll of boxing's most exciting fighters.

He had trainers who tried to change him, convince him there was another way to box that would hurt less and bring greater rewards, but Maddalone was Maddalone, just a big, tough guy who liked to fight and, at 38, nobody was going to change him now.

This looked to be a sideways step for Fury, but still, a good match.

Maddalone was slow-footed and hittable, made for the new Fury.

Fury trained for the fight in Belgium 'to keep out of the way', but still, drama followed him.

He was pulled over by police while driving to camp and arrested on suspicion of murder and robbery following a hold-up nearby in which a man was shot dead. Fury and four members of his team were subjected to a nine-hour interrogation after being forced to strip to their underpants in a local police cell.

Fury said, 'When we were stopped on the way to the gym, I thought I must have been driving too fast.

'But they ordered us out of the car, told us to kneel at gunpoint, handcuffed us behind our backs, put forensic gloves on us and then made us lie face down in the dirt. I heard a police helicopter arrive overhead.

'They were shouting at us in Dutch. I didn't understand a word. I kept telling them I was a boxer in training for a big fight but they wouldn't listen. We were taken to the station and had to strip.

'Apart from the shock, I wasn't too worried because I knew it was mistaken identity.

'We had just happened to fit the description of the gang of large men they were desperate to catch.'

'They stopped us at nine in the morning and they eventually let us go at eight in the evening. They apologised and gave us flip flops and paper sheets to wrap ourselves in so we could walk back to the car.

'We got our clothes back three days later. It was startling, but strange things do happen in life.'

Fury reported that, despite the disruption, he was 'in the best shape of my life' and when he got on the scales, he weighed 17st 7lbs 8ozs, the lightest of his professional career.

The fight with Maddalone was held in Clevedon, in Somerset, in what Channel 5 commentator Dave Farrar remembered as 'a cow shed'.

He added, 'There was a young farmer's party in an adjacent building and it was dark, there were no lights. It was an edgy night.'

Not for Fury it wasn't. He hit Maddalone at will with jabs, body shots and uppercuts, opening a gash on his left cheekbone in the fourth before the referee decided the fight had become too one-sided in the next round.

Fury had been thoroughly dominant, walking Maddalone on to accurate punches and on the rare occasions the American did get inside, Fury stopped him working.

'My job is to not let them get close,' Tyson said afterwards, 'and if they do get there, 17½ stones leans on them and pushes them down until the referee says, "Break" and they get nothing off.'

FURY didn't have to fight to make headlines.

Channel 5 spotted him – he was hard to miss – at ringside when stablemate James DeGale defended his European super middleweight title against hard Frenchman Hadillah Mohoumadi and, of course, Tyson was happy to give his opinion on David Price's 82-second blast-out of Audley Harrison earlier that night.

'Watch this,' he whispered to Clifton Mitchell, sitting next to him as the interviewer approached.

Tyson described Harrison as 'the biggest bum inside boxing' and stabbing a finger at the camera, he turned his attention to Price and said, 'I'm going to do you some serious harm, you big, stiff idiot.

'You are getting it for sure and you know your gay lover Tony Bellew, I will fight him in between rounds.'

The interview was terminated before he could say anything else, but not before Fury had stolen a few headlines from Price.

CHAPTER 8

Into World Class

'I'M GOING to be heavyweight champion of the world,' Tyson Fury told a friend with complete confidence.

He stretched his arms out to reveal a reach that was measured from finger to fingertip at 85 inches. 'With arms this long,' Tyson reasoned, 'who's going to be able to hit me ?'

The mission for Fury was to rid boxing of the Klitschko brothers, Wladimir and Vitali.

From Kazakhstan, part of the former Soviet Union, Vitali was the elder sibling, a fighter considered the less talented of the brothers but who nonetheless had two spells as heavyweight champion.

Under Emanuel Steward, Wladimir, a gold medallist at the 1996 Olympics in Atlanta, had tightened his defences and developed what Steward described as 'a magic left hand' to keep opponents under control.

They had been the world's dominant heavyweights since the retirement of Lennox Lewis. It was a cuts win over Vitali in 2003 that convinced Lewis the time was right to retire. After six rounds, Klitschko led on two scorecards but two cuts over his left eye were deemed too bad for him to continue.

The brothers were cerebral, well mannered and good for boxing – or so most thought.

'I don't like either Klitschko,' said Fury. 'They are bad for boxing. I can't stand them and the sooner I get rid of them, the better.

'They jab someone to death and when they have them hurt, they don't jump on them and finish them.

'Wladimir is a disaster waiting to happen. Now Emanuel's gone, he has no proper advice in his ear.'

Steward died in October 2012, leaving one of his fighters, heavyweight Johnathon Banks, in charge.

Klitschko boxed only two weeks after Steward's death and outpointed Poland's Mariusz Wach in Hamburg.

The rumours were, Vitali would retire to concentrate on his political career before Fury could get his hands on him and with Wladimir approaching his 37th birthday, the world wondered who the next dominant heavyweight would be.

American fight fans, without a world heavyweight champion since Shannon Briggs held the WBO belt for seven months in 2006–07, pinned their hopes on former footballer Seth Mitchell and 2008 Olympic bronze medallist Deontay Wilder, while in Britain, it was Price and Fury.

Ever since the fight with Price fell through, Fury had been bombarded with unpleasant messages on Twitter and they became more regular following his outburst on Channel 5. Fury estimated that '99 per cent' of the messages he received on social media were abusive.

He was obviously keen to provoke, but much of his abuse was racist.

'It's no secret that gypsies ain't the most liked race in the country,' he said. 'In fact, they are probably the most hated. When people say, "What do you know about gypsies?", the words that come out are, "Dirty, rob people, steal stuff" – that's the persona people think about.

'They think we steal children, put spells on you and will take anything.'

Fury confessed that living on the fringes of society had its advantages for a professional boxer.

'People are scared of Travellers,' he said. 'No one wants to go out there and have a bareknuckle fight with one. They'll stand there and have it for ten hours non-stop.'

Of Fury and Price, Fury was closer to a world title shot. He was ranked number three by the WBC and there was talk that should he beat the fighter ranked one place below him, Denis Boytsov, in Belfast in December 2012, Fury would then meet the winner of the forthcoming Bermane Stiverne–Chris Arreola fight with the vacant WBC title on the line, should, as expected, Klitschko retire.

Boytsov was pulled out of the fight by his promoters four weeks before the show, leaving Hennessy with a headache.

THE answer to his headache proved to be Kevin 'Kingpin' Johnson, a 33-year-old from Atlanta, Georgia, beaten only by Vitali Klitschko, in a challenge for the WBC title in Switzerland in December 2009, and Tor Hamer in 31 fights (one draw).

The loss to Hamer came over the three-round distance in *Prizefighter*, which didn't really suit Johnson, a boxer who didn't fight with a lot of urgency and whose focus was on defence rather than attack.

'It was hard to hit him,' said Klitschko after dominating him over 12 rounds. 'He was very defensive.'

Johnson put his negative showing that night down to a bicep injury that was aggravated early in the fight.

He won his next five, including a bubble-bursting stoppage of Aussie slugger Alex Leapai, before entering *Prizefighter*, a tournament he might have won had he really wanted to.

Johnson stood 6ft 3ins tall – so around six inches shorter than Fury – but had beaten an opponent bigger than Tyson.

Julius Long, outpointed by Johnson over eight rounds, was a towering 7ft 1in, but a long way off world class. Johnson took the Fury fight at only three weeks' notice – and did his best to sell it.

'I'll beat Fury so bad, he'll want to retire,' he promised. 'Fury's just not in my class.'

Johnson did look to be the best opponent Fury had faced yet. He had had only had 16 amateur bouts but learned much from Larry Holmes in the gym. Johnson would claim his jab was the best the heavyweight division had seen since Holmes was in his 1980s pomp and he developed a cross-armed defence that was hard to penetrate.

The only question mark about him was his desire. Johnson was in demand as a sparring partner and as sparring partners have to, he learned how to keep himself safe and get through rounds. There were times during the Klitschko fight when it seemed Johnson had settled for keeping himself safe and losing on points. He didn't show much desire to win the rounds.

Still, he was a seasoned, quality operator and such were his credentials, the WBC made his fight with Fury an eliminator for its world title.

'Johnson is just the kind of opponent that I want at this stage of my career,' said Fury.

'We needed a world-class fighter and we have got one, and when I take him apart the world will sit up and take notice.

'I'm not going around getting opponents out of graveyards, fighting guys well past their best, like some other heavyweights in Britain. I'm taking on Kevin Johnson, who has fought for a major world title and been the distance with Vitali Klitschko.

'I am getting closer to a shot at Klitschko myself and I'm going to show Vitali why he has to fight me because when I do a number on Johnson and get him out of there, I'll have done a better job than Vitali did on him.'

The remark about 'fighting guys well past their best' was aimed at David Price.

The night before Fury took on Johnson, Price defended his British and Commonwealth titles against 45-year-old Matt Skelton.

Price took less than two rounds to overpower Skelton and the expectation was that Fury would be made to work much harder by Johnson.

FURY set up camp for the fight in Essen, on the border between Belgium and the Netherlands, where Peter had a spacious house with a swimming pool and tennis courts which, in Clifton Mitchell's estimation, was worth around £750,000.

Mitchell described the house as being 'in the middle of nowhere, surrounded by fields' and the Furys would drive to a weights gym and another where they would spar kickboxers such as David Ghita and Rico Verhoeven.

'They are very good in their boxing ability because they are top, world-level fighters,' said Peter. 'It's excellent work.

'I think a lot of people are going to be shocked by just how good he [Tyson] looks and the performance he gives. It's going to be a world-class performance and every other fighter in the heavyweight division will see that.'

Fury had told his followers on Twitter six weeks before the fight that he was weighing 18½ stone, with 8.4 per cent body fat.

BOXING News, and just about everyone else, fancied Fury to beat Johnson on points. Johnson was known for being negative and durable,

Fury was known for his skills rather than his punch. Every story ever written about Johnson made mention of his jab, but Fury had a better one.

Tyson came out at the opening bell firing his left hand at Johnson and though he didn't land everything he threw, the steady stream of punches gave Johnson enough to think about to stop him firing much back.

There was a bit more urgency from Johnson after he felt Fury hit him with some rabbit punches in the second.

Johnson had a spell of pressure, let his right hand go, but again, Fury won the round with his jab.

Johnson turned to ringsiders at the end of the third round and said, 'I got him, I got him,' but that wasn't how it looked. Fury's fists and feet were flowing – and Johnson was struggling to land anything. 'He's long,' Johnson would say afterwards, 'very long, longer than you think.' Because of that, Johnson's punches were falling short and Fury kept peppering away with jabs and combinations, keeping Johnson guessing where the next attack was coming from.

There was a bit more from Johnson in the fifth. He got his feet closer and sent right hands fizzing just past Fury's chin, and in Tyson's corner at the end of the round there was some concern.

The feeling was, Fury was letting Johnson into the fight and Fury's response was to start the sixth with a two-fisted bombardment.

Johnson did a good job of keeping his chin out of harm's way but still, there was no question who was in control of the fight at the halfway stage.

Fury was docked a point in the seventh for punching on the break but otherwise won the session with his jab.

Such was Fury's grip on the fight at this stage, the only question appeared to be whether Tyson would tire.

That seemed to be Johnson's only hope, to pray Fury would capitulate the way Leapai had against him.

The pace remained the same in the eighth. Fury's punches were still sharp and he kept them coming in threes and fours.

There was much to admire about Fury's boxing, his movement, jab and combinations, but the Belfast crowd wanted more drama.

There were boos during the ninth that were surely aimed at Johnson, for what was presumably perceived as a lack of effort.

The truth was, Fury had stopped him fighting.

Fury wouldn't stand still long enough for Johnson to hit him and when Fury did stand still, he was too far away to hit.

Nevertheless, referee Howard Foster reminded both ahead of the tenth round, 'You're being paid to fight.'

Johnson looked like he wanted to fight. He quickened his feet and looked to press Fury back, but whenever he shaped to let his hands go, Fury beat him to the punch and moved off.

The advice to Fury ahead of the 11th was, 'Take no chances – he's desperate.' Tyson fired off combination after combination to keep Johnson on the defensive and went back to his stool smiling.

The job was almost done.

Johnson wasn't exactly desperate in the last but did throw more right hands. They missed and Fury countered with flurries of punches.

The decision was a formality, the three judges giving the fight to Fury by scores of 119-110 and 119-108 (twice).

'I boxed to a game plan,' said Fury afterwards. 'I outboxed him.'

The following morning, Peter boarded an aeroplane to Armenia, where his son, Hughie, was boxing in the final of the World Junior Championships.

Hughie had reached the final with four wins in seven days and came home with the gold medal after boxing his way to a 10-6 win over Narender Berwal, from India.

CHAPTER 9

The Big Apple

NEXT WAS what Fury described as 'the pinnacle' of his boxing career.

Tyson was a boxing obsessive and would claim to know more about the sport, and heavyweight boxing especially, than any other fighter.

The 24-year-old knew whose footsteps he was following in when he fought former IBF cruiserweight champion Steve Cunningham at Madison Square Garden on 20 April 2013.

The first fight to ever be held at the original Madison Square Garden in 1882 involved a British fighter.

The prize to anyone who could last four rounds with the formidable bareknuckle champion John L. Sullivan, the most famous sportsman of the day, was $1,000 and a share of the gate receipts.

Unlike most Irish-Americans, Richard Kyle Fox, proprietor of the leading sports paper the *Police Gazette*, was no fan of Sullivan's and wanted to find someone who could last the four rounds with him, or better still, beat him.

Fox turned to England and in Leicester he found an old prizefighter and street scrapper called Tug Wilson.

Wilson accepted the challenge but when he arrived in the States, Fox's heart sank.

Wilson – real name Joseph Collins – looked pudgy and confessed he had not fought competitively for years.

But he was smart. Wilson ducked and dodged, barely threw a punch and when he felt he had no other option, he threw himself on the floor to eat up a few more seconds.

The crowd booed but Wilson made it through the four rounds, collected his money and earned more on the vaudeville circuit around America, telling audiences of how he fooled the mighty Sullivan. By the time he returned to England, Wilson had earned several thousand dollars, enough to open a boot and shoe store in his home city.

Wilson did promise Fox he would return to America for a rematch with O'Sullivan, but that was never his intention.

Jack Dempsey gave Madison Square Garden fans rather better value for money in the 1920s and half a century on, Muhammad Ali and Joe Frazier shared two fights there, setting up *The Thrilla In Manila*. Gerry Cooney was an Irish-American heavyweight who was always a big attraction at Madison Square Garden and he left-hooked former champion Ken Norton to defeat there in only 54 seconds in May 1981, securing a shot at WBC champion Larry Holmes.

Cooney was beaten in 13 rounds.

Ahead of Fury–Cunningham, Cooney met Fury and gave him advice on how to deal with fame.

Tyson Fury, it seemed, was going to be famous.

THE fight with Cunningham wasn't anywhere near the magnitude of the Ali–Frazier duels and was held in the Garden's theatre rather than the main arena, but still, it promised to have a significant bearing on the immediate future of the heavyweight division.

With Fury ranked number eight by the IBF and Cunningham four places below him, the sanctioning body made the fight an eliminator for their number two spot.

The expectation was the winner of Fury–Cunningham would go on to face Kubrat Pulev for the right to meet Wladimir Klitschko.

Almost as importantly for Fury, given his need for attention, the fight would be screened live on free-to-air television in both America and Britain. NBC was hoping for an audience of ten million and Channel Five expected two million to tune in.

Fury would give viewers what he later described as 'a real gun fight'.

REPORTERS squeezed into Jack Dempsey's Irish Bar in New York for a press conference and they mostly listened to Fury.

The opening exchanges were cordial enough.

Cunningham accepted the size of the task in front of him.

He stood 6ft 3ins tall and weighed barely 15 stones, while Fury was 6ft 8¾ins tall and was expected to scale around 18 stones.

'A lot of guys don't want to get in the ring with a giant, but I'm a fighter,' said Cunningham, nicknamed USS in recognition of his time spent in the Navy.

'I grew up in Philly. I had the threat of getting shot going to school. We still went to school. There's no fear in me. I don't fear getting hit. I don't fear losing.'

Fury insisted on a round of applause for Cunningham for taking the fight but then said, 'This is a heavyweight v a light-heavyweight. I'm going to retire you, Steve. This is a three-hit fight. I hit him, he hits the floor, Tyson Fury hits New York.

'I was wondering if the bottom of Steve's boots have been sponsored. As there's going to be a lot of people watching around the world, I would like to put my Twitter account on the bottom of them.'

Cunningham rolled his eyes while reporters laughed and responded, 'The guys who talk a lot, they're chumps.

'The only reason he's winning fights is because he's big. Shrink him down to 6ft 4ins, 6ft 3ins, 6ft 2ins and he's garbage. I've been in camp with the Klitschkos and they're big, but they work hard, they are skilful. If they were normal size, they would still be champions. But this dude is just winning fights because he's big. He leans on guys, he gets them tired. I get better.'

Fury replied that as well as being tall, he was also 'dark and handsome' and got on his feet for a stream-of-consciousness rant.

'I'm the best fighter in the world at all weights,' he said. 'There's not a man born from his mother can beat Tyson Fury. I don't care if he's 7ft or 3ft.

'Steve Cunningham is in big trouble. I haven't come here to play games and talk nonsense.

'You talk a good game – "I'm a tough guy from Philly, a gangster" – but fighting is in my blood.

'You're not a heavyweight, I am and you're in trouble. I mean business. I came here to do demolition jobs on cruiserweights.'

Cunningham hadn't been knocked out in 30 previous fights, but Fury told him, 'You're small, you're chinny, you're getting knocked out.'

Fury had earlier conceded Cunningham promised to be the toughest opponent he had faced.

The 36-year-old had two spells as IBF cruiserweight champion and won four of his eight world title fights. He had beaten opponents of the calibre of Guillermo Jones, Krzysztof Wlodarczyk, Marco Huck and Wayne Braithwaite, world champions all, without getting the recognition he deserved. 'America doesn't know me,' he said.

To be recognised beyond boxing's hardcore fans and earn better money, cruiserweights have always had to go up to heavyweight and following defeat to Cuban southpaw Yoan Pablo Hernandez in their rematch in February 2012, that's what Cunningham did.

He said he wasn't interested in fighting 'C-grade heavyweights' but he did fight small heavyweights, outpointing tough trialhorse Jason Gavern and dropping a disputed split decision to Tomasz Adamek, a former champion at light-heavyweight and cruiserweight.

The points loss to Adamek was close enough for Cunningham to stay in the IBF rankings.

Fury reckoned Cunningham deserved the decision over the Polish hero. The heaviest Cunningham had weighed was 14st 11lbs, for his win over Gavern, and the expectation was that Fury would outweigh him by around three stones.

That, reckoned Cunningham's trainer Naazim Richardson, wouldn't be enough to beat his fighter.

Richardson, who at the time was coming up with the tactics that kept Bernard Hopkins near the top of the pound-for-pound rankings well into his forties, reckoned it was Cunningham's brains, rather than Fury's size, that would prevail.

The lively exchanges created interest in the fight but the British Boxing Board of Control decided Fury had gone too far in his social media attacks on David Price and Tony Bellew and handed him a £3,000 fine.

Fury said, 'I was told to behave myself. If I do it again, I'll be in big trouble. People like outspoken people – and I am outspoken. But when you are getting hit for three grand, it's time to maybe quieten down a bit.'

Tyson was lying.

FURY would be without his trainer for the fight.

The Furys set up their training camp in Canada and Peter said, 'I first thought there might be a problem entering America when my visa application was declined ahead of the first press conference.

'People were supposed to be looking into it, so I'm very disappointed. We had enough time to get it sorted through the proper channels. I found out at the 11th hour what I needed to do, which meant me spending six hours talking to the customs police when I tried to travel from Canada.

'My previous criminal convictions and the fact I've spent time in prison means I will automatically be refused the standard ESTA [Electronic System for Travel Authorisation] document – I need a special waiver from the US government and that can take up to two months to get.'

In Peter's absence, Clifton Mitchell, who was his assistant and cut man, was put in charge.

Mitchell had been a solid heavyweight himself, good enough to challenge for British and European titles. At the start and end of his 20-fight professional career, he fought out of Brendan Ingle's gym in Sheffield.

Ingle gave him the ring moniker 'Paddy Reilly', hardly fitting for a man of Jamaican heritage who lived in Derby.

'I wasn't very happy about it to start with,' admitted Mitchell.

'But at the time, Brendan was giving a few of his fighters daft names – and it got me publicity, which was the idea.'

Mitchell went on to be a manager, promoter and trainer of fighters – and he went about his business the same way Ingle went about his.

'Some trainers get given Olympians, but Brendan never has,' he said, 'and neither do I.'

Ingle once described the characters who turned up at his Sheffield gym as 'head bangers, nut cases and no-hopers' but he turned them into 16 British champions, eight European champions, three Commonwealth champions and four world rulers.

Dave Ryan was one of the first through the door when Mitchell opened his own gym in Derby city centre and went on to be one of his biggest success stories. The Midlands title appeared to be the rather negative Ryan's ceiling before, with Mitchell's encouragement, he reinvented himself as a hard-as-nails fighter who could grind out wins over the championship distance. Ryan won the Commonwealth super lightweight championship and was also world-ranked for a spell.

Mitchell knew fighters and how to communicate with them, but as he tried to get his message across to Fury in the changing room before the Cunningham fight, he sensed there may be trouble ahead.

PETER Fury rang Mitchell in his changing room minutes before he was about to walk to the ring.

Mitchell passed on his advice to Tyson, who had tipped the scales at 18st 2lbs the previous day to Cunningham's 15 stones.

'Let's take our time and have a look at him,' Mitchell told Fury before the opening bell.

Mitchell suspected Fury wasn't going to follow his instructions. 'Tyson started smashing his gloves together,' said Mitchell, 'saying, "Come on!"

'I was thinking, "I might have a problem here."'

There was another sign of the mayhem to come when, on referee Eddie Cotton's instruction to touch gloves, Fury slammed his right glove down hard on Cunningham's waiting fists.

Fury came out jabbing, keeping Cunningham on the outside, from where he launched a few right-hand swings that sailed harmlessly wide.

'Come on, Steve,' said Fury, a maniacal look etched on his face. He dropped his hands invitingly and when Cunningham made his move, Tyson leaned back and connected with a check left hook.

At the bell, Fury followed Cunningham as he headed for his corner and gave him what he would later describe as 'a shove of encouragement'.

It had been a good opening round for Fury and he came out for the second looking confident – over-confident, as it turned out.

He had his hands dangling by his sides and swung a sloppy left and right from his waist. Cunningham put his head down and slung a right hand over the top. Cunningham wasn't even looking at his target when he let the punch go, but still it connected – and flung Fury on to his back. 'When you don't see them coming, you go down,' explained Fury afterwards.

'Please, not on my shift!' thought Mitchell, but he remembered, 'Tyson was lying there brushing his hair, so I knew he wasn't badly hurt.'

Around the referee's count of 'five', Fury started to stir and by the time Cotton had reached 'eight', he was on his feet and ready to fight.

There was more than two minutes left in the round – and Cunningham went for the finish.

He forced Fury to the ropes and launched a left and right that glanced off his chin. Tyson grabbed. The referee separated them and, his head clearing, Fury started pumping out jabs. The crisis appeared to be over and Cunningham looked disorganised himself for a split second after Tyson crashed a double jab and right hand off his jaw.

Fury started the third round fast, firing jabs and rights at Cunningham, who responded by hurling rights that missed. The action was messy. There was lots of missing and Fury was warned for holding and hitting.

The best punch thrown in the round came in the dying seconds. Cunningham smashed a short left hook off Tyson's chin – and he barely blinked.

Inside the opening 30 seconds of the fourth, Cunningham landed cleanly again and this time the effect was rather more dramatic.

Fury made the same mistake he had made in the second round. He fell in behind his jab and Cunningham whipped over a right hand that crashed into Tyson's face and had him stumbling. Fury grabbed and was warned for holding, the referee's lecture giving him priceless extra seconds to gather himself.

After the fight restarted Fury got his hands up and set about walking Cunningham down. Cunningham fired rights at Fury and grabbed.

Hennessy screamed at his fighter, 'Lean on him.'

Tyson set about Cunningham in the fifth and was docked a point for rubbing his head in his opponent's face, but the way the fighters started swinging at each other, it seemed unlikely the scorecards would be needed. The crowd screamed as the pair let their hands go like a pair of Saturday-night revellers settling a score. It seemed the fight could end at any moment.

Fury delivered a rat-a-tat burst to body and head that made Cunningham give ground. He fired a right hand but couldn't stop Tyson marching forwards and ended the round under fire.

Mitchell told Fury in the corner, 'Keep it simple. Don't punch with him. Cover up and when he's finished punching, you start punching. He's too fast and too fresh at the moment. Let's see what he's got after a couple more rounds.'

Before the sixth, Tyson looked into the crowd and screamed, 'Come on' as he waited for loose tape on Cunningham's glove to be tidied up.

The fight resumed and Cunningham looked to be getting desperate. He hurled punches at Fury, who just walked through them.

Mitchell sensed the end may be near.

He asked Fury after the sixth, 'Is he slowing down?' Fury gave a one-word answer.

'Knockout,' he said, a maniacal look fixed on his face.

Cunningham was hurt, tired and sensing the fight was perhaps becoming a lost cause. With around 40 seconds left in the seventh, Fury found a punch that did more to break his spirit.

He dug a hard right uppercut into the pit of Cunningham's stomach. The American took a couple of steps back and then sagged into the ropes.

Fury didn't rush in. He looked where the openings were before deciding what to do next. Tyson grazed his chin with an uppercut, half landed a couple more punches and when Cunningham put everything into a right hand, Tyson put his hands up to block it.

Finding himself too close, Fury stuck his left forearm under Cunningham's jaw, leaving his chin exposed.

Tyson took his chance, detonating a short, clubbing right hand on his target to send Cunningham crashing. He landed on his side, then rolled on to his back. Around the count of 'six', Cunningham thought about trying to beat the count, but there was no fight left in him and he stayed where he was.

Fury jumped for joy in celebration and the adrenaline was still pumping when he was interviewed by NBC a few minutes later. He asked the crowd to 'show your appreciation for an absolute war of a fight' in the manner of an unhinged street preacher and then burst into song.

Fury would say that before he discovered boxing, he thought he would be a singer and claimed a lineage to Irish folk band The Fureys, who had a worldwide hit with their heartbreaking version of 'When You Were Sweet Sixteen'.

Tyson chose another tune to charm the millions watching, later admitting it wasn't his best vocal performance.

'HE did what a big man is supposed to do to a smaller guy,' shrugged Cunningham afterwards. 'Lean on him, put his weight on him.'

Others in the American's camp were unhappy with Fury.

During the fight, Richardson had complained about Tyson's use of his head and elbows and at the post-fight press conference, Fury's answers were interrupted by shouts of, 'If you don't shut up, you won't make it back to the airport.'

To members of Fury's family and his supporters, that sounded like a challenge and it was decided the press conference should be aborted.

In the early hours of the following morning, Fury was spotted marching through the streets, shirtless and proud, the new king of New York.

CHAPTER 10

Heartbreak

THE CUNNINGHAM fight made Fury a star.

No question Wladimir Klitschko was the best heavyweight in the world, but Fury was the heavyweight everyone wanted to see.

'It wasn't very good for me as a boxer,' said Fury of his 21st straight win, 'but it was very good for entertainment and TV in America and everyone watching.

'As far as I'm concerned, everything went perfect on the night. I got an emphatic knockout at Madison Square Garden, New York, New York. Just the king of the world now. I'm the man to beat.'

From a business perspective, the fight was just about perfect for Fury.

Every American television channel that showed boxing wanted to screen his next fight and because he had looked so vulnerable against Cunningham, opponents would not be hard to find.

But he wouldn't be fighting Kubrat Pulev any time soon.

The IBF had ordered an eliminator between Fury and Pulev, the unbeaten European champion from Bulgaria, but Tyson withdrew, his uncle Peter explaining the fight 'wasn't financially viable'.

Mick Hennessy felt that following the drama of the Cunningham fight, Fury was now in the market for 'worldwide superfights' and wanted a fight that would bring greater rewards.

There was little interest in the David Price fight after American veteran Tony Thompson had burst his bubble with a two-round stoppage, but there was another fight that, to the Furys, made perfect sense.

TYSON reckoned a fight with David Haye would be 'the biggest build-up and fight to happen in a British ring'.

At the time, Haye, Amir Khan and an emerging Anthony Joshua were the most well-known fighters in Britain, boxers whose appeal stretched beyond the sport's core audience and into the mainstream.

Haye was back-page news, sometimes front-page news, and Fury fancied beating him would put him in the same company.

He had good reason to think so.

Like Haye, Fury looked good, could talk and his fights were mostly exciting.

Because of his honesty and vulnerability, Fury had an everyman quality that Haye didn't possess.

But as a fighter, Haye had achieved more.

Haye, an athletic, streetwise south Londoner, had rebuilt from an early stoppage loss to the tough veteran Carl Thompson to win world titles at cruiserweight and heavyweight – and he'd done it the hard way.

He became the world's best at 14st 4lbs with stoppages of Jean-Marc Mormeck in France and Welsh puncher Enzo Maccarinelli – and answered those who said he wouldn't be as effective up at heavyweight by beating the biggest heavyweight champion of them all in Nikolay Valuev.

The Russian was 7ft tall, weighed around 22 stones and held the WBA title until Haye overcame a seven-stone weight disadvantage to take it off him, following trainer Adam Booth's 'sting and be gone' tactics to dethrone him in Nuremberg in November 2009.

The belt was lost on a rainy night in Hamburg, where Wladimir Klitschko comfortably outpointed Haye, who later blamed a toe injury for his failure to close down the IBF and WBO champion.

As he always said he would, Haye retired from boxing on his 31st birthday – 13 October 2011 – but had a rethink and made WBC champion Vitali Klitschko his target.

Frustrated at his failure to make the fight happen, Haye quizzed Klitschko during the press conference that followed Vitali's successful defence against Chisora in February 2012.

Understandably annoyed, Chisora went to confront Haye and when the ensuing mayhem was over, Don Charles, Chisora's trainer, had a broken jaw, Booth bled from a wound on his scalp and Haye and Chisora were headline news around the world.

The British Boxing Board of Control withdrew Chisora's licence but couldn't punish Haye because he wasn't licensed.

He hadn't reapplied for his licence because he had intended to retire.

Nothing sells quite like a grudge fight and knowing a match between Haye and Chisora would surely fill a football stadium, promoter Frank Warren set about finding a way around the fact that neither fighter was licensed by the Board and therefore unable to box on one of its shows.

The Luxembourg Boxing Federation was happy to ignore the fighters' indiscretions and sanction a fight between Haye and Chisora, which Warren announced would go ahead at West Ham United's Upton Park ground in July 2012.

'I want this win on my record – not my police record,' said Haye. He told Chisora at a press conference where they were separated by a wire fence, 'You talk a lot. The best thing that's ever come out of your mouth is my fist.'

Haye went on to knock out Chisora in five rounds in front of 30,000 fans, confirming his status as one of British boxing's biggest stars.

For Fury, a fight with Haye could generate a possible £5 million purse – his biggest pay by a distance – increase his profile further and, given that Haye was naturally a cruiserweight rather than a heavyweight, Tyson saw it as a very winnable fight.

This was a potentially life-changing bout for Fury, a shot at boxing superstardom.

'Nobody knows Pulev outside Bulgaria,' replied Tyson when asked why he had chosen to fight Haye rather than an eliminator for the IBF title.

'I'm not here to take punches in the face for nothing.

'David Haye has a big reputation and once I knock him out, his reputation becomes mine and my ego gets bigger.

'I can't think of a fight people would rather see.'

'I HATE Haye,' said Fury. 'When I was a kid of 18 at the ABAs, I went over to him to say "Hi" and he looked at me like I was a dickhead and he was God.

'I was a kid who liked watching him box and it made me feel really bad. I thought, "I'd never do that to a kid when I'm champ."'

Fury had first called for a fight with Haye after beating Dereck Chisora in 2011.

'I've heard David Haye is going to retire from boxing this year and be a movie star,' he said. 'Well, I want to be a rock star but that's not going to happen either, is it?

'He should stick to boxing and give me my chance.'

The fight didn't happen then, but 18 months on there was talk of a fight between Fury and Haye.

One of the problems with making the fight was that Manuel Charr was supposed to be fighting Haye next.

Charr was lined up as Haye's comeback opponent in Manchester on 29 June before Haye was ruled out with a hand injury.

'David Haye is fighting me, not Tyson Fury,' Charr, beaten only by Vitali Klitschko in 24 fights, had said.

It was Fury who would fight Haye next, live on Sky Sports Box Office.

Negotiations were as difficult as they were always likely to be. Haye had achieved more in his career, while Fury was a rising star in demand in both Britain and America.

Fury appeared to have more options than Haye and he would also do more to sell the fight after a 50/50 deal was agreed.

Haye had originally asked for a 60/40 split, while Fury made a tongue-in-cheek 80/20 demand on social media.

Fury told *Boxing News* his personality meant he was worth an equal share.

'I've had 21 unbeaten fights,' said Fury, 'but anyone can get that just by fighting bums.

'I've fought good opposition but it looks the same on paper.

'It's the personality behind the record. People know me because I'm so vocal and I say what I think.

'You don't need to be able to fight to be a star. If you can talk a good game and entertain people, then everyone will tune in and watch. I say what I say and I deal with the consequences later and you can be sure there will be repercussions after this fight because there will be a lot of crazy shit going down.'

In his next breath, Fury set about selling the fight.

'I have no respect for Haye as a fighter, not one per cent,' he said. 'His strength is his speed and power. He's explosive. His weaknesses are his punch resistance – it's quite low – and that against the bigger guys, he tends to box.

'I think I can win because I will go in there and give everything. I believe myself to be a super champion and if I can't deal with another blown-up cruiser, then I never was any good.

'I'm blowing Haye out of the water, the heavy-duty weapons are coming out. I'm going to try to get him out of there from the word go. I'm knocking him out.'

The press conference to announce the fight was as entertaining as it always promised to be.

Haye's opening remark that he was handing Fury a payday got under Tyson's skin.

'It's the other way round,' replied Fury, explaining that Haye wasn't going anywhere until the fight came up.

Throughout the following half an hour, during which Fury was honest and passionate, Haye appeared disinterested.

Haye gave the impression he didn't think Fury was his equal, or anywhere near his equal, while Fury accepted defeat was possible.

Not that he thought it very likely he would lose to someone he described as 'a big tart' and 'a little girl'.

Fury promised to take Haye into the trenches and knock him out, while Haye said he would fight like 'a sniper', the style that had brought down the 7ft tall Valuev.

This was a fight the public wanted to see. All 20,000 tickets were sold out within 24 hours of going on sale and trade paper *Boxing News* regularly made mention of the fight on its front page.

The bookmakers made Haye a clear favourite, but this was still a good fight. The proof lay in the fact that a good case could be made for both fighters winning.

Haye thought he was too good for Fury, Fury thought he was too big.

'The fella punches harder than me and is faster than me,' admitted Fury, 'but on the other hand I'm bigger and I have bigger balls, and I don't need any more than that.

'His balls are like peas compared to mine.

'He is not as awkward as Steve Cunningham. I see me getting on top of him and beating him up.'

The press joked that as soon as Cunningham was counted out, Haye was asking to fight Fury. The version of Fury that fought Cunningham would surely run into trouble against Haye – and even with Peter in his corner, there was a chance Tyson would be reckless.

He was fiercely proud and wouldn't want to be seen backing off from a cruiserweight.

Haye loved fighting as much as Fury – and had done since he was a boy.

'You just want praise when you're a kid,' he said, 'and I used to get praise by beating people up. Some people are good with numbers and others are good with words. I've always been good at knocking people out. All the other kids at school used to roll around on the floor pulling each other's hair, but I used to get the job done with one punch.

'I would find out who the toughest kids were at all the neighbouring schools and then fight them after school on Friday. I was always fighting guys older than me. I would get as many people as I could to come along. It was like a boxing match. I used to get the same adrenaline then as I do now. There were so many of my mates going to watch me fight that I knew I couldn't lose and I never did. Nobody would fight me after a couple of years. They all knew about my reputation and wouldn't go near me. I refined my skills on the streets of Bermondsey. I learned a lot about co-ordination and timing in those fights.'

As an amateur, Haye won silver at the World Championships in Belfast in 2001 before turning professional after injury ruled him out of the Commonwealth Games in Manchester, which he seemed certain to win.

Haye went on to become only the seventh British fighter to win a version of the world heavyweight championship with that victory over Valuev.

Fury decided the championship was no longer his goal.

'Titles and belts mean nothing,' he said. 'It's not all about sanctioning bodies. I just want to be in great fights and I could let the public decide who I fight after Haye.

'They demanded the Haye fight and made it happen, so I might ask the public who they want me to fight after I've beaten him.

'I see myself fighting Haye, Klitschko, Klitschko and there's nobody else after that. Maybe Lennox Lewis if I can tempt him back into the ring.

'If George Foreman can box at world level when he's nearly 50, why can't Lennox? Beating him would prove I am the greatest ever heavyweight to come from Britain.'

Lewis had retired more than a decade earlier and seemed content to stay retired. 'I have definitely achieved what I wanted to do,' he said and, unlike many other fighters, he never became restless in retirement.

HAYE had seen much in his boxing career but had never seen anyone quite like Fury before.

He appeared mildly amused and then bored by Fury's presence at the press conference to announce their fight and when Sky Sports brought Fury and Haye together on their *Ringside* programme, it was always going to be very watchable.

Haye spent most of the programme with an arched eyebrow, as though he was struggling to hide his disdain for this unworthy adversary.

He smirked and rolled his eyes when Fury claimed he would break him down with his infighting and would also prove to be way too good for Wladimir Klitschko.

At that point, Haye decided he had heard enough.

'I can beat Usain Bolt at 100 metres,' he responded, his point being that Fury's words didn't mean an awful lot and didn't show any genuine confidence.

Haye scoffed at the suggestion he had once been like Fury. Yes, Haye had been young and confident, but he added, 'I was realistic. I knew about the world.'

Haye did sense Fury was trying to outsmart him by promising to take the fight to him.

From that, Haye concluded Fury would get on the back foot.

Either way, Haye, oozing confidence as always, predicted a comfortable win.

'I will knock him out,' said Haye, 'when I want to knock him out.'

The back-and-forth undermining of each other continued in separate interviews. Haye claimed his sparring partners, including Deontay Wilder, would beat Fury. Tyson said he regarded Haye as 'a stepping stone' to a big fight against Wladimir Klitschko.

Fury sparred former opponent Steve Cunningham and Eddie Chambers – but it was all for nothing.

EIGHT days before the fight was scheduled to go ahead, Haye suffered a cut over his left eyebrow while sparring that required six stitches, ruling him out.

At first, the severity of the wound wasn't clear and for a few hours, there was even hope the fight would still go ahead until Sky Sports came to the realisation it was off.

This was a crushing disappointment to Fury, who had invested so much of himself in a fight he felt sure would change his life.

There was the huge payday and what's more, beating Haye could have made Fury a crossover star.

Hennessy had spoken of his hope that in the fight's build-up, the public would get to see the 'generous and loyal' Fury he was so fond of.

Tyson was also funny, charming and fond of singing and dancing.

The words Hennessy found to describe Fury's mood after Haye pulled out were 'very upset, annoyed and frustrated', but many of the words Tyson used after news of Haye's pull-out reached him were unable to be broadcast on Sky Sports.

His interview was transcribed, sent to lawyers and chunks of it were deemed unfit to be shown.

Tyson's rage was understandable.

He had put everything into the previous 11 weeks to prepare for a fight that now wasn't happening – including a lot of his own money.

Fury estimated the cost of his preparations for the fight could have reached £250,000.

Several sparring partners had to be flown in, paid up to £2,000 per week and fed, and there were other team members who needed paying and feeding.

Tyson would later ask Haye to compensate him for his outlay.

Peter said the fight would not be rescheduled.

'We move on from Haye now and look to better things,' he said. 'This has put a bad taste in our mouths, so we're moving on and the fight will not be rearranged on our side.'

There was more diplomacy from Hennessy and Adam Booth, Haye's trainer.

Booth said he hoped Sky Sports would find a new date for the fight and while Hennessy expressed similar hopes, he was unable to hide his disappointment.

He said, 'Tyson would not have been sparring a week from the event, so close to the fight.

'Tyson would not cancel a fight under any circumstances. We'd have to drag him out of it.

'I believe this fight should happen. We genuinely believed Tyson was going to do a major job on Haye and then go on and fight for a major title.

'This is a crazy situation, getting an injury so close to the fight.

'Tyson was in the best possible shape physically and mentally for this, nothing could have been better.

'That's why I would like to see this fight happen.'

THE fight was too big for Fury and Haye to walk away from and with Sky keen to televise it on pay per view, a new date was found: Saturday, 8 February 2014.

Again, it didn't happen.

Haye felt a niggle in his right shoulder while training and on his doctor's advice, he went for an MRI that revealed surgery was needed.

Not only was the Fury fight off again, it seemed Haye's career was over.

'The boxing gods keep hinting that maybe enough is enough and that it's time to finally hang up my gloves,' he said.

Fury was as angry, as he had every right to be, taking to social media to hurl abuse at Haye, while, as ever, Peter was rather calmer.

'I think Haye will let the dust settle and then he'll get "challenged", so he can say, "I was retiring, but I'll give it one more go,"' he predicted.

'I don't think it's about bottling it. They just looked at Tyson as a big risk and if Haye loses, his career is over. But losing to a Klitschko – he's got a chance against Vitali – there's no shame and if he wins, he's a world champion and he's into the big bucks.'

So what next for Fury?

CHAPTER 11

On the Brink

FURY WAS looking for a fight to pay the bills.

He estimated Haye's pull-outs had cost him around £5 million in lost earnings and, on top of that, he had paid sparring partners in preparation for the fight.

Fury only earned money when he was fighting and in 2013, he only fought once.

He still had bills to pay, like everyone else, and the frustration at his lack of fights was obvious.

Tyson was forced to apologise to the WBC after criticising its decision to pair Bermane Stiverne with Chris Arreola for the title vacated by Vitali Klitschko.

Fury insisted on fair play and he was desperate to fight.

Hennessy had a contract with Channel 5, but now Fury was boxing in world class, their budget wasn't big enough to pay for Fury and his opponent.

Frank Warren contacted the Furys and offered Tyson a spot on his show at the Copper Box Arena in February 2014, which could be followed by a rematch against Dereck Chisora, a fighter Warren promoted.

Chisora was also boxing at the Copper Box, defending his European heavyweight title against Andriy Rudenko, and provided both he and Fury won, there was the prospect of them fighting each other again, possibly in a world title eliminator.

Chisora had chalked up four straight knockout wins to earn top ten rankings with the WBC, IBF and WBA.

He was also number 13 with the WBO.

At the press conference to announce the Copper Box show, Fury let off steam.

Understandably, he was still furious with Haye, accused Vitali – or 'grandpa robot', as he called him – of retiring to avoid fighting him and then turned his attentions to his younger brother, Wladimir.

'I can't wait to get the rematch in the summer against Chisora and then take Wladimir's head off,' Fury told the press.

For the rematch to happen, Fury and Chisora had to win at the Copper Box.

The show was only five weeks away when Tyson agreed to go on the show – and he was weighing a hefty 22 stones.

Peter took his nephew to train in Cannes in the south of France.

'I really like it when we train in Cannes,' said Tyson, 'because you can train on the beach and it's red hot, you can go running with no shirt on, all the girls are there in their bikinis.

'When you're not training, you can go for a nice walk down the [Promenade de la] Croisette, have a look in the shops, that sort of stuff.'

Given that the fight was only a few weeks away, Fury was only going to get down to around 19 stones, but for a fighter of Joey Abell's capabilities, the Furys reckoned Tyson wouldn't have to be at his very best.

Abell was a 32-year-old southpaw from Minnesota who either got the knockout or got knocked out himself.

The record showed he carried power – 28 of his 29 wins had come inside the distance – and that when he stepped up in class, he usually lost early himself.

Fury was licking his lips at the prospect of what he would later describe as 'a gunfight'.

He reckoned he had 'a gunslinger's mentality where it's going to be him or me', but for all the anticipation of the forthcoming fight, Fury also seemed tired of the boxing business when interviewed by *Boxing News* in the weeks before the Abell match.

'Given the right opportunities, I do believe I can be the heavyweight champion of the world,' he said.

'But it's not going to be easy because these opportunities don't seem to be coming to me, for whatever reason. This is why I've got to talk bullshit. To try to force people to fight.

'I don't want to talk bullshit all the time, I don't want to be the bad guy all the time.

'But sometimes I feel like I have to be because without being the underdog or the person people want to lose, then I don't seem to get many opportunities.

'If I do win the heavyweight championship of the world, they will say it was the most terrible, worst era the heavyweight division has ever seen, that it was nothing like the seventies or the Klitschko era.'

Reporters found Fury to be a moody, but honest interviewee. His answers would change from day to day.

Boxing News had found him to be weary and contemplative and what happened in the week leading up to the Abell fight did little to lighten his mood.

Tyson took Paris and their children, Venezuela and Prince, to his camp in France and while they were away, the family received a telephone call telling them that two cars outside the family home, a Volkswagen and BMW estate, had been set alight.

Paris also had to go into hospital for surgery and Tyson suffered a cut when sparring American 'Fast' Eddie Chambers.

Fury posted a photograph of the nick above his left eye on social media and in a clear swipe at Haye, gave the message that real fighting men fight with cuts.

Fury was looking forward to fighting again and savoured every moment of his walk to the ring at the Copper Box Arena, singing along to every word of 'Wonderwall', the hit by Manchester scruffs-turned-global stars Oasis.

Peter told his nephew ahead of the fight, 'Let's have a look at him. He can punch. Don't do anything to start with and let him see what it's like to be in with a world-class heavyweight.'

Tyson was also a big world-class heavyweight and by the final minute of the opening round, 6ft 4ins Abell was showing irritation at his inability to get past Fury's jab.

Abell landed his first punch of note in the second, a left hand connecting during an exchange with enough force to rock Fury's head back.

Abell followed through with his head, earning a telling-off from referee Jeff Hinds, and any chance he had of jumping all over Fury when he may have been dazed was lost.

By the end of the round, Fury's jab had raised a swelling over Abell's right eye.

Fury felt comfortable, possibly too comfortable. Abell took advantage of a sloppy moment to find his chin with another back hand, but Tyson was untroubled, firing straight back with one of his own to instantly seize back control.

Moments later, Abell was on the floor, a low blow leaving him on his knees. 'It was a body shot,' protested Fury to referee Hinds.

The next time Abell hit the floor, it was the result of a moment of class from Fury.

He opened up the American's guard with a double jab and then drilled a right hand through the gap to dump him on the seat of his trunks.

Abell got up, tried to take the fight to Fury and in the dying seconds of the round, both hurled southpaw lefts at each other. They landed simultaneously – but it was Abell who ended up on the floor.

The bell rang during the count before Fury could finish the job and he went back to his corner content he had his man where he wanted him.

Abell wasn't finished yet, however.

Early in the fourth, Fury shipped a right hand that stiffened his leg briefly. His balance was quickly restored and Fury really set about Abell, determined to finally put him in his place.

Within seconds, Fury had bludgeoned him to his knees with a two-fisted counter attack.

Abell still wouldn't accept the inevitable and hauled himself to his feet. He slung a few all-or-nothing punches at Fury – and one of them landed. That switched Tyson on and with a contemptuous fury, he opened up to pound Abell to the floor for the fourth time and the fight was over.

THE fight that followed Fury's thumping of Abell was between Chisora and Kevin Johnson, who stepped in after Andriy Rudenko was ruled out through injury.

Put another way, it was a fight between heavyweights Fury had previously beaten, as he was quick to remind Box Nation viewers.

He added that he beat both 'easily really'.

Chisora's stock had risen since Fury had handed him a boxing lesson around two and a half years earlier.

He was widely considered unfortunate not to take the European title off the towering Robert Helenius and went on to push Vitali Klitschko harder than expected in a world title challenge.

Following a knockout loss to Haye in a hugely hyped grudge fight at Upton Park, Chisora put together four straight knockouts.

Chisora looked short of motivation against flabby journeyman Hector Alfredo Avila and laboured to a ninth-round stoppage, but Malik Scott, Edmund Gerber and Ondrej Pala had a combined record of 90-4-1 and Chisora stopped them all.

The difference between that Chisora and the version well beaten by Fury was his weight.

On the insistence of his mother, Chisora had removed biscuits from his diet and found he was way more effective at 17 stones than 18 stones. He was lighter on his feet and therefore able to close the gap quicker.

Chisora wasn't a big heavyweight – he stood only 6ft 1¼ins tall – and was very much a front-foot fighter.

The combination of Chisora's improvement and Fury's inactivity led some to lean towards Chisora should they fight again, possibly at a football stadium that summer.

The rematch would happen if Chisora got past Johnson at the Copper Box Arena.

The result wasn't in doubt from the early rounds. The only question would be whether Chisora would find the punches to stop Johnson. He did have the satisfaction of handing Johnson the first knockdown of his career – courtesy of a fifth-round right hand – but otherwise lacked the imagination to find a way through the American's defences. For round after round, Chisora chugged forward throwing the same punches.

Johnson only fought when he had to – and when he knew the end of the fight was near.

In the final minute, Chisora clearly felt a body shot but Johnson couldn't follow it up and lost widely on the scorecards.

THE rematch between Fury and Chisora would go ahead at the Manchester Arena on 26 July – provided Fury didn't get banned by the British Boxing Board of Control.

At the press conference to announce the fight, Fury tipped over a table and walked out.

That was followed by a furious outburst at a press conference a couple of weeks before the fight.

Fury swore and threatened Chisora throughout. 'Every time he thinks of Tyson Fury in the future, he's going to wish he'd never heard that name,' he said.

'I'm going to annihilate him. He's going to sleep for good. There's no doubt in my mind. I'm flattening his big, fat, ugly face.'

Chisora tried to calm Fury down. 'I don't give a fuck how many women and children are in the audience,' Tyson answered. 'If you don't like the station, change the channel. This is my show, I do what I want. This is boxing. It isn't tap dancing. If anyone doesn't like that, they shouldn't be here.'

Fury and Chisora did agree on one thing, that the winner of their fight for Chisora's European and the vacant British title should pay the loser £100,000.

Fury had originally offered a £10,000 wager before deciding that wasn't enough.

Cynics wondered whether all this had been done to drum up interest in a fight that was in danger of being overshadowed by the forthcoming football World Cup.

More likely, it was Fury in 'fight mode' – the fight was less than two weeks away – but still, Tyson accepted he had gone too far.

He took to social media to apologise, posting on Twitter, 'No bad feelings or intentions. Just a show, forgive me.'

The fight was only five days away when the Furys got a phone call telling them it was off.

Chisora had a fractured hand. 'He got injured on the last day of sparring against [Alexander] Ustinov,' revealed trainer Don Charles. 'He's devastated. I feel numb.'

At least Fury would still be fighting.

Peter insisted he didn't want his nephew to 'stagnate' and asked for a replacement to be found.

Fres Oquendo, narrowly beaten by Ruslan Chagaev for the vacant WBA belt a few weeks earlier, priced himself out of the fight, highly ranked Christian Hammer wasn't interested and Australian brawler Lucas Browne was otherwise engaged.

There was another leading heavyweight who was in the gym and in the country – and Ustinov agreed to fight Fury.

Beaten only once in 30 fights, Ustinov, from Belarus, was ranked number nine by the WBA, number 14 by the IBF and stood a towering 7ft1/2in tall.

Still, the fight didn't happen.

On the day of the fight, Fury's uncle, and former trainer, Hughie was rushed to intensive care.

He had undergone routine surgery to place a pin below his knee after breaking his leg and a blood clot developed, leaving him fighting for his life.

THE British Boxing Board of Control handed Fury a £15,000 fine for his outburst at the Chisora press conference.

Fury said the Board would have to wait until after the fight finally went ahead before it got its money.

The fight was rearranged for 29 November at the ExCel Arena in London's Docklands on the same bill as another hugely anticipated grudge fight, between British, Commonwealth and European middleweight champion Billy Joe Saunders and Chris Eubank Jr, a fighter who, Saunders believed, needed putting in his place.

Fury said, 'If they can wait until after the fight, they can have it gladly.

'I'm not going to run away from £15,000. But if they can't [wait] – come and arrest me. Take me to jail for it.

'At one stage, I was rubbing my hands together with [the equivalent of] a Lottery win [the payday from the Haye fight] and today I'm as broke as a joke. I could have been sat here £5 million strong and who knows what else with other big fights?

'But instead I'm sat here in a pair of tracksuit bottoms that I've had on for two weeks and a fine to pay that they are going to suspend me for – but I haven't even got the money.

'I explained this but nobody seems to listen. So whatever they are going to do they are going to do.'

Fury explained he had spent money preparing for fights that didn't happen.

'All these sparring partners, planes, hotels, food, on more than two occasions, it all comes out,' he explained.

'What do you do? Do you be stingy and think this fight is not going to happen and then not prepare properly?

'Or do you put your heart and soul into something to get the reward? That's what I've done and that's why I'm in this brassic ['brassic lint' is rhyming slang for 'skint'] state at the moment.

'It's hard. My wife says to me, "Why do you keep spending our money on sparring partners and training camps when you don't fight?"

'I'm like the man who is always supposed to fight but never ends up fighting. He just spends money.

'I've not been paid millions of pounds for any fights. I've never made any money out of boxing.

'It's only get-along money and all that's been spent.

'All I care about is providing and living every day. I don't care about world titles, being a legend or being a hero.

'I just want to make money, get on with my life and be involved in good fights. If I'm not going to be involved in good fights, then what's the point [of] being a boxer?'

To avoid any further fines, Fury went to a press conference for the Chisora rematch with tape across his mouth and answered journalists' questions with hand gestures. Asked how long the fight would last, Tyson stuck up his middle finger before rethinking. He stuck up two fingers and pointed them at Chisora.

Chisora had sympathy for him, saying, 'He has never offended me. This is boxing. We can sit here and be nice and shake hands, but when you're close to the fight, after doing all the training, you're in a different frame of mind.'

The fight was around seven weeks away when Tyson learned his uncle Hughie, after three months in intensive care, had died as a result of complications resulting from surgery to insert a pin in his leg. 'Tragic loss for the fury [sic] family,' tweeted Tyson. 'Uncle Hughie Fury. Forever in my heart & life. RIP. Gone to see Jesus.'

THE views of Fury and Chisora ahead of their rematch were as different as you would expect them to be.

Fury could only envisage a repeat of their first fight, while according to Chisora, he had improved in the three years and five months since they first shared a ring and Fury hadn't.

Of their first fight, Chisora said 'the fittest man won' and much had changed since then. 'He isn't fit enough to be in the ring with me,' said Chisora. 'We are going to set the pace.'

Charles said Chisora would 'be on him like a rash' and as well as fitness, there was also the issue of activity when trying to pick a winner of the fight.

In the previous 19 months, Fury had only boxed once, the four-round thumping of the outgunned Abell, while Chisora had four wins and looked to be in the best form of his career.

Fury was unbothered. He told Peter his aim was to win the fight without taking a single punch and gave his reading of the fight to the press.

'He's going to come forward with his cross-armed defence trying to chop down the tree from the base working the body more than he did last time – and he's going to walk on to clean, accurate shots on the way in that do ultimate damage and send shockwaves down his legs,' was Fury's prediction.

If that happened, Chisora's trainer promised to 'sack himself'. Don Charles explained that defeat to Fury would be the fifth time Chisora had fallen short in world class and that would be proof he needed a new trainer to help him break through at the highest level.

Chisora weighed in at 17st 3lbs 8ozs, a good weight for him, with Fury 17st 12lbs.

The atmosphere was charged by the time Fury and Chisora made their way to the ring.

Saunders had just held off Eubank's drive in the closing rounds to beat him on a majority decision and the sizeable contingent of Travellers among the crowd who celebrated his win then got behind Fury.

Tyson gave them plenty to cheer.

Chisora struggled to get into range and when he did get close enough to Fury to hit him, his punches strayed below the belt and referee Marcus McDonnell gave him a telling-off.

In the second, Fury turned southpaw, putting as much distance as possible between his chin and Chisora's dangerous right hand. Chisora tried a left hook that sailed past Fury's chin and Tyson raised his arms above his head in triumph. Fury jabbed and moved and won the round clearly.

The third followed a similar pattern and the instructions from Peter to his nephew at the end of the session were, 'Don't set [your feet] so he can get the big overhand right over. Play with him like a cat playing with a ball.'

Chisora did get Fury where he wanted him in the fourth, but again, he ate punches. Tyson, he discovered, could fight on the inside as well and when Fury put more distance between them, he sent a shiver down Chisora's legs with a looping left hook.

Fury started the fifth round boxing out of the orthodox stance and Chisora half landed a right-hand clump. Fury had a rethink, turned southpaw and for the rest of the round he barely took a punch, while Chisora shipped jabs and uppercuts.

Chisora told his corner before the sixth he couldn't find his rhythm and matters didn't improve for him – or the crowd. There were boos in the final minute of the session. This wasn't the fight they had paid to see. Fury was winning the rounds while boxing well within himself and there seemed to be nothing Chisora could do to turn the fight around. Every time he got into range to let his hands go, Fury either beat him to the punch and moved or grabbed him.

Charles asked Chisora before the seventh, 'Do you want to be in there?' and that brought a response from his fighter.

He quickened his feet at the start of the round but just ran on to punches as Fury adjusted and put extra weight into his combinations to leave Chisora's right eye swollen and his mouth bloodied.

The only possible reading of the fight seemed to be that Tyson had won every round.

More boos from the crowd during the seventh led to the referee asking for more from both fighters, but really, what could Chisora do? When he tried to put Fury under pressure, he got picked off and on the rare occasions he tried to stand off and walk Tyson on to punches, Fury drilled him around the ring. It seemed that whatever Chisora did, Fury punched him in the face.

Chisora had the look of a beaten fighter as he sat on his stool after the eighth and he was sent out for the tenth with Charles telling him, 'It's now or never... no regrets tomorrow morning.'

The last thing a shattered and disheartened Chisora wanted to see when he looked across the ring moments before the tenth round started was Fury bouncing on the balls of his feet across the ring, eager to hear the bell and continue piling on the punishment.

Chisora did rouse himself to apply pressure early in the round but it brought him no reward and he resorted to backing up and waving Fury forward, hoping he might walk into the path of a desperate swing.

Fury just teed off on him with long, straight punches. After a crisp, two-fisted salvo thudded into Chisora's battered face, Tyson turned to the referee to enquire if he wanted to stop the slaughter.

McDonnell let the fight continue but his corner knew Chisora's cause was hopeless.

He wanted to come out for the 11th round but once he stopped arguing with Charles, his trainer brought over the referee to signal Chisora's retirement.

Chisora ended the fight with his nose broken and right eye swollen shut.

THE win over Chisora put Fury exactly where he wanted to be.

He was the mandatory challenger for the WBO heavyweight championship, held by Wladimir Klitschko.

This was what Tyson had been working towards since he made his professional debut six years earlier – or even further back.

As a boy, Fury was fond of drawing cartoon stories that ended with him being crowned heavyweight champion of the world.

He was on the brink of getting his chance – and decided to risk it against a fighter who was ranked just two places below him by the WBO at number three.

This looked foolhardy – or an extreme show of confidence.

Fury explained he took the fight to 'preserve my ranking', but there looked to be another reason.

Klitschko agreed a three-fight deal with American broadcasters HBO following a five-round knockout of Kubrat Pulev and the fear of the Furys was that Klitschko, if possible, would look to fight in the States against opponents more recognisable to their audiences.

Fury wanted to ensure he couldn't be avoided and beating a fighter ranked number three would further strengthen his case.

This seemed to be a sizeable risk – to everyone apart from Fury.

Fury never did think there was any possibility he would lose a fight. If he couldn't outbox opponents, he would out-tough them. The way Fury saw it, nobody was as big as him and nobody wanted to win as much as him.

Christian Hammer was 6ft 2ins tall, weighed around 17½ stones and though beaten three times in 20 fights, he had won his previous ten, including a close points win over common opponent Kevin Johnson.

No wonder promoter Frank Warren called the show *Risky Business*. Warren confirmed ahead of the fight that he had spoken to the teams behind heavyweight champions Klitschko and Deontay Wilder about the possibility of bringing them to a football stadium in the summer to defend against Fury, and the way Tyson was talking he had already beaten Hammer.

He didn't make too much mention of him at press conferences, instead spelling out how he would beat both Klitschko and Wilder.

'I can beat Klitschko before he enters the ring,' said Fury. 'It's like how Mike Tyson used to beat people. Klitschko's mind will be boggled before he fights me.

'The other fella, Deontay Wilder, doesn't need to be boggled at all. I just need to hit him with a right hand and it's "Goodnight Vienna."'

Fury promised a 'spectacular performance' against Hammer and said he had been aware of him since they were both amateurs.

Fury and Hammer, then boxing under his real name Cristian Ciocian, had both competed in the World Junior Championships in Morocco in 2006 and were on course to meet in the final.

Fury was beaten in the last four and Ciocian went on to win gold.

The Romanian missed out on the 2008 Olympics in Beijing after losing to Fury's big rival David Price.

Price remembered Ciocian losing interest in trying to win the fight after breaking his nose in the first round with an uppercut. (Fighting as Christian Hammer, he would get his revenge on Price in the pros.)

Fury also towered over Hammer and to emphasise his point, he stood on his tip toes.

He was heavier by 1¼lbs at 18st 8lbs.

Fury was sung into the ring by an Elvis Presley impersonator. 'Trouble' was the song, appropriately enough, and at ringside was John Fury, days after his release from prison. The last time he had seen his son box, Tyson outpointed Zack Page in Canada for his 13th straight win, and he said this Tyson Fury was very different.

He circled the ring, let Hammer come to him and then slammed hard, fast punches into his face.

Fury appeared to be enjoying himself. He smiled at Hammer and talked to him after making him miss.

During the second, referee Marcus McDonnell decided he had heard enough from Fury and asked him to stop talking.

Fury allowed himself a smirk of satisfaction in the fourth after making Hammer miss, countering with a flurry and then disappearing before Hammer could hit him back.

Later in the round, Hammer smiled back at Fury after narrowly missing with a right hand, but any confidence he took from that was dented by a moment of class from Tyson in the fifth.

Fury shaped to throw a left hand and sneaked a right uppercut on to Hammer's chin. The punch took something out of Hammer and moments later, Fury clobbered him to his knees with a right hand.

There was still a minute to go and somehow, Hammer made it through to the bell.

Hammer finally got close to Fury in the sixth, but it was Tyson who landed all the punches, short, jolting blows.

Hammer picked up a final warning for using his head in the seventh and the end of the fight wasn't far away.

In the dying seconds of the eighth, Hammer put everything into a right hand, but Fury beat him to the punch with a short southpaw left. Fury pounced to land two more to propel Hammer into the ropes and had the bell not sounded, he may well have finished the fight.

As it turned out, they were the last punches of the fight. Hammer's corner decided their fighter couldn't continue.

CHAPTER 12

King of the World

PARIS FURY reckoned her husband had '20 different personalities'.

He was streetwise, yet in some ways sheltered; he was hard to his core, but vulnerable; he could outwit better educated people but at other times his lack of education would let him down.

Fury had been radicalised by his uncle Earnest, a born-again Christian and preacher, and social media gave Tyson the platform to air his Old Testament views of the world that alienated many.

Although he was daft as a brush sometimes and genuinely nice, Tyson could also say things that came across as downright nasty.

John Fury tried to explain his son.

'We all have crazy days and say things that seem like a good idea at the time,' he said.

'Tyson is his own man. I try to steady the ship. But he sees people for what they are. I am a man of few friends and it does not bother me, either.

'Sometimes, people don't like proper people, do they? They like you to say things to please other people, but we don't roll that way.

'The gypsy man pays homage to nobody. It's a cultural thing. Our culture is different to yours. We have our own beliefs and standards.

'This kid has come up the hard way. He has poured his heart out for this mongrel race, this island in the middle of the ocean, this postage stamp that's worthless, this dumping ground for the world.

'He has given his all for this country and what has he got in return? Someone on Twitter [saying], "I hope you die, you pikey bastard." What's all that about?

'Tyson is a good lad, he has never been in trouble. But people don't want to see a Travelling champion. We are hated people.'

TYSON showed several of his many personalities in the build-up to his challenge for Wladimir Klitschko's WBA Super, IBF and WBO titles, set for Dusseldorf on 24 October.

Fury had promised from early in his career that he would 'give press conferences like nobody else's' and the press conference at a West London hotel for the Klitschko fight was unlike any other.

Fury made his entry dressed in a Batman costume and sat at the table deadpan while Johnathon Banks, Klitschko's trainer, talked.

Adam Smith, head of boxing at Sky Sports, introduced Fury and at that moment his cousin, Hughie, burst into the room dressed as Batman's arch enemy, The Joker.

Fury – or should that be Batman? – jumped off the table and wrestled The Joker to the floor.

He then pointed his finger at Klitschko and promised, 'You're next, you old fool' before turning his attention to Banks.

'You took too many punches,' Fury told the former cruiserweight and heavyweight contender. 'I didn't understand a word you said.'

Fury would explain later that his intention wasn't just to entertain and make headlines.

'My fooling around outside the ring takes my opponents' eyes off the ball inside the ring,' he said.

'They look at my antics instead of my boxing. That's a good thing for me. That is my unpredictability.

'Wladimir has seen everything before – fast footwork, the fast right hand, every punch in the book. There's nothing a man can do in that ring that he hasn't seen, normally.

'But when he doesn't know what's going to happen, that's unsettling.

'He will be waiting for something to happen. It might happen and it might not.

'He cannot prepare for someone like me and since he's a control freak, that's his worst nightmare. He's fighting the unknown.'

The joking stopped during an intense head to head that followed the press conference.

Fury half joked, 'I better back off Wladimir Klitschko before he gets the jitters and doesn't turn up, like his comrade David Haye.'

Two days later, the fight was off.

On his way home from London, Klitschko strained a calf muscle. The fight would have to be postponed.

The Furys felt this was 'a stunt'. Peter believed the Klitschkos wanted Tyson to overtrain for the fight.

Fury kept himself in the headlines following the postponement by declaring his intention to become Morecambe's Member of Parliament.

He said, 'Morecambe was a booming place back in the '40s, '50s and '60s. Today it's mainly for old-age pensioners, heroin addicts, crackheads and thugs, and I want to clean the place up.'

As a way of connecting with his public, Fury invited residents to join him on his early-morning runs along the beach. 'I want to be the people's champion,' he told those who ran with him. On one occasion, he stopped to give food and drink to a homeless man. 'It was quite upsetting to see my fellow man lying on the floor,' he said.

The fight was rearranged for 28 November at the ESPRIT arena in Dusseldorf and by the time the opening bell sounded, there were thousands who should have been supporting Fury but weren't.

The *Mail On Sunday* ran an interview with Fury in its 8 November edition that turned many against him.

As ever with Fury, his message was mixed. In parts, he came across as well-intentioned, but they weren't the parts that made headlines.

Fury described himself as 'anything but straightforward' in the interview with the newspaper's chief sports writer, Oliver Holt.

The headline read, 'Vile homophobic slurs, ranting about devil worshippers and Armageddon... is this man fit to fight for the world heavyweight title?'

Fury said he saw himself as 'awkwardness to the utmost, highest level. Whatever is conventional, I am the opposite. So if you want to walk in a straight line, I am going to walk in zigzags. If you want to throw a one-two, I'll throw a two-one. Whatever is back to front, that works for me in life because I don't want to be an ordinary person because ordinary, [if] you do ordinary things, you are on an ordinary level. I always aim for high levels in everything I do.'

The subject then turned to darker matters.

'We live in an evil world,' said Fury. 'The devil is very strong at the minute. Very strong. And I believe the end is near, just a little short [sic] few years away, I reckon, from being finished.'

Fury was predicting Armageddon and when asked why, he said, 'Abusing the planet, the wars in the Middle East, the famines, the earthquakes, the natural disasters. All these things are talked about 2,000 years ago. Prophesised. So now it is all coming true.

'It says there will be a time when men lay with men and women lay with women and that's accepted, and it's only in 1967 that these things were OK: abortion, being homosexual in public. So from 1967 until now.

'There are only three things that need to be accomplished before the devil comes home. One of them is homosexuality being legal in countries, one of them is abortion and the other is paedophilia.

'So who would have thought in the '50s and early '60s that those first two would be legalised? When I say paedophiles could be made legal, that sounds like crazy talk, doesn't it?

'But back in the '50s and '60s, for them [sic] first two to be made legal, [I] would have been looked upon as a crazy man again.

'All these things that happen in the world, wise men already know they are going to happen and they see what they really are.

'Foolish people follow the system, get caught up in media news, what the government want you to believe and the world and all the higher powers want you to believe and want you to be in the system, want you [to] go down the same path as all the sheep in the cattle market.'

Fury said the Bible was his guide. 'My faith and my culture is based on the Bible,' he said. 'The Bible was written a long time ago, wasn't it? From the beginning of time until now. So if I follow that and that tells me it's wrong, then it's wrong for me. That's just my opinion.'

Fury saw his fight with Klitschko as a clash of good versus evil, like David and Goliath.

He said, 'Goliath was a big monster of a man and a champion of a man who had never been beat and beat everybody and killed everybody and then this young guy come forward, child, who believed in God and done it and God gave him the power because of what was right and what was wrong. What was right will always prevail over wrong in the long run. Good will always prevail over evil, no matter what it is, not necessarily right now, but as time goes on it will always come back round.'

He went on to describe Klitschko as 'a devil worshipper', explaining, 'They are involved in bigger circles and stuff like that and they do magic tricks.'

Fury came across as rather muddled but every fighter's mood darkens as a fight approaches and it seemed he was also finding ways to get as much as possible out of himself. By his own admission, there were days when the heavyweight championship didn't mean as much to him as it once had and he was disinterested in material possessions, so in his mind, Fury had painted his fight with Klitschko as a battle between good and evil.

He went on to give a better explanation of how he saw himself and the Klitschko brothers.

'They live for this world,' he said. 'I don't.

'The be-all and end-all of everything is their careers and money and what they can do and what they can achieve in life.

'My be-all and end-all is passing through here, trying to do a few good things on the way, helping people. It's all about a test to me, going to a different place, a heaven, where we are promised a better life. If I can make it there, that's my ultimate ambition. It ain't about winning titles for me.

'People think success is being rich and having a nice house and driving nice cars and being Mr Flash. Success isn't that. Success is being happy and content in yourself, in what you are doing in that period of your life.'

Fury said that should he beat Klitschko, he would spend his time 'spreading good news, doing good things, setting up charities, rehabilitation centres'.

The *Catholic Weekly*, an Australian publication, did its best to unravel Fury's religious views.

They wrote his faith was 'genuine' and added, 'Outwardly religious, his opinions are not – unsurprisingly – theologically sophisticated. Instead, they seem to represent a composite of ideas made up from personal interpretations of scripture informed by the kind of evangelical Catholicism that has become increasingly prominent within Travelling communities in recent years.'

Fury was quoted as saying, 'I try to go to church every Sunday and I read the Bible quite a lot, although not as much as I should do.

'Religion is complicated and hard. People have practised it for thousands of years and still not understood, so it's hard for me to understand it all after only a few years. I'm always trying, always looking to be a better person, although sometimes the media pushes your opinions a certain way and people can misunderstand. Yes, I'm a controversial character, but am I a good person? Of course.'

He added, 'I pray for my opponents before fights, praying that they are strong and healthy and put up a good fight, but I'm doing a job like everyone else. It tells us in the Bible we need to work, and boxing is just a sport at the end of the day.'

Tyson did, however, once threaten to kill Dereck Chisora.

That, he would explain, was to sell tickets.

'Doing controversial things in life is what you'll be remembered for, not for how kind or how nice you were,' he said. 'People want to listen to what I say, whether it's rubbish or facts. And not everyone is as gifted as me in being able to talk rubbish. Anybody can be Mr Boring and sit in the corner and be nice and quiet.'

AS fighters, champion and challenger were as different as it was possible to be.

Klitschko was a methodical, thinking boxer, while Fury appeared to put complete faith in his instincts.

Tyson talked of being spontaneous when he fought, the last thing Klitschko would ever be.

Away from boxing, Klitschko spoke four languages and played chess, while Fury spent his spare time reading the Bible and watching boxing and Western movies.

Fury said he planned to be 'the most colourful and controversial champion since Muhammad Ali' and told Klitschko he had 'as much charisma as my underpants'.

He had respect for the Klitschko brothers and their achievements, but said the public demanded more of their heavyweight champions.

'The Klitschkos are up there, if not better, than any heavyweights because of their size, athleticism, ability to stick to a game plan and conditioning – no one had all that in the past,' he said.

'They're true professionals at what they do, so they have to be admired, embraced and celebrated, but, on the other hand, this is a dull moment [era] for the heavyweights.

'If you go back to the 1980s, that was a dull moment, too. Ali and [Larry] Holmes were followed by Trevor Berbick and Pinklon Thomas and then we ended up with some random people as heavyweight champions of the world before Mike Tyson came along to shake things up.'

Fury felt it was his job to 'shake things up', saying, 'If I didn't play up a bit, what would you talk about down the pub?'

Millions would be talking about Fury if he could topple a fighter who had been at the top of heavyweight boxing for around a decade.

Klitschko had held a version of the world championship since 22 April 2006, when he beat Chris Byrd for the IBF belt.

Only Joe Louis, who was champion for 12 years when there was only one title, had worn the crown for longer.

Louis had 27 world title fights between 1937 and 1950, a record Klitschko would break when he fought Fury.

Klitschko was 39 years old, 12 years older than his challenger, and Fury said, 'Age is the key to victory.'

Fury was giving himself confidence but didn't want to devalue his forthcoming victory.

'I don't see that he's gone backwards,' he said. 'When I beat him, I don't want people to say I beat a faded champion because he's not.

'When I beat him, I will be shouting, "I am the greatest!" I will be whipping a guy who hasn't been beaten for 11 years.

'I will be shaking up the world.

'I will say something original.'

Fury was borrowing his quotes from Cassius Clay, who had screamed, 'I shook up the world' after taking the heavyweight title from the seemingly indestructible Sonny Liston in February 1964.

So deluded had Clay been considered before his challenge, his mental condition was evaluated by doctors before it was decided he was fit to fight.

Clay was acting, Fury wasn't.

'He's bipolar,' Klitschko said of him. 'He has mental issues.'

Klitschko added, 'Tyson has a couple of loose screws that need tightening up.

'His brain is the size of a squirrel's or a walnut. Some of what he says makes me sick. It's disgusting and he should keep such stuff to himself.'

Fury was clearly way more emotional and vulnerable than Klitschko, who spoke with the icy detachment of a villain from a James Bond film.

He described himself as 'a professor of the noble science' and said that 'beating people up for a living is most enjoyable'.

Klitschko made the comments during a press day at his training camp in the Austrian Alps, where on three sides of the ring, screens showed Fury fights on a continuous loop.

Klitschko admitted it was hard for him to find sparring partners of Fury's size.

Sheffield's Richard Towers was one of those who got a call.

He stood 6ft 8ins tall and though he couldn't move like Fury and didn't have the same jerky style, Towers was athletic and could punch. He had won 15 of his 16 fights, 12 by knockout.

Towers said of Klitschko, 'When he throws a punch, nine times out of ten it lands and he's always in position to throw shots. He may be 39 now but there's no deterioration, believe me.'

Towers had also sparred Fury and fancied Klitschko would keep his titles either with a late stoppage or on points.

Sky Sports doubted Fury would make it past the opening rounds and *Boxing News* editor Matt Christie wrote, 'Try as I might, it's hard to visualise any kind of victory for Fury.'

Fury didn't just predict victory, he predicted an easy victory.

'This is going to be, will be, one of my easiest nights,' he said. 'That might sound crazy as he is a super champion, a world champion for 11 years, but I see so many chinks in the armour and I am going to expose them very quickly.

'There is nothing that I see that Wladimir does that makes me afraid or makes me think I can't win against this guy.

'Everything Wladimir does attracts me to him. If I could pick from every other champion to fight, I would still pick him because I can expose what he doesn't do very well.'

Surely Fury was foolish to see the fight this way? Either that or he wanted people to think it.

Nobody else seemed to see the fight, or indeed the world, the way Fury did.

He seemed to have an almost childlike, naive confidence in himself, but he was also smart.

He knew how to get opponents to underestimate him, how to mislead them and that appeared to be his intention when he gave Johnny Nelson some 'insight' into his tactics during an interview for Sky Sports.

Tyson said he would block Klitschko's jab, get inside and beat him up with uppercuts. 'Thanks Tyson,' said Nelson, 'but I don't believe you.'

There were other rumours that Fury would use his head and elbows to unsettle Klitschko.

Surely, Fury would box on the move, try to frustrate Klitschko the way he had frustrated Chisora in their rematch and Hammer? But with Fury, you could never be quite sure *what* he was going to do.

Klitschko didn't appear to know quite what to make of Fury when they came face to face across a table for a Sky Sports *Gloves Are Off* programme.

Klitschko treated his challenger with a mixture of bewilderment and curiosity. At one point, he narrowed his eyes and said, almost in the manner of a father addressing his son, 'I think this has come too soon for you.'

Fury turned that argument on its head, insisting that it was his youth that gave him the advantage.

Klitschko found other reasons to believe he would win. 'I've checked his record,' he said. 'His past six or seven fights have not been at a good level.

'But I am expecting one of my most difficult nights. He is a big man with a big ego and big plans.'

For years, Klitschko had been turning back the challenges of fighters with big plans, fighters with better CVs than Fury's, such as Alexander Povetkin and Kubrat Pulev.

This was no golden age of heavyweight boxing, but for years, the gap between Klitschko and the rest had been sizeable.

There were those who saw traces of decline in Klitschko's most recent defence, a points win over Bryant Jennings seven months earlier, and that was one of the reasons why commentator Dave Farrar went for Fury to beat him.

Farrar was well placed to predict the outcome having watched both fighters for years.

'I felt Tyson would be too big, too clever and on top of that, there had been signs of deterioration in Klitschko and I felt he was underestimating Fury,' he said.

'The Germans laughed at me.

'So many times they had come along to basically watch an execution and they expected the same again, but Fury wasn't there for that.

'He really didn't care who Klitschko was or what he had done. He was a fighting man – and he was there to win.'

There were others, former champions Carl Froch and Richie Woodhall among them, who gave Fury a good chance of pulling off what would be one of the best wins by a British fighter overseas, up there with John H. Stracey dethroning Jose Napoles in Mexico in 1975 and Lloyd Honeyghan upsetting Donald 'The Cobra' Curry in Atlantic City 11 years later.

THE Furys were in enemy territory and suspicious.

They picked and poked at the food in their hotel and because of fears the water might be contaminated, someone Tyson described as 'my mate Dave' drove water over from England.

Tyson would later describe the Klitschkos as 'cheats' and wanted it known he would have everything the way he wanted it – or he would pull out of the fight.

Fury rejected the gloves he was sent, saying they hurt his thumbs. He found a new prototype more to his liking, but they had yet to be made. Hennessy made it clear that if Fury didn't get the new gloves he wanted, there would be no fight.

The Furys kept themselves to themselves. Tyson, Peter and John would sit in a corner of the hotel's dining room talking boxing, particularly Klitschko's previous fights.

For all his suspicions, Fury was a happy figure around the hotel.

Peter told a reporter, 'This is the nicest and friendliest he'll ever be because he's got something to look forward to and he feels good within himself. He's fit, he's healthy, he's eating well. But you wait until the fight is over and he's been home a few days. That's a different Tyson altogether. It's hard being around that Tyson.'

At the weigh-in, Fury received a confidence boost, if he needed one, when Klitschko was unable to look him in the eye.

The suspicion in the Fury camp, and among several reporters, was that Klitschko had worn heels at the press conferences to make himself appear closer to Fury's 6ft 8¾ins.

The weigh-in revealed Klitschko was, in fact, his official height of 6ft 6ins and on the scales there was only a pound between them.

Fury had claimed just before the weigh-in that he would weigh around 18st 3lbs, but instead he came in at a lean 17st 8lbs, the lightest he had been since beating Maddalone around three and a half years earlier.

Tyson gained further motivation on the eve of the fight when Paris told him she was expecting their third child.

'WHAT the fuck is this?'

The Furys had just stepped on to canvas at the arena – and couldn't quite believe it.

'We're not boxing on a beach,' Peter told Bernd Bonte, Wladimir's manager. Farrar reckoned what followed had a bearing on the outcome of the fight.

He wandered into the arena in mid-afternoon and saw Hennessy standing on his tip toes shouting furiously at Vitali Klitschko.

'He was shouting, "Pull it all out – or we're not fighting. I'm fucking serious.

'"We don't need the money, we will go home."

'The issue was the amount of padding under the canvas.'

Clifton Mitchell was with Hennessy.

'There's a minimum amount of layers [of padding],' he said, 'but no maximum and they had six layers of sponge underneath the ring.

'Put it like this, it was like training for a match on grass and then being told you were playing on sand. After two rounds jumping around on that, your legs would be fucked. It would have been like fighting on a mattress.'

Farrar said, 'Vitali was protesting but Mick wouldn't back down and he won the argument.

'I saw three men taking away three trolley-loads of padding each.

'They seemed to take out a lot of padding.

'The Klitschkos always had so much control over their shows and I still can't believe Mick got his way.

'Psychologically, that was a big victory.'

Later, Vitali went into the changing room to watch Fury have his hands wrapped.

He was a large, potentially unsettling presence, but Fury saw the funny side. 'I want you next,' Tyson told him.

Fury said later, 'I told him to put some kisses on my wraps and he said, "I'll do better than that" and put two lovehearts on.'

Fury continued his rather cavalier approach to what appeared to be his own public execution on his way to the ring, singing and seemingly enjoying the occasion.

'He was singing and messing around,' said Farrar. 'The feeling among the German broadcasters was, "Who is this guy?" They thought he was a nutter – and they thought I was a nutter for picking him to win.'

FURY acted like 'a nutter' throughout Michael Buffer's introductions.

He paced up and down, talking to Klitschko in the opposite corner.

One of the things he appeared to be saying was that Wladimir wasn't as tall as he had made himself out to be at the press conferences.

At the opening bell, there was a surprise.

The likelihood was Fury would box as a southpaw, but he came out in the orthodox stance. He stood off where Klitschko couldn't quite reach him, feinting and trying to land his jab.

The best moment from either fighter in a quiet opening round came from Fury. He put his hands behind his back and while Klitschko wondered what to do, Tyson snapped a jab into his face.

This was an astonishing display of confidence. Fury was letting it be known that he could do what he wanted with the best heavyweight of the last decade.

There was more flippancy from Fury in the dying moments of that opening round. 'Nearly,' he said to Klitschko after he fell short with a jab.

Klitschko knew he had to get closer and at the start of the second, he quickened his feet and tried to put punches together. Fury dodged them and then stepped in with a burst of his own. He smiled with a maniacal glee after landing a jab in the final 30 seconds.

Fury felt in control and during the third, he turned southpaw and walked around the ring with his hands down, waving Klitschko forward. Still, Klitschko couldn't let his hands go. He was unwilling to take a risk for fear of the consequences and the less Klitschko did, the more Fury's confidence grew. Again, he put his hands behind his back. Klitschko did nothing.

Klitschko did go for him in the dying seconds of the round – and missed with a right hand.

'Enjoy it,' Peter told his nephew in the corner. 'Take him to school.'

It wasn't until the final seconds of the fourth that Klitschko landed a right hand – but Fury ignored it.

The Klitschko corner implored him to throw more punches and not allow Fury to 'steal' the rounds. Fury wasn't throwing a lot of punches himself, but he was throwing more than the champion.

With Tyson forever feinting and moving, Klitschko was struggling to set himself.

Heads banged together in the fifth, leaving Klitschko cut on his left cheek. It was another frustrating round for the champion. He had tried to get his jab working – the punch that had put challengers under his control for around a decade – but missed with every one.

There was too much missing and not enough punches thrown for it to be an exciting fight, but it was hugely engrossing nonetheless.

The sixth was another quiet round and the only punch that landed was Fury's jab.

'I'm giving him a boxing lesson, this kid,' Tyson told his corner at the end of the round, clearly happy with the way the fight was going.

He was confident enough to try a left hook-right hand combination in the seventh and it was enough to win another quiet round.

Fury had another opponent in the eighth. He swatted away a wasp.

Mostly the round was one of missed punches and tangles. There was applause from Fury's corner in the last minute of the round after he landed a jab, but Peter wasn't entirely happy. Tyson had been standing in front of Klitschko, relying on his reflexes and judgement of distance to make Klitschko miss. Peter wanted to see his nephew move his feet more.

Fury held his feet long enough in the ninth to ship a right hand that he shrugged off with a shake of his head and after being told off by referee Tony Weeks for holding, Fury finished the round well.

Klitschko ended up with his back to Fury after they untangled themselves once again and, with no intervention from the referee, Tyson went for him. He swept a left hook over the champion's shoulder and on to his chin and got through cleanly with an uppercut before a dazed Klitschko was able to wrap his arms around him. For the judges, that burst of action in a quiet session was enough for Fury to win the round.

In Germany, it was notoriously hard for an away fighter to gain a points decision, but after nine rounds, British and American television both had Fury ahead. The feeling was the fight was running away from Klitschko and seldom had he faced such a dilemma before.

Up to that point in the fight, Tyson hadn't got it wrong many times, but he got it wrong in the tenth. He gave Klitschko a sight of his chin – and took a right hand. Fury saw the punch coming at the last split second and turned away from it, lessening its impact, and then tapped his chin, indicating to Klitschko all was well.

Klitschko didn't come close to hitting him again for the remainder of the round and by the dying seconds, sections of the crowd were chanting, 'There's only one Tyson Fury.' The challenger won the round on all three judges' scorecards.

The mood in Klitschko's corner was becoming desperate. 'You gotta go get him,' said Banks, and the message got through.

Klitschko launched a lead left hook early in the 11th that had everything behind it – but it missed. Klitschko did connect with what looked like a deliberate head butt, but it went unpunished by the referee.

Heads bumped accidently moments later, leaving Klitschko cut along his right eyebrow. Fury landed a pair of left hooks on the fresh wound and as a confused and dazed Klitschko half turned away, Tyson landed a right hand to the back of his neck. For that, Fury was docked a point. How important would that prove to be?

Even though every ringsider seemed to have Fury in a sizeable lead, there was a chance that, given so little had happened in some rounds, the judges would have it close.

Peter told his nephew he needed to win the last round and the feeling across the ring was the same.

Weeks told them to 'keep it clean' as they flung themselves at each other at the start of the 12th round. Klitschko landed cleanly with a couple of shots, but each time Fury responded instantly and at the bell, both fighters raised their arms.

The celebrations in the challenger's corner looked more convincing.

Fury and Hennessy asked at ringside and discovered Sky Sports and HBO both had the challenger winning, while punch stats revealed Fury landed 86 blows to Klitschko's 52.

Fury found a quiet spot in the ring and stood with his head in his hands. 'Please don't rob me,' he prayed, while Klitschko had his wounds tended to.

Master of ceremonies Michael Buffer announced that both Cesar Ramos and Raul Caiz Sr had scored the fight 115-112, with Ramon Cerdan marking it 116-111.

'The winner by unanimous decision,' he said, 'from the United Kingdom...'

The remainder of the sentence was drowned out by the screams of joy from Fury and those with him.

Fury had done it, he had achieved what he had set out to achieve. He had put his name alongside those he had idolised since he was a boy.

He was the heavyweight champion of the world.

Fury sobbed while his family jumped all over him. A few tried to hoist the new champion on their shoulders – but decided against it.

Tyson dedicated the victory to his late uncle, Hughie, and then produced what American commentator Jim Lampley said was 'if not the strangest moment in the history of heavyweight championship fights, it was certainly one of them.'

Fury took a microphone off Lennox Lewis, apologised to him for what he had said in the past and started singing to his wife, Paris.

He chose 'I Don't Want To Miss A Thing', a ballad by ancient rockers Aerosmith – and sang it well while Paris sobbed.

There really was only one Tyson Fury.

CHAPTER 13

Trouble Ahead

'BOXING IS the only thing I wanted to do with my life,' Tyson Fury said once. 'I didn't want to be anything apart from being heavyweight champion of the world.'

Now he was and as he made his way back to his hotel room on the tenth floor, Fury shook his head as he tried to come to terms with what he had achieved a few hours earlier.

Once inside, he dropped to his knees and thanked God.

The following morning, after Fury woke, he said aloud, '*New* heavyweight champion of the world.'

He thought about it for a few moments before concluding, 'That's got a nice ring to it.' The former heavyweight champion of the world had some explaining to do.

Klitschko had been heavily fancied to keep his world titles but instead was handed a boxing lesson.

'It's difficult to fight a fighter that switches from southpaw to regular [style],' he told the press.

Asked why he didn't let more right hands go, Klitschko said, 'I couldn't find the right distance to land those shots.

'Tyson was quick with his hands and body movement and his head movement.

'I couldn't land the right punches.'

Fury made quite an entrance for breakfast at the hotel the morning after the fight. He wore a suit – and flip flops on his feet. Because he wore a new pair of socks for the fight, Tyson's feet were badly blistered and plasters covered his wounds. He said that, before he fought again, he would have to invest in new socks.

If he fought again.

'As far as I'm concerned right now, if I never win another fight I don't care because I've achieved what I set out to achieve,' Fury told the press.

'I'm a winner and I've had a lot of bumps in the road, but I stuck with it and it shows that determination and dedication pays off.'

One of the questions was, what's next?

There was a rematch clause in the Klitschko–Fury contract that stipulated a return had to be held where it made the most financial sense.

A football stadium in Germany looked the most likely venue, but London or Manchester were also possibilities.

One thing was certain: Fury wasn't going to fight David Haye next – or ever, for that matter.

Haye stole a few column inches from Fury in the British press by announcing that after three and a half years out of the ring, he would return to face Mark de Mori, a Croatian-based Australian with a record of 30 wins, one defeat and two draws, the following January.

'David Haye will never get a fight against Tyson Fury after what he did to me, what he put me through mentally, physically. He tortured me,' said Fury.

'If he gets to be mandatory for the WBA, he can have the WBA. Let him go and fight Fred Flintstone or Joe Bloggs and make no money.

'Whatever title he gets mandatory for, I will vacate.

'He is a pretender, a fraud, let him fight the next in line.

'I'm not giving him a payday. I don't care if he says I can make ten million. I'm not here about the money because, let's face it, the next fight with Wladimir Klitschko is going to be for a lot of money.'

Tyson excused himself and drove to Rotterdam to catch the ferry to Hull.

'Tyson drove back from Germany and we went through Scotland,' remembered Peter. 'There was snow in a field, so he [Tyson] got out and had a snowball fight.

'Where do you draw the line?

'The undisputed champion of the world is having a snowball fight after driving himself back – no return flights, nothing like that.

'He is happy go lucky.'

Tyson knew the laughter would end. 'After the fight, I'm going to be in a very depressed mood, for sure,' he said. 'It's such a high when you box and win, but after, I will crash and hit the floor completely.

'I will go from the ceiling to the floor and will not be allowed to be around anybody for a week to ten days because I'll be murder to live with.

'That's what usually happens.

'After ten days, I'll come back to normal again and can start to properly enjoy what I've done.

'I'm not the nicest person to be around after a fight. I probably need locking in a room.

'I won't start getting moody until I get home, be by myself and all the people have gone.'

Melancholy would set in after Fury came to the realisation that being heavyweight champion of the world wasn't quite what he had imagined it would be.

'When you build something up,' he said years later, 'and you want it very, very much and you get it, sometimes it's not what you expected.'

There were signs that achieving his goal may have taken away Fury's appetite for boxing and there was also the feeling he wasn't getting the recognition he deserved.

'There wasn't much in the papers,' remembered John, whose son had to share the headlines on Monday morning with the Great Britain tennis team.

Captained by Andy Murray, they had won the Davis Cup for the first time in 79 years.

'It was like it didn't take place,' said John.

'I used to say to him, "Don't expect the same treatment as the man next to you. Travelling people have been talked down for centuries. If you win the heavyweight championship of the world, be prepared for a stormy ride." It was all a mess and became trouble.'

The trouble started less than 48 hours after the Klitschko fight when the IBF ordered Fury to defend its belt against Vyacheslav Glaskov, his mandatory challenger.

The promoters were told they had 30 days to reach an agreement or the fight would go to purse bids. Clearly, this was unrealistic and anyway, it was expected Klitschko would enforce the rematch clause in his contract and Fury would have to fight him again.

The IBF stripped Fury of its belt and Tyson discovered that his every move was now news.

In the days following the Klitschko fight, he was photographed shopping in bargain store B&M and out walking his dog.

The headline above the latter read, 'Tyson Fury is in the doghouse.'

Fury quite liked that. 'I am a typical dog,' he said, 'placid most of the time and though I can bite, there will never be any slyness. If the world had more men like me, it would be a better place.'

Not everyone was in agreement.

THE Oliver Holt interview wouldn't go away.

Scott Cuthbertson, a lesbian, gay, bisexual and transgender campaigner, started a petition to have Fury removed from the BBC's *Sports Personality of the Year* (SPOTY) shortlist.

Fury claimed on Irish radio, 'It's all misquotes. It is newspapers trying to sell papers on writing bad things about me. I don't have any hate for anybody. I'm not homophobic, I'm not racist and I'm not against any people. All I have for people is love because at the end of the day, we are all brothers and sisters in God. What people do is none of my business. God bless everybody.'

A couple of days later, a video was released that undid any goodwill. The video was filmed ahead of the Klitschko fight and showed Fury threatening Holt.

'See big Shane there,' he said. 'Have a look at big Shane. He's 6ft 6ins and 25 stones. He's going to break his jaw completely with one straight right hand. I ain't going to do it because I'll get in trouble. But the big fella there – he'll annihilate him, won't he? So, Oliver, take a good look at him because that's the face you're going to see before you hit the deck.'

Fury then pointed at another member of his group.

'That's the face you're going to see when he's jumping on your head,' he said. 'What are you going to do to him, Cliff?'

Cliff replied tongue in cheek, 'I'm going to fuck him up.'

The threat to Holt clearly wasn't going to be carried out by Fury or any of his associates.

Even Paul Hayward, of the *Daily Telegraph* and no fan of Fury's, described the threats as 'cartoonish'.

The video also showed Fury being asked what he thought of women in boxing.

'I think they're very nice when they're walking around that ring holding them cards,' he said. 'I like them actually. They give me inspiration when I'm tired and I see a good sort walking, wriggling about.'

Even more controversially, Fury added that 'a woman's best place is in the kitchen and on their back. That's just my personal beliefs. Making me a cup of tea, that's what I believe.'

The subject turned to Jessica Ennis-Hill, the Olympic champion heptathlete who was surely Britain's best-known sportswoman at the time.

Earlier that year, she had returned from the birth of her first child to win world championship gold, making her another contender for the BBC's SPOTY prize.

'That's the runner, isn't it?' said Fury. 'She's good. She's won quite a few medals. She slaps up good as well. When she's got a dress on, she looks quite fit.'

This was tame compared with comments made in boxing gyms all over the world every day, and Mick Hennessy jumped to his fighter's defence.

'Tyson is a playful character,' he said, 'and he often says these things tongue in cheek. He likes winding people up, being controversial for the sake of it and, more often than not, what he says is in jest.

'I can tell you he's a really good, genuine guy who means no one any harm.'

Fury seemed genuinely puzzled by the storm his comments caused. He sent Ennis-Hill a message on Twitter that read, 'If I'm going to get in trouble for giving a woman a compliment, what has the world come to, I said u look fit in a dress?'

Ennis-Hill presumably wasn't flattered and, asked to explain himself, Fury said, 'Men don't look good in dresses. Women do. And what? Why is that bad?

'Why should it be bad for a sportswoman to look nice in dresses? Are they not allowed to do that? Do they have to be treated like men all the time?

'I'm a little bit backward. I didn't really go to school, so which part of "a woman looks good in a dress" is sexist?

'I stand up for my beliefs.

'My wife's job is cooking and cleaning and looking after these kids, that's it. She does get to make some decisions – what she's going to cook me for tea when I get home.'

ON THE WAY UP … *Tyson Fury makes short work of Mathew Ellis in April, 2009*

BREAKING THROUGH … *Tyson Fury slams a right hand off Dereck Chisora's chin on the way to a breakthrough win in July, 2011*

KING OF NEW YORK … *Fury urges Steve Cunningham to let his hands go at Madison Square Garden in April, 2013*

TAMING TYSON … *Peter Fury (foreground) pictured with his nephew at a press work-out in April, 2014*

BANG ON THE CHIN … Fury catches Joey Abell cleanly during their fight in February, 2014

CLOSING IN ON KLITSCHKO … Fury hands Chisora a painful boxing lesson in their rematch in November, 2014

BY THE LEFT … *Tyson slams a jab into Christian Hammer's face during their fight in February, 2015*

SHAKING UP THE WORLD … *Tyson Fury lands a punch on the befuddled and soon-to-be-former world champion Wladimir Klitschko*

BANG ON THE BUTTON ... Klitschko eats a right hand from Fury as his world titles slip away

AND THE NEW ... Fury with his world championship belts after dethroning Klitschko. His father, John, is on his left and behind him on the right is his younger brother, Tommy

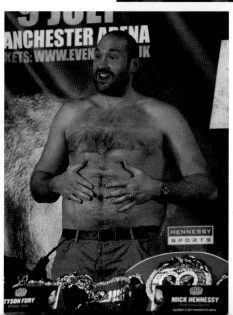

"YOU LET A FAT MAN BEAT YOU" ... Fury taunts Klitschko at a press conference ahead of their scheduled rematch

BIG FRIENDLY GIANT … Fury pictured in April, 2017, weighing around 25 stones

ON THE WAY BACK … Fury hits the pads with new trainer Ben Davison at a public work-out in Manchester in July, 2018

THERE'S ONLY ONE TYSON FURY … Who else would pick up his opponent at the weigh-in? Here he gives Sefer Seferi a lift before his comeback fight in June, 2018

THE COMEBACK … Tyson smacks Sefer Seferi on the nose in Manchester in June, 2018

CATCH ME IF YOU CAN … Tyson taunts WBC champion Deontay Wilder during their fight in Los Angeles in December, 2018

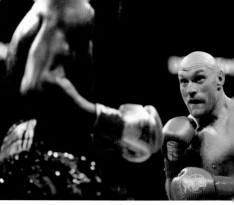

WHAT WILL HE DO NEXT? … Fury keeps Wilder thinking during their world-title fight

THE FIGHT IS OVER … or so everyone thought after Wilder dropped Fury in the 12th round

IT'S A DRAW … referee Jack Reiss raises the hands of Tyson Fury and Deontay Wilder after their fight

WIN NUMBER 29 … Fury, blood dripping from two wounds around his right eye, wades into Otto Wallin

The number of signatures on the petition to have him removed from SPOTY grew and the next time Fury was interviewed, he was in truculent mood.

He said everyone who had signed the petition could 'suck my bollocks' and took a swipe at the other contenders for the SPOTY award, Formula One driver Lewis Hamilton and Andy Murray.

'I've got more personality in my little toe than they've all got put together,' he argued, 'so if it comes to personality, there's only one winner. If it comes to sporting achievement, there's only one winner.

'What personality does it take to drive a car around a track 100 times or hit a ball back and forth? That's not very personality [sic], is it?'

The sporting establishment wondered if the straight-talking Fury was welcome among them.

THE British sporting establishment was possibly best represented by the BBC's *Sports Personality of the Year* award.

Every British sporting great had lifted the trophy since its inception in 1954, including fighters Henry Cooper (twice), Barry McGuigan, Lennox Lewis and Joe Calzaghe.

In 2015, the bookmakers reckoned Murray was the favourite, ahead of Ennis-Hill.

Fury stayed on the shortlist – despite 130,000 signatures on Cuthbertson's petition to have him removed.

Nick Pitt's signature wasn't among them. He had interviewed Fury for the *Sunday Times* ahead of the Klitschko fight and said, 'He talks a weird mixture of boxing and religion, but I actually quite like the fellow. He's quite genuine. He shoots from the mouth. He is who he is and it's ridiculous to expect him to be a modern man. He genuinely believes all that Jesus stuff he spouts, so he'd probably take a win at Sports Personality to put some of us straight. It could be hilarious.'

Fury was aware he had caused genuine outrage, however. He was reminded of that when he walked into a Manchester bar one evening.

Paul Cole approached him and screamed in his face, 'I can't stand you.'

Cole was a 27-year-old homosexual who had been incensed by Fury's comments.

Fury hugged him, kissed him on both cheeks and posed for a selfie.

'I've changed my mind about him,' said Cole afterwards. 'He would definitely float my boat if he was gay.'

That was a moment captured only by those who were there and Fury made a public statement to clarify his views.

It read, 'I would like to put on record that I am not homophobic. I have homosexual friends and I do not judge them because of their sexuality. My comments you may have read are from the Holy Scriptures and that is where I live from.'

Fury admitted on Twitter, 'Hopefully I don't win @BBCSPOTY as I'm not the best roll [sic] model in the world for kids, give it to someone who would appreciate it', but the BBC decided Tyson should stay on the shortlist for the award.

They explained, 'The Sports Personality shortlist is compiled by a panel of industry experts and is based on an individual's sporting achievement. It is not an endorsement of the individual's personal beliefs, either by the BBC or members of the panel.'

On the night, there was polite applause for Fury and an apology from him. 'I have said a lot of stuff,' he said, 'and none of it is with the intention to hurt anybody. I'm not a serious sort of person. I apologise to anyone who's been hurt. It's not my intention.'

He finished fourth, with Andy Murray winning the award.

'THERE are seven billion people in the world,' said Fury, 'and there's only one heavyweight champion of the world – and that's me.'

Except, boxing being boxing, it wasn't as simple as that and in January 2016, Fury flew over to New York to watch two fights for versions of the championship.

Even in the States there wasn't too much interest in the fight between Charles Martin, a southpaw from Phoenix, Arizona who had come through the All-American Heavyweights programme designed to find future heavyweight champions, and Glaskov for the vacant IBF title.

In Deontay Wilder, Fury possibly had a more worthy adversary.

For a while, Wilder had looked like the heavyweight the world, not just America, had been waiting for.

He was a puncher with a loud personality and a good story.

In his teens, Wilder had shown promise as a basketball player and American footballer, but he left sports college when he was 19 after daughter, Naieya, was born with spina bifida. He worked a job delivering beer to fast-food restaurants to help support her and only took up boxing in October 2005, around the time of his 20th birthday, after discovering there was a gym in his home city, Tuscaloosa in Alabama.

Wilder was a spindly 6ft 7ins tall, athletic – and learned quickly.

Less than three years after he took up boxing, Wilder won bronze at the 2008 Beijing Olympics.

He lost in the semi-finals to world champion Clemente Russo by a 7-1 scoreline that looked closer, and was the only member of the nine-man USA team to win a medal.

Wilder turned professional later that year and was thrown some limited opponents early on.

Only one of his first nine opponents made it past the opening round but when he stepped up to face veteran trialhorse Harrold Sconiers, Wilder was down and close to defeat before bludgeoning his rival to defeat in four rounds.

Wilder went on knocking out everyone he faced without always impressing. For all his power, he was often sloppy and ungainly. He threw himself off balance at times and would swing wildly and excitably like a novice once he had opponents hurt. He hurt everyone he hit with his right hand. Once that punch landed, the fight was either over or close to being over.

Wilder would say he was unconcerned about trying to impress people. To him, a boxing match was like a street fight and all that mattered was that he was the last man standing.

As he stepped into the fringes of world class, the knockouts kept coming. Audley Harrison was pounded into retirement in little over a minute, ex-WBO champion Siarhei Liakhovich was dispatched in similar time and Malik Scott, once a prospect, folded tamely inside a round.

After 32 straight knockouts, Wilder got a shot at WBC champion Bermane Stiverne in January 2015 – and the chance to become the first American to claim a version of the world title since Shannon Briggs held the WBO belt for seven months in 2006–07.

For the first time in his professional career, Wilder heard the final bell, but victory was his. Wilder had to rely on his jab after hurting his right hand in the fourth round.

Wilder came through a wobble in his first defence to stop Texas schoolteacher Eric Molina, rather laboured against the average Frenchman Johann Duhaupas and didn't have things all his own way against Polish southpaw Artur Szpilka either.

Earlier that night, Fury had seen Martin claim the vacant IBF title without landing a significant blow.

Glaskov had settled into the fight more quickly, but after his right knee gave way in the third round, he was unable to continue and Martin was declared the new champion.

Wilder then struggled to get to grips with Szpilka before finding the exclamation-mark finish he wanted in the ninth round.

Both loaded up and swung their back hands. Wilder landed first, sending Szpilka crashing heavily. For a few moments, Wilder feared Szpilka was dead and it took him a few minutes to get to his feet.

Once he had, in a scene reminiscent of American wrestling, Fury climbed into the ring and got hold of a microphone.

'Any time, any place, anywhere,' he boomed at Wilder and they went nose to nose.

Fury peeled off his jacket and stormed around the ring, while Wilder took the microphone and said, 'You're not a real fighter. I don't play this. This ain't acting, this ain't WWE.'

That reaction would have pleased Fury. The signs were Wilder was underestimating him. Fury found another rival a few weeks later, one who was much closer to home.

ANTHONY Joshua was a heavyweight blessed with a knack for being in the right place at the right time.

From Watford, he struck super heavyweight gold at the London Olympics in 2012 after winning a couple of close decisions that may not have gone his way had the Games been held elsewhere. Now, after 15 straight knockouts as a professional, there was an opening to fight for the world heavyweight championship.

Joshua had come through a crisis, the first of his paid career, against Dillian Whyte in his previous fight, but still, promoter Eddie Hearn fancied IBF champion Charles Martin was very beatable.

He suggested the fight to Joshua by text. Joshua replied instantly, 'Let's roll.'

Fury and Joshua had sparred back in 2010 when Tyson was preparing for his rematch with John McDermott and Joshua was still an amateur.

Their accounts of the spar varied wildly.

Fury said, 'Amateur boxer he was at the time. He had a good couple of rounds, then I started hitting him round the body.

'He was like this, lifting his legs up in the corner, there were ten people in the gym who saw it.

'I'm there with my hands down, he's coming forward with big swings. How's he going to hit me? I said, "Go on then, I'll stand still."'

Joshua said, 'I didn't know who Tyson Fury was.

'I remember reading that Tyson Fury is going around different gyms sparring and if anyone can knock him out, they get to keep his Rolex.

'I was hungry. Those assets and stuff were so out of reach to me.

'I remember him popping in the gym and then coach says, "All right Josh, you're sparring." In the boxing gym, there is no word called "No".

'I just got my headguard on, gumshield in and we just cracked on. Me and him just had a straight war. What I learned about Fury is, we've got the same heart. We're both fighting people and we go to war.

'I didn't manage to knock him out. We both hit each other with some big shots, powerful shots.

'He predicted, "Watch out for this kid, he'll be heavyweight champion of the world one day."'

Fury later dismissed that as the sort of encouragement he would give to any young amateur. He would call Joshua 'a poor man's Frank Bruno' but he also accepted the possibility that a 'fickle' boxing public could one day put Joshua ahead of him in their affections.

He gave the public a reminder of the heavyweight hierarchy the day Joshua fought Martin.

It was announced the rematch between Fury and Klitschko would take place at the Manchester Arena on Saturday, 9 July.

The news stole a few column inches from Joshua and was a reminder that it was Fury who was the true world heavyweight champion and that the biggest fight in the division was his rematch with Klitschko, not a fight between Joshua and Martin.

The following day, hours before the Martin–Joshua fight at London's O2 Arena, which would be shown live on Sky Sports Box Office, Box Nation announced it would be screening the Fury–Klitschko rematch.

Fury reckoned that without a decent jab and footwork, Joshua would need 'a miracle' to beat Martin. He backed his judgement with a £1,000 bet for Martin to win by knockout. Fury picked up winnings from the bookmakers after Rule The World won the Grand National horse race that afternoon, but Martin rather let him down.

Joshua beat him early, as most expected him to do. After a quiet opening round, Joshua got his feet a bit closer, his timing right – and Martin went down twice in the second round.

THE focus turned to Fury and Klitschko later that month at a press conference in Manchester, where Fury was at his most outrageous and contradictory.

Fury brought cheerleaders with him and danced – but it was Klitschko who threw the first verbal punch.

He spoke of his disgust at some of Fury's previous comments and said, 'To all the people who say the same and think the same out there, and to you Fury, I want to say, "Fuck off".'

Fury mocked Klitschko and lifted his shirt to reveal a sizeable stomach. He turned to Klitschko and said, 'Shame on you, you let a fat man beat you. I don't even live an athlete's life. It's a disgrace to call me an athlete. Wladimir lives a strict lifestyle, but what's the point in being professional for all those years if you can't beat a fat man? I could beat Wladimir if I was 30 stones and fat as a pig. I don't need to turn up in shape.

'Boxing doesn't mean an awful lot to me. If it did, I wouldn't have eaten all the pies, drunk every pint of beer in Lancashire and gone into camp four stone overweight.

'I wish I wasn't a boxer. I hate every second of training and I hate speaking to all of you idiots [the press].

'I'd rather be at home with the kids watching television and eating sweets. But I'm just too good at it [boxing] to stop. It's easy money, knocking over a few bums.

'I'm not motivated for the fight. I hope he winds the clock back and puts me into next week. Then I can retire, get fat and go on loads of holidays.'

None of this made much sense to Klitschko. 'What comes out of his mouth is not right,' he said. 'I will knock him out.'

Fury went back to belittling Klitschko, saying, 'If a so-called super champion can't land [punches] on a big, fat, lazy gypsy with a loud mouth, what kind of a super champion is he?'

Fury stayed in the headlines after an interview with a video channel was aired. During it, he said of Jews, 'Everyone just do what you can, listen to the government, follow everybody like sheep, be brainwashed by all the Zionist, Jewish people who own all the banks, all the papers, all the TV stations. Be brainwashed by them all. You're all going to heaven. Oh, sorry, there isn't a heaven in the modern-day world. So just crack on.'

He also said of transgender people, 'It's like you're a freak of nature if you're normal. You're the odd one out, nobody else. What's normal? I'll just get myself changed into a woman. That's normal, isn't it? Today, [I'll] call myself Tysina or something like that, put a wig on. I don't think it's normal. I think they're freaks of nature.'

Fury seemed to despair of the world in which he lived.

'I think it'll be perfectly normal in the next ten years to have sexual relationships with your animals at home,' he said. 'You know, your pets, your cats and dogs and all that. So that will be legal.

'You are already allowed to marry your kids and stuff. It is going to happen, though, isn't it?

'Whatever you think of that's bad will be made legal because that's what the devil wants. So if you want to shag your animals, it will be made OK. It's legal, it's normal. In a world that's changing its morals daily and lowering the bar of daily morals, then it is OK to do all this sort of stuff.

'I'm probably going to get into a lot of trouble for this interview, for talking sense and the truth.'

He did get into trouble. Complaints were made to the British Boxing Board of Control and Tyson was forced to apologise.

He said in a statement, 'I apologise to anyone who may have taken offence at any of my comments. I said some things which may have hurt some people, which as a Christian man is not something I would ever want to do. Though it is not an excuse, sometimes the heightened media scrutiny has caused me to act out in public.

'I mean no harm or disrespect to anyone and I know that more is expected of me as an ambassador of British boxing and I promise in future to hold myself up to the highest possible standard.

'Anyone who knows me personally knows that I am in no way a racist or bigot, and I hope the public accept this apology.'

The statement added, 'As a man of Traveller heritage, Mr Fury has suffered bigotry and racial abuse throughout his life, and as such would never wish anyone to suffer the same. He has many friends of a wide range of backgrounds and races and wishes no ill to anyone of any race, religion or sexual orientation.

'Mr Fury is a devout Christian and a family man. However, he accepts that in the past, he has said things publicly which are misrepresentative of his beliefs and usual good character. He appreciates he has a duty as the heavyweight champion of the world. He knows it comes with certain responsibilities and anything he says publicly will be heavily scrutinised. Mr Fury now wishes to move past this and instead concentrate on what he does best, which is boxing.'

FIVE weeks later, it was a very different Fury who met the British press at his training camp in Steenbergen, in the southern part of the Netherlands.

He looked rather more like an athlete.

'No one is knocking on the door,' Tyson explained, 'none of my friends are here. It's solitude. Train, eat, sleep, repeat. I'm really getting into it.'

He also made a change to his diet. Fury revealed he no longer ate meat, usually considered a crucial part of a fighter's diet given it is such a major source of protein.

'It's got to the point where I don't like meat any more,' he said. 'If I am sitting in a restaurant and I am looking at the man next to me and he is eating a big juicy steak, I'm like, "Urgh, that's disgusting." I'm not a vegetarian, I'm a pescatarian and I think I will stick to it.

'I don't feel bloated after eating fish and don't want to lie down like a lion after it has killed something.'

CHAPTER 14

Falling Apart

THE KLITSCHKO fight was only 15 days away when it was announced that Fury was injured and would have to pull out.

He explained in a statement, 'About ten days ago I was running up in the Lake District and I went over on my ankle and sprained it. I've been to the hospital and had X-rays and MRI scans. They say it is not broken, but it is badly sprained and to keep off it for six or seven weeks.

'I tried to train on it and had a second opinion a week later and I've had the same advice. So the fight will be postponed.'

Fury said the fight would be rearranged 'as soon as possible'.

Surely it wasn't a coincidence the announcement was made the day before Anthony Joshua defended his IBF title against American Dominic Breazeale. Fury knew the news he wasn't fighting was bigger news than Joshua fighting.

Joshua kept his title by breaking down the stubborn, but limited Breazeale in seven rounds at London's O2 Arena, but the following day, the headlines were all about Fury.

THE *Sunday Mirror* claimed that both Tyson and cousin Hughie had been found with 'unacceptable levels of nandrolone' after a drugs test.

Nandrolone was treated as an anabolic steroid and on the banned list of the World Anti-Doping Agency.

It is a male sex hormone that can be created naturally in the body, particularly if the subject has eaten large quantities contaminated with the substance.

It can help to increase an athlete's muscle size, strength and power, aids recovery from injury and allows them to train harder for longer.

The story claimed Tyson and Hughie had both been brought to a meeting to explain themselves the previous September, around eight weeks before the Klitschko fight.

Promoter Mick Hennessy released a statement. 'We are baffled by the story in the *Sunday Mirror*,' he said. 'Tyson Fury absolutely denied any allegation of doping.'

It seemed bizarre.

The test Fury failed was conducted by the Voluntary Anti-Doping Association. Fury himself volunteered for the testing and then failed, which seems highly unlikely.

Fury gave the explanation that he had eaten offal from uncastrated wild boar, the same explanation previously given by cyclists and swimmers after they failed a similar test.

There was always the possibility he had taken it unknowingly in a supplement, as fellow heavyweight Dillian Whyte did.

Surely this was a genuine mistake.

That Fury himself volunteered for the test strongly suggests he had nothing to hide and to take drugs would be an admission that he needed help to win a fight.

It would be the equivalent of taking a weapon to a bareknuckle fight and would go against the code of a proud fighting man like Fury and bring shame on his family.

Fury was outraged. He said he planned to sue.

Peter Fury gave a straightforward defence of his nephew and son. 'It's a load of bollocks,' he said. 'I don't see anything in all of it.'

Peter also had to defend what happened next.

Tyson headed to France to support England's football team at the European Championship.

He was filmed buying a round of 200 jagerbomb drinks – a mix of alcoholic and energy drinks – for supporters and leading them through the streets, conducting chants of, 'There's only one Tyson Fury.'

Peter was quizzed about his nephew's behaviour and said he understood. 'The fight game,' he explained, 'a lot of it's mental. Whatever it takes for him to be in a good mood, let him do it.

'If he wants to go out and have a party, if he wants to go out and enjoy himself and be around crowds of people, let him do it. He's isolated in a training camp, so if he wants to do the opposite and flip that coin and he's not doing anything wrong anyway, go and do it.'

Fury had more reason to celebrate that summer when his son was born.

He was named Prince after the former world featherweight champion, Prince Naseem Hamed.

IF you want a happy ending, the history of the heavyweight championship isn't the best place to look.

One of the biggest prizes in sport has often proved to be a poisoned chalice.

Norman Giller's book *Crown of Thorns* told of the troubles that had engulfed fighters who held the title, including Leon Spinks.

He was arrested six times in the seven months between his win over Muhammad Ali and the rematch in 1978.

'There's a lot on your mind when you're heavyweight champion,' admitted Spinks. 'Maybe I didn't know how to deal with it.'

Fury was equally ill-equipped to deal with the attention holding the belts brought and in the summer of 2016, months after he had taken the world heavyweight championship off Klitschko on one of the great nights in British boxing history, Tyson decided he couldn't take any more.

'I hit the drink, I hit the drugs and I was out all night with the women of the night,' he said.

'I just wanted to die and I wanted to have fun doing it. But when the drink wears off, it just leaves you with a bad hangover and even worse depression.

'When you have a goal in your mind from being a child and you achieve it, I was lost, I didn't know what to do.

'I was waking up and I didn't want to be alive. I was making everyone's life a misery. No one could talk any sense into me at all.

'I would get very, very low at times and start thinking these crazy thoughts.

'I bought a brand new Ferrari convertible in the summer of 2016.

'I was in it on the highway and I got the car up to 190 miles per hour and was heading towards a bridge.

'I didn't care what anybody was thinking. I didn't care about hurting my family, friends, anybody. I didn't care about nothing. I just wanted to die. So bad. I had given up on life. As I was heading towards that bridge in this Ferrari, which would have been crushed like a Coke can if I had hit it, I heard a voice saying, "No, don't do this, Tyson. Think about your kids. Think about your family. Think about your little boys and girls growing up with no father and everybody saying their dad was a weak man, who left you and took the easy way out."

'Just before I turned into the bridge, I pulled on to the motorway and I was shaking. I pulled over and I was all nervous and I did not know what to do. I was so afraid. And I thought to myself, "I will never, ever try – or even think about – taking my own life again.'''

THE Klitschko rematch was rescheduled for 29 October in Manchester.

There was a press conference for the fight in London on 12 September but Fury wasn't there.

The explanation given was that Fury and his travelling companion got stuck in traffic and then ran out of petrol. Fury telephoned Hennessy to tell him the news just as his mobile phone battery was dying.

'This is the first press conference Tyson has ever missed,' said Hennessy. 'He's normally very early and very entertaining at press conferences. So this is not the norm and we are not making it up.'

Klitschko rolled his eyes at the news, but Warren assured there was 'no danger' of the fight not going ahead.

Fury did still have the UK Anti-Doping investigation hanging over him, but a judge ruled the hearing would not take place until after the fight and Warren promised, 'If Tyson's car breaks down on the way to the arena, I'll pick him up on my motorbike.'

Still, Peter Fury confessed the last few weeks had been 'chaos'.

He added that Tyson was training twice a day and estimated he would weigh around a stone more than he did for the first fight with Klitschko.

Twelve days later, the fight was off.

Doctors decided Fury was 'medically unfit' to fight and in a letter to Klitschko, he was told Tyson would be 'unavailable for the foreseeable future'.

Hennessy released a statement. 'Medical specialists have advised the condition is too severe to allow him to participate in the rematch and that he will require treatment before going back into the ring,' it read.

'Tyson will now immediately undergo the treatment he needs to make a full recovery. We and Tyson wish to express our sincerest apologies to all those concerned with the event and all the boxing fans who had been looking forward to the rematch.

'Tyson is understandably devastated by the development.'

Peter wrote in a post on Twitter, 'He will not and should not be stripped of his belts.'

The WBO was set to meet for its annual convention in Puerto Rico on 17 October, when it would discuss what to do with its heavyweight belt. The WBA also had to decide what to do next. Worse was to follow.

Six days later, ESPN declared they had seen a letter saying Fury had tested positive for cocaine.

The test had taken place on 22 September, two days before Fury pulled out of the Klitschko rematch.

The letter, from Voluntary Anti-Doping Association president Margaret Goodman to Fury, Klitschko, the British Boxing Board of Control and the United States' Association of Boxing Commissions, stated that Fury's 'A' sample had traces of benzoylecgonine, the central compound found in cocaine.

On 1 October, Fury posted a photograph on Twitter with his head superimposed on the body of Tony Montana, the drugs baron from the *Scarface* film.

In front of him was a pile of white powder, presumably cocaine.

'#Tysonmontana' read the tagline.

ON Monday, 3 October 2016, Tyson Fury announced his retirement from boxing.

'Boxing is the saddest thing I ever took part in, all a piece of shit,' he wrote in a tweet. 'I'm the greatest & I'm also retired, so go suck a dick, happy days.'

Three hours later, he reversed his decision, again on social media.

'Hahahaha u think you will get rid of the Gypsy King that easy!!!' he wrote. 'I'm here to stay. #The Greatest just shows u what the medea [sic] are like. Tut tut.'

Fury added later, 'Soon as I get better I'll be defending what's mine: the heavyweight throne.'

The following day, Billy Joe Saunders was asked about Fury at a press conference to publicise his defence of the WBO middleweight championship against Artur Akavov that was scheduled for later that month.

He had known Fury since he was a teenager and said, 'I'm very concerned he won't see 30 years old. If the public don't get behind him and he doesn't get the help he needs, it could affect his and his family's lives forever.

'The Travelling community's behind him. But [others] need to give him a pat on the back. I'm not saying everything he's done is right. But he needs an "It'll be all right, don't worry about it, chin up." Give him a bit of that and perhaps he might see a bit of light, it might give him a bit of confidence.

'He's very down. He's not in a mood to talk to anybody. He's mentally not there. Nothing shocks me at the moment because he's not mentally right. He needs help. He's in an extremely bad place.'

Saunders gave an insight into the sort of abuse Fury suffered.

He said, 'It's easy to say, "Just ignore it" if you are not on the receiving end all the time.

'It isn't every so often [that Tyson was receiving abuse on social media], it is every day. After a bit, you get to think, "This is true."

'I know some people say things to get certain reactions. I put it to the back of my mind. With Twitter and Facebook, you can chuck that phone out of the window if you want and never have to look at it again, but not when it's night and day walking down the street, when you can't get away from it. You can be sitting in a restaurant and someone is giving you abuse.'

Saunders revealed that in the previous couple of days, a van driver had hurled abuse at him.

FURY gave readers of *Rolling Stone* magazine's website an insight into his troubled mind in an astonishing interview published on Tuesday, 4 October.

'It's been a witch hunt ever since I won that world title,' he said. 'Ever since I got a bit of fame for doing good, there's been a witch hunt on me because of who I am and what I do.

'There's hatred for Travellers and gypsies around the world, especially in the United Kingdom, especially with the British Boxing Board of Control and some of the sanctioning bodies of the world titles.

'I had to fight one of the best champions in history. No one gave me a prayer. I finally prevailed over the guy, beat him and I get treated like shit.

'Within a week, the IBF, the International Boxing Federation, stole my belt and give it to somebody else, knowing full well I couldn't defend it in a week because I had a rematch set with Klitschko.

'From then on, it's been nothing more than a witch hunt. From then on, they've tried to get me chucked out of boxing because they cannot tame me, they cannot hire me, I'm not for sale, no one can turn a key in my back.

'No one can do nothing to stop me, so now they're saying I took some cocaine, for what they've done to me. It's a travesty what they've done. I want to expose them for what they are. The British Boxing Board of Control is in on it too. They're all in it together. The drug testing companies are in on it as well.

'If I tested positive in February 2015, for drugs, why let me fight the long-reigning champion and leave [sic] of all his belts in November? Why not strip me in February?

'I come from a Travelling background and we suffer the biggest racism and discrimination in the country. I've been refused in restaurants because I'm a Traveller. I'm the heavyweight champion of the world and I've been to restaurants and been told, "Sorry mate, you can't come in. No Travellers allowed."

'So you can see my frustration with it all. I get no credit for defeating the second-longest-reigning champion in history. Even my own country where I was born and raised hate me. The only thing the press wants to write is negativity.

'As soon as I won the title, I got back off the boat and picked up the newspaper. "Tyson done something controversial." It wasn't, "He's dethroned the best man." It was that he's done this and done that. Anything to try and take credit away from me.'

That was followed by a startling admission.

'I've done lots of cocaine, lots of it,' admitted Fury. 'Why shouldn't I take cocaine? Plenty of people have done cocaine as well. What the fuck has that got to do with anything? That ain't a performance-enhancing drug. Am I not allowed to have a life now as well? Do they want to take my personal life off me, too?

'I've not been in the gym for months. I've not been training. I've been going through depression. I just don't want to live any more. I've had total

[sic] enough of it. They've forced me to the breaking edge [sic]. Never mind cocaine. I just didn't care. I don't want to live any more.

'So cocaine is a little minor thing compared to not wanting to live any more.

'I only started to take cocaine in the last few months.

'I was a lot happier when I wasn't the world champion because people wasn't [sic] giving me as much shit. People wasn't [sic] wanting me to do all these bad things so much.

'Listen, I've been pushed to the brink. I can't take no more. I'm in a hospital at the moment. I'm seeing psychiatrists. They say I've got a version of bipolar. I'm a manic depressive. All from what they've done to me. All this shit through boxing, through taking titles, through writing me off. I beat the man, but I'm still shit.

'I used to love boxing when I was a kid. It was my life. All the way through it was my life. You finally get to where you need to be and it becomes a big mess and that's it.

'I hate boxing now. I wouldn't even go across the road to watch a world title fight. That's what it's done to me. I don't even want to wake up. I hope I die every day. And that's a bad thing to say when I've got three children and a lovely wife, isn't it?

'But I don't want to live any more and if I could take my life – and I wasn't a Christian – I'd take it in a second. I just hope someone kills me before I kill myself. I'll have to spend eternity in hell.

'I don't know if I'm going to see the year out if I'm honest. I am seeking help, but they can't do nothing for me. What I've got is incurable. I don't want to live. All the money in the world, fame and glory, means nothing if you're not happy and I ain't happy. I'm very far from it.

'Boxing, I would say, is the most corrupt organisation in the whole of sports. My face didn't fit. I don't belong in boxing, people like me. They only want people that they can tell what to do and wind the key in the back. Robots.'

Tyson went on to explain the cause of what sounded like paranoia.

'Last week, they came to my house at 1.30 in the morning, tested me, and came back at 9am to test me again,' he said. 'What is this?

'Do you understand the treatment I'm getting off these people? They're driving me mad. It is crazy that's what's going on, but listen, I don't really care. They've won, they've got what they wanted. That's it. I'm as fat as a pig. I'm 285lbs, 290lbs, I've been an emotional wreck.

'My wife says she can't live with me because I'm a lunatic. I'll lose my family, my wife, my kids, everything. All due to boxing. I wish to God on everything that I never got into boxing as a child.

'I wish this never happened and I had just done a routine job and a routine life. It's shoved wedges between my team, my uncles, cousins, relatives, everyone who was involved in boxing. Everyone was unhappy with all of this and it's all because of me. I feel like I'm the one who's done all this. It's my burden to carry. Why should everybody else have to carry it around with them just because they trained me?

'I feel more racism now in 2016 than any slave, any foreign immigrant, ever did in the 1800s.

'Listen, when Muhammad Ali threw his gold medal away in the 1960s for being mistreated and abused, this is what I'm doing today. I'm throwing all my world titles in the bin because I ain't accepted in society for being a Traveller in 2016. What does it mean to be a world heavyweight champion when you cannot go into your local restaurant, sit down and have a dinner? It doesn't mean nothing, clearly.

'No one can say a good thing. Whatever I do. If I won over 30 fights and knocked out everybody, it would be no good. If I was the best maths teacher in the world, it would be no good. If I was the United States president, I'd be no good. I can't do anything in my life that's any good to the general people because I'll never be accepted for who I am and what I am.

'You could go and ask 100 people about Travellers and they've got nothing good to say about them. I don't know where it comes from.

'I always thought, "Once I get to the top it will all change." But I know, deep down inside, it would never change.'

Tyson was adamant he 'never took a performance-enhancing drug ever. The only person that can beat me is me.'

Fury was falling apart.

'I've not been in the gym since May,' he admitted. 'I went over to Holland to do a training camp and was crying every night. I said to Peter, "I cannot do this any more." I said, "I'm breaking down, there's something wrong with me, I want to go home. Take everything and chuck it in the bin. I don't want it no more."

'From that day forward, I've never done any training. I've been out, I've been drinking. I'm on the verge of becoming an alcoholic. I'm drinking Monday to Friday to Sunday. I can't deal with it and the only thing that helps me is when I get drunk out of my mind and that's it. I don't tell lies, I've no need to tell lies. I've taken drugs, cocaine, on many, many occasions for the last six months. Not to enhance my performance – because I haven't been performing.

'I've been out drinking, drugging, acting like a lunatic, being a fool, all to try and feel better in myself. But nothing can suffice [sic] my thirst no more. I'm finished. All the drugs and drink in the world ain't going to make me happy no more. Nothing makes me happy any more because I have gone past the point of happiness. There is no returning for me any more. I am finished.'

Fury did say he had given up drink and drugs. 'I just want time alone with my family,' he said. 'I've got demons on me, I'm trying to shake them off. I want a normal life. I don't want to box any more.'

Following the interview, Fury rang the reporter back to retract his retirement and added, 'Nothing can ever, ever mean more to my family, my history of people, than winning those titles. We are bareknuckle champions – boxing champions. All that matters to us is fighting.'

THE British Boxing Board of Control was set to hold its monthly meeting on Wednesday, 12 October when Fury's immediate future would be discussed.

On the same day, Tyson decided to relinquish the WBA Super and WBO championship belts.

He said in a statement, 'I now enter another big challenge in my life, which I know, like Klitschko, I will conquer.

'I won the titles in the ring and I believe that they should be lost in the ring, but I'm unable to defend at this time and I have taken the hard and emotional decision to now officially vacate my treasured world titles.'

The following day, it was announced that the Board had suspended Tyson's licence to box.

Peter insisted his nephew would fight again.

'Boxing is in his life,' he said. 'It's in his blood. It's in his veins. He doesn't know anything else.

'He's just frustrated. When you lose interest in everything and you can't see the meaning of anything, clearly you've got a problem.

'He's addressing it now and we spoke for three and a half, four hours yesterday. The treatment he's had already is doing him a lot of good. He hasn't got a drug addiction. He just did a stupid thing. He's not going into any clinics for drug abuse; he's got manic depression, which is a version of bipolar. They did have a name for it, but I can't think of it. They said over a period of the next few months, he should start to respond and progress.

'The Board needs to understand that he's got a severe depression problem. He's got all of his reports to go with it. He's attending the necessary clinics. Once Tyson Fury produces all of his records of what he's been through, the boxing board I don't think will have any option but to give him his licence back because this is a guy that's needing medical treatment.

'Once the powers that be say he's fit to box and he's OK, there's no reason why he can't be reinstated [as a professional boxer].

'He is controversial, he lights up boxing, whether it be good or bad.

'He is the world champion, the true world champion. I think when he does come back, he'll be welcomed with open arms. Especially [because of] the way he's voluntarily relinquished the belts.'

STORIES started to circulate among Morecambe's homeless community.

In the early hours, a giant figure was walking among them handing out bundles of notes adding up to £1,000.

The mystery figure was Tyson Fury.

Given his wealth and status, he might have been expected to be found in fashionable nightclubs drinking with celebrities.

Fury instead found companionship among those who couldn't cope and reached out to help them.

Those close to Tyson never questioned the goodness of his heart.

His late uncle, Hughie, ranted at me after Tyson decided to be trained by his brother, Peter.

There had been a fall-out with Peter years earlier and therefore Hughie would have nothing more to do with his nephew. He still wished him all the best.

'Tyson's a lovely lad,' said Hughie once he had emptied himself of his hurt, 'and I do hope he becomes world heavyweight champion.'

Fury did become world heavyweight champion and though it didn't spoil him, it brought him trouble, as it had done many more before him.

He had described himself as 'a misfit' and felt winning one of the most prestigious prizes in sport would bring him happiness and acceptance.

It hadn't.

It had always been Tyson Fury against the world and even now he was heavyweight champion of the world, it still was.

Fury argued that those who judged him simply didn't understand his culture and that Travellers were the victims of dreadful prejudice.

Katie Hopkins, considered worthy of having a column in the *Daily Mail*, went as far as to describe gypsies as 'feral' on social media and for Fury, verbal abuse was daily.

ONE family friend described Tyson Fury as 'a heart attack waiting to happen' around the time Anthony Joshua and Wladimir Klitschko fought in front of 90,000 fans at Wembley Stadium on 29 April 2017.

Fury's exile had cleared the way for such fights to happen and as he sat down to watch the fight, he was as far away from facing the winner as it was possible to be.

At the time, he estimated he was drinking around 20 pints most nights and washing them down with shorts.

The fight between Joshua and Klitschko gave Fury something to focus on other than his own self-destruction.

David Kidd of *The Sun* went as far as to describe it as 'an authentic fight to stop the planet – the brightest young heavyweight on Earth against the veteran who has dominated the division for a decade and is desperate to win back his crown.'

Somehow, the fight lived up to its billing.

Not an awful lot happened until the fifth, when Joshua got in first with a right hand and kept punching until Klitschko slid to his knees.

He was up immediately but still looked dazed and worse still for Klitschko, there were more than two minutes left in the round.

Joshua unloaded right hands and left hooks as the crowd screamed, but Klitschko was hard to nail cleanly and the flow of punches from Joshua slowed after Klitschko found his chin with a leaping left hook.

Only a clean punch from victory a minute or so earlier, Joshua was now on rubbery legs. He grabbed, blocked and slipped as Klitschko, blood dripping from a wound under his left eyebrow, went after him. Joshua tottered around the ring unsteadily, but he stayed on his feet until the bell.

The minute's break wasn't enough for Joshua to recover fully. Midway through the sixth, he was on the floor. Joshua got up and had to find a way to get through the one minute 40 seconds left in the round.

There was no rush from Klitschko. He was content to take his time, pick his punches. Most of them missed and when he did land, Joshua grabbed and got through to the bell.

It looked only a matter of time before an exhausted Joshua was knocked out, but with Klitschko either unable or unwilling to go through the gears, he got through the crisis and by the end of the ninth was re-energised and ready for a big drive in the last nine minutes.

Joshua made his breakthrough in the 11th with a huge right uppercut and it proved to be the final twist in a compelling fight. This time, there was no way back for Klitschko. Joshua kept pouring on the punches to drop him twice before the fight was stopped.

In the euphoria of victory, Joshua asked the crowd if they wanted to return to Wembley to watch him fight Fury.

The answer was overwhelming. Fury had two replies on social media. 'Welldone [sic], good fight,' he tweeted, 'you had life & death with Klitschko and I played with the guy, let's dance.'

He added, 'Challenge accepted. We will give the world the biggest fight in 500 years. I will play with u [sic]. You are a boxers [sic] dream.'

Fury was asked later how he had felt when he saw Joshua dropped in the sixth round.

'I was willing him to get up because me against him is the biggest fight ever,' he said. 'It's the Achilles and Hector of today.'

BY September 2017, Tyson Fury was growing impatient.

There had been an anti-doping tribunal planned the previous month to decide his future, but it was halted after one day because one of the lawyers involved had a conflict of interest.

'How long must I be held up and kept out of action?' he tweeted. 'It's been 15 months since I've been under investigation. You're keeping an innocent man from fulfilling his destiny and from providing for his family. Everybody else is dealt with in a few months, why must I be treated differently? Surely there must be a human rights law preventing this from happening to people.

'Either ban me or set me free as I've been in limbo for a long time! I want to move on with my life! Clear my name and let me return to my former glory.'

One of the fighters to benefit from Fury's absence was his cousin Hughie.

TYSON Fury once said he would win all the heavyweight belts and then vacate one to allow his cousin to fight for it.

That wasn't quite how things worked out, but still, Hughie got his shot against Joseph Parker for the WBO title in Manchester in September 2017.

Parker had claimed the WBO belt vacated by Tyson with a points win over chubby American Andy Ruiz and so became New Zealand's first holder of a world heavyweight championship.

Parker was always likely to be a boxer. His father was named after Jack Dempsey and from the age of three, Joseph was hitting his hands in preparation for a boxing career.

Parker went on to win bronze at the World Youth Championships and while still a teenager, he reached the quarter-finals of the 2010 Commonwealth Games in New Dehli.

He turned professional and made an exciting rise up the world rankings before reining himself in to outpoint Ruiz for the vacant WBO title.

The fight was close and had Ruiz not won the last round, it would have been a draw.

Parker was set to make his first defence against Hughie Fury in May 2017, but the challenger was ruled out through injury.

Parker went on to defend against sparring partner Razvan Cojanu and the fight with Hughie was rearranged for September, in Manchester.

Hughie, a quietly spoken character, had jabbed his way into world title contention.

He turned professional aged 18 after winning gold in the world juniors and he was kept busy fighting on his nephew's undercards and small-hall shows.

Fury made his move into world class by outpointing Andriy Rudenko in Monte Carlo in February 2015.

Rudenko was a hardened gatekeeper beaten only by Lucas Browne on a disputed points decision in 25 previous fights, but by the middle rounds against Fury he was shaking his head.

Rudenko simply didn't know what to do with Fury as he jabbed, moved and smothered on the inside.

Fury won unanimously on the scorecards and cemented his place in the world rankings by turning what looked like a tricky test against Fred Kassi into a glorified sparring session.

In his previous fight, Kassi had held veteran gunslinger Chris Arreola to a draw, ruining his hopes of a shot at Deontay Wilder, but he barely laid a glove on Fury.

Hughie had previously turned down chances to challenge Wilder and Joshua for versions of the world title and it was felt that fighting Parker in Manchester was a much better opportunity for him.

Parker hadn't sparkled since reaching world level, while Fury had developed a style that was hard to beat.

Tyson was there throughout the build-up to the fight and revealed a kinship with Parker.

He was full of praise for the champion, while at the same time rooting for his cousin.

Tyson was at ringside for the fight, big enough at 25 stones to fill two seats.

The fight itself was a dull spectacle. There were no knockdowns, no exchanges and no real drama.

Fury did a good job of jabbing and moving and frustrating Parker, but in too many rounds he didn't throw enough punches.

Two of the judges had it a landslide for Parker at 118-110 and the other couldn't separate them at 114-114.

The Furys offered a different interpretation. They celebrated wildly at the final bell, apparently convinced Hughie had done enough to win the belt, and there were bemused looks when the decision was announced.

At ringside, there were those who had Fury winning, while others had it a draw or scored for Parker.

Tyson, who had previously been in playful mood that night, was furious. He ranted at Board officials, certain this was further proof of a conspiracy against his family.

TYSON went on to join Parker as he celebrated keeping his portion of the world championship.

They headed to the fashionable Ice Cave Club in Manchester and later posted footage of them with their shirts off performing the haka, a tribal dance made famous by the New Zealand rugby team.

The following night, Tyson went out again.

Photographs that appeared in *The Sun* newspaper showed him leaving an Italian restaurant wearing a T shirt that barely stretched over his stomach and later, he was spotted in the Neighbourhood nightclub.

An eyewitness told *The Sun*, 'I went over to ask if I could get a photo with him, but the two blokes that seemed to be looking after him said, "No" and were laughing about the state he was in.

'Then, when he got up to leave, he could barely stand and had to be helped out.

'It looked like he had been on a two-day bender as I had seen pictures of him wearing the same stuff after the fight on Saturday, and by Sunday his jeans were all ripped.'

THE following month, Fury reached something of a turning point. 'I was out at Halloween dressed as a skeleton,' he remembered, 'but I was 29 and everyone else was younger. I thought, "Is this what I want from my life?"

'I left early and went home into a dark room, took the skeleton suit off and prayed [to] God to help me.

'I'd never begged God to help me before and I could feel tears running down my chest. I know I couldn't do it on my own.

'I almost accepted that being an alcoholic was my fate, but after praying for ten minutes I got up and felt the weight was lifted off my shoulders. For the first time in my life, I thought I was going to be OK.'

CHAPTER 15

Fighting Back

IN NOVEMBER 2017, Tyson Fury posted footage of himself training at Ricky Hatton's gym in Hyde, Greater Manchester.

One of Hatton's assistants was there and couldn't quite believe what he was seeing.

'The punches he was throwing were sharp and snappy,' said Mike Jackson, who had learned his job under Brian Hughes at the Collyhurst and Moston Lads' Club.

'But his arms were attached to this huge, fat body. Physically, he didn't look great, but his speed and skills were still there.'

'It was strange to see.'

Jackson estimated Fury was weighing around 25 stones. Tyson said he had lost two and a half stone in the previous two weeks and added in social media posts that his 'head is on it'.

Jackson was hugely impressed by what he saw. 'Tyson got in there and sparred [domestic contender] Dave Allen and you waited for him to tire,' he said, 'but Tyson just kept getting better. He is a freak of nature.'

Hatton posted a photograph of himself and Fury shirtless on social media. Both were flabby, but Hatton wrote, 'Don't let Tyson Fury's look fool you. What I've seen the last few weeks. Trust the Hitman.'

Anthony Joshua was less impressed, writing on Twitter, 'Get fit, you fat fuck.'

Peter Fury had said a few days earlier that Tyson would be looking to fight again in April, but he wasn't holding the pads for his nephew at Hatton's gym.

With him was Ben Davison, a trainer remembered for his corner work with Billy Joe Saunders when he defended his WBO middleweight title against Artur Akavov in Scotland in December 2016.

Days before the fight, Saunders had split from trainer Jimmy Tibbs, turning what appeared to be a routine defence into chaos.

Twenty-four year-old Davison stepped in to run the corner and though Saunders got through the fight and won unanimously, he was poor.

As he expected, Davison was criticised afterwards by a press and public who didn't understand the problems leading up to the fight.

Saunders had returned to the gym weighing 218lbs – 58lbs above the middleweight limit – and only just made the weight.

Davison said, 'That fight was all about round management because we knew Billy Joe didn't have a full 12 rounds in him. The thing is, I knew Akavov had only been 12 rounds once, so he'd have his own concerns about going the distance.

'It was a close fight and the textbook may say "Pick it up and put it on him", but I couldn't because of the situation we found ourselves in. It wasn't until rounds seven, eight and nine that I told Billy to step it up a bit so we could increase the doubts in his opponent's mind. That would allow Billy Joe to cruise the rest of the fight. I had to make the best of a bad situation because I knew Billy Joe didn't have a full tank of gas.'

Who, wondered the boxing public, was Ben Davison?

His father had boxed as an amateur and so did Ben, who also showed promise as a footballer.

He had a spell with Stevenage Borough without breaking into the first team, but boxing was his passion and he learned about the sport from Jimmy Tibbs, a trainer with around four decades of experience to pass on.

Tibbs regarded Saunders as one of the best talents he had worked with and took him to British, Commonwealth, European and WBO world honours.

Once, Saunders asked Davison for a spar, he obliged and their friendship was forged.

Fury would later say Davison 'saved my life'.

He explained, 'He was working with Billy Joe Saunders in Spain and Billy invited me over.

'I was a 27-stone mess and thought a trip to Marbella would be a good way to get on the lash.

'But then I started doing pads with Ben to see if he had balls.'

Fury discovered Davison did have what he was looking for and decided to set him another test.

'There were two gorgeous girls walking by one day and I said, "Get their numbers and you can be my trainer,"' said Fury. 'He did a swagger and came back with both, so I said, "You're hired."'

THE pair went their separate ways until a few months later, when Tyson contacted Davison and asked him to be his trainer on one condition.

Davison had to move into Fury's Morecambe home. Davison agreed, but secretly, he wanted to train Fury in Marbella.

'One morning we set out for a run in Morecambe and Tyson's kids wanted to come,' said Ben.

'They had their scooters, then one of the scooters broke. We had to fix the scooter, the wind's blowing, the rain starts coming down. I said to Tyson, "Look, I've told you we have to go to Marbella if you want to get this done." I'm thinking, "There's no way I'm going to get him over there."'

'Later on, out of the blue, he turns round and says, "Right, I've booked it. We leave tonight."'

'The journey over was a nightmare and he wanted to turn back every five minutes. We stopped off in Paris and he said, "Let's go to Disneyland Paris and I'll pay you whatever." But the next day, we were driving, the sun hit the bonnet and he was like, "I can't wait to get over here and train." I knew then that we'd made the right decision and having the family over there was good for him too.'

Davison set about getting the best out of his new fighter.

He believed the keys were 'routine and structure' and to 'keep him mentally stimulated'.

Davison found ways to keep Fury engaged. 'In sparring, I might say to him, "You're only allowed to counter punch with two shots" or, "You're only allowed to use your left hand,"' he said.

'It keeps him switched on with a target in mind, and that's how you get the best out of Tyson.'

Davison saw similarities between Fury and Saunders. Both were easily bored, but he also admitted Fury was unlike anyone else.

'We asked him to walk up a mountain and he ran,' he said. 'We were thinking, "What is this lunatic doing?" because he was still 26 stones.

'I thought he would stop after a minute, but a minute went by so I gave him another two minutes, and then another five, but he was never stopping.

'We got to the point where all fighters stop and I said we were finished, but Tyson being Tyson, he kept going to the top of the mountain.

'He puts himself in these situations to show that he's different.'

By appointing Davison as his coach, Fury was showing he was different, that he did things his way. As the former heavyweight champion of the world, he could have chosen any coach he wanted – and he picked a young unknown.

Fury explained later, 'I needed a change in my life and career and Ben was knowledgeable, ambitious and fun to be around. You get sick of going in the gym when it's dull and boring, and it's just the same repetitive bullshit. Ben changed things up and I started to enjoy training again. We've got a great relationship and we're close friends.

'In terms of boxing, he reads a fight very well, plus he's got youth on his side. One of the best things about Ben is his youth. There's more to being a trainer than just training a man into the floor. It's a thinking game and you've got to be willing to learn and to listen. You need to understand your fighter, know what he likes and what he doesn't like. That's what Ben does great; he's a good communicator.

'I need someone to be there 100 per cent of the time and Ben dedicated that part of his life to me.'

Davison also had to prove he could take a punch.

Tyson remembered a pad session with him that went wrong.

'I thought, "I've killed the trainer!"' said Fury. 'We were pouring water on him. He was out for about five minutes. When he came round, he said, "What happened?" and I told him, "You slipped, that's all."'

The other question was, what had happened to Tyson Fury?

TYSON Fury had his heroes. He talked about John L. Sullivan and Muhammad Ali and was immensely proud to follow in their footsteps.

Fury was without a world championship belt but because he hadn't lost them in the ring, he retained a claim to the title.

He was the lineal champion, the true champion whose succession could be traced back through the pages of boxing's record books.

'I hold it with pride, respect and honour and it means more to me than any belt anyway,' he said once. 'To have that great lineage going back to the days of John L. Sullivan all the way to today, to have my name among those greats is a very big achievement.'

Possibly Fury's biggest hero was his father.

John Fury was a proud, strong man who bowed to nobody and despite the prejudices he faced as a Traveller, he used his charm, his wits and, when he felt it was necessary, his fists to prevail.

If anyone could get through to Tyson, it was his father.

John Fury decided he had seen his son struggle enough. He took a caravan to Tyson's house in Morecambe, told him to pack some belongings and took him away for six weeks.

Father and son talked things through and the Tyson Fury who returned to Morecambe was rather more positive about his future.

Because of the emergence of Joshua and Wilder, Fury had targets and something to prove. Surely, after everything he had been through, Fury couldn't come back and beat them?

This was similar to the position he found himself in before the Klitschko fight.

Klitschko had been the best for years – and hardly anyone gave Fury a chance of beating him.

There was the suspicion that had his titles fallen into the hands of fighters with lower profiles, Fury may well have stayed retired, his social media activity giving him the attention he craved.

But in Joshua and Wilder, Fury had a pair of rivals to remotivate him.

'I've got a massive opportunity to go down as one of the best heavyweights of all time,' said Fury after his comeback was announced. 'I have the dance partners to achieve that.'

FURY was reunited with promoter Frank Warren for his comeback.

'Suddenly I got a phone call from him,' said Warren. 'We got together and done [sic] a deal. It was quick. We shook hands and it was done.'

Warren had known Fury since the first Chisora fight, back in July 2011.

Warren was with Chisora but admitted, 'I quite took to him [Fury]. I liked him from the off. What you see is what you get with Tyson. He was funny.'

Warren estimated Tyson would need 'three or four' fights before stepping up to fight for the world championship again.

There was speculation he would fight in Belfast on 21 April 2018, and Fury told dinner audiences that Shannon Briggs was a possible opponent.

That seemed unlikely. Though he was a crowd favourite for his pantomime behaviour and constant repetition of his 'Let's go champ' catchphrase, Briggs was 46 years old and had taken so many beatings that he was unlikely to be given a licence by the Board.

Fury had been relicensed after accepting a two-year backdated ban from UK Anti-Doping (UKAD).

There had been a delay hearing the case against Fury after UKAD sought to carry out further research into nandrolone.

Fury protested his innocence and had he been cleared, he would have been in a position to sue UKAD for loss of earnings, possibly bankrupting them.

UKAD decided to drop their claim against Fury for failing to take a test in September 2016, when he was in the depths of depression, and he accepted the backdated ban, freeing him to resume his boxing career once the Board agreed to give Tyson his licence back.

Fury was interviewed by the Board in January 2018 and they decided to relicense him 'subject to receipt and clearance of all medical requirements'.

The April date came and went and instead it was announced Fury would fight at the Manchester Arena on 9 June.

The question most asked of Fury was, what had brought him back to boxing?

As he is known to do, he gave several different answers.

One of them was, 'Deontay Wilder spurred me on. He said I couldn't do it. Definitely not. He said I was finished. I was walking along the canal with my dog at the time and I thought, "I'm a fat pig, look at the state of me." I felt like jumping in.

'I had to turn it around. I had to come back and knock him out.'

On another occasion, Fury said, 'I'm not coming back for money. I've had money and it didn't make me happy. Having something to live for makes you happy.

'Looking back, boxing has helped me through all those hard times, the good times and the bad times. I feel comfortable in the ring.'

The boxing ring was possibly the only place where things made sense to Fury.

IT wasn't just Fury who was fighting back.

The same was true of his promoter.

Frank Warren was born on 28 February 1952 and brought up in an eight-storey block of council flats on the Priory Green estate in the Angel, north London.

He drifted through several jobs after leaving school and whatever he did, Warren showed street smarts and worked hard. He made money out of selling pool tables to pubs around London, but didn't show any interest in boxing until he went to a show to support his cousin, the fearsome Lenny McLean, who he once described as 'a terrible bully'.

McLean lost a fight that, in Warren's opinion, he really ought to have won. He convinced McLean to take on a trainer – and he won the rematch inside a round. Warren said he won £25,000 that night betting on his cousin.

The beaten fighter's manager asked for a deciding third match and Warren told them, 'Why should you put it on and get all the money? He can fight anyone, he doesn't need you.'

Warren had a sharp eye for business – and spotted an opening.

Unlicensed boxing was popular and Warren felt that if he could polish its image, he could make money.

There was nothing illegal about unlicensed boxing. The term referred to professional boxing that existed outside the jurisdiction of the British Boxing Board of Control, which had run the sport since 1929.

In Warren's National Boxing Council (NBC), they found a rival.

He attracted crowds of up to 2,000 to his shows and though the boxing wasn't always of the highest quality, the fights were entertaining and the crowds kept coming back for more.

The Board, and major promoters Mickey Duff, Mike Barrett and Jarvis Astaire, became aware of the huge threat Warren posed to them when he applied for membership of the World Boxing Association, then one of the sport's two governing bodies.

It was a bold move and, if accepted, which seemed unlikely, Warren's NBC would be legitimised and the Board of Control would have to share power for the first time in half a century.

Ray Clarke was general secretary of the Board at the time and remembered, 'Warren had run those [unlicensed] shows, more or less sticking up two fingers at the Board of Control, saying he didn't need the Board, and set up his organisation, which later fell by the wayside.

'We were worried at the image of unlicensed fights, splashed across the front pages of the tabloids, who were usually calling for them to stop.

'It was bad for the image of boxing.

'He [Warren] wasn't actually invited to make an application, but word got out to him, you know, "Why don't you go legitimate? You won't get anywhere running this sort of rubbish?"'

Warren had taken on the establishment and won, and his first show under the Board's auspices, in December 1980, was a huge statement of intent.

He brought in world-class heavyweight Jerry 'The Bull' Martin to fight Otis Gordon at The Bloomsbury Hotel.

'I couldn't get TV,' Warren remembered years later, 'and on the night, the place was half empty. I lost £17,500.'

Still, Warren had made his intentions clear. He was aiming high.

Warren kept losing money on shows before he made the bold move to bring Joe Bugner out of retirement.

The British public had never forgiven Hungarian-born Bugner for sending Henry Cooper into retirement with a controversial points win in 1971. Bugner didn't find redemption in going the distance with Muhammad Ali (twice) and Joe Frazier and a decade on from the Cooper fight, Bugner remained a villain, albeit one of the pantomime variety.

One night, when he fought at Alexandra Palace on a Warren show, a huge banner was unfurled as Bugner made his way to the ring that read simply, 'Boo.'

But as the saying goes in boxing, it doesn't matter why they buy tickets, just as long as they do, and people did buy tickets to watch a 32-year-old Bugner.

That brought Warren to the attention of ITV and he secured a deal that would see his shows screened on its channel.

The relationship with Bugner didn't last, but Warren built other fighters with the help of someone described as his 'trusty lieutenant', the hugely knowledgeable trainer and matchmaker Ernie Fossey.

Fossey was dubbed 'a left-hand expert' by *Boxing News* during a professional career that peaked with a loss to Ron Hinson in a final eliminator for the British lightweight title in 1958.

Warren decided to take aim at 'the cartel' that had a grip on British boxing.

'The cartel' consisted of Jarvis Astaire, Mickey Duff, Terry Lawless and Mike Barrett and between them, they appeared to have the sport tied up.

Astaire had the finances and was vice-chairman at the Wembley Pool venue. Duff and Lawless had the best fighters in their stable and Barrett had a contract with the Royal Albert Hall.

Astaire, Duff, Lawless and Barrett decided it would be in their best interests to work together – they could tie up the best fighters and venues and split their profits, though their working relationship wasn't publicly declared.

Their shows were screened by the BBC.

Other promoters approached the channel – and were turned down.

'The cartel' were determined to hang on to power.

The Board had a 14-day rule that prevented two major shows being staged in London within 14 days of each other. The intention was to prevent crowds being thinned out, but 'the cartel' realised that if they spaced their shows correctly, they could prevent any other major promotions being held in the capital.

'The cartel' appeared to have British boxing sewn up and they became lazy.

There were some poor matches on their shows. On one infamous night at the Royal Albert Hall in October 1980, Charlie Magri, Cornelius Boza-Edwards, Dave 'Boy' Green and Jimmy Flint took a combined total of 16 minutes 20 seconds to dispose of their Mexican opponents.

It was known as 'The Night of the Tijuana Tumblers'.

Warren took on 'the cartel' – and he won.

His lawyers questioned the Board's 14-day rule and said that should the matter go to court, the Board would surely lose under the terms of the Restrictive Practices Act.

The Board decided against going to court. Warren had scored a significant victory.

The Board were unhappy with shows being screened on television either live or on the same night, believing attendances would suffer. Again, Warren took them on, knowing he had the law on his side.

Against the Board's wishes, he went ahead with a show screened live on ITV's regional channel, Thames, knowing that if they objected, he could take them to court under the Restraint of Trade law.

Warren made another huge breakthrough when he got hold of a signed document that was proof of the working relationship between the four members of 'the cartel' which, though never openly declared, was obvious.

This was front-page news.

'It's A Fix!' screamed the *News of the World*. 'Exposed: The Secret Deals of Boxing's Mr Bigs.'

The rather more sombre headline in the *Sunday Times* read: 'Revealed: The secret cartel behind boxing.'

Fighters such as John H. Stracey and Charlie Magri complained that because of Lawless's conflict of interests – he was manager, trainer and promoter – they didn't earn as much as they might have done.

The job of a manager and trainer was to secure his fighters as much money as possible, while a promoter wants to keep the cost of shows down. Magri fumed in the *Sunday Times*, 'I'm very upset about this. I've worked very hard for them and now I realise that I've been earning peanuts.

'I know Lawless had good offers for me to fight abroad, but never took them. It seems they only wanted me to fight at the Albert Hall or Wembley.'

Lawless dropped out of the group. The remaining three formed National Promotions.

The Board saw nothing wrong with what Duff, Barrett, Astaire and Lawless had done. To them, it was merely a case of a successful group protecting their interests and they took no action, but no question, this was a victory for Warren.

WARREN had said once, 'Boxing is supposed to be this big, heavy Mafia number, but if that's the case, why hasn't Mickey Duff shot me or why haven't I got him shot?

'I've had some silly phone calls, idiots, but gangs of heavies, definitely not.'

But as he got out of his car outside Barking Theatre on 30 November 1989, Warren was approached by a masked man and shot. The bullet missed his heart by an inch and though in terrible pain, he was able to flee while the gunman made his escape.

Warren survived and though he had half a lung removed, within a few days he was sitting up in bed, giving out instructions to his staff.

Fifteen days after he was shot, Warren held a press conference to declare business would go on as usual, but he would later admit the shooting had left him feeling 'humiliated' and that he could think of nothing worse.

TO the shock, and excitement, of the press and public, one of Warren's former fighters, Terry Marsh, was arrested and charged with his attempted murder.

Marsh was apprehended at Gatwick Airport on his return from the States, where he had kept Nigel Benn company ahead of his fight with Sanderline Williams and even talked of fighting again.

His arrest really was a sensation.

Marsh was a skinny, frail-looking firefighter and former Royal Marine from Essex who said he won fights by 'breaking their hearts'.

Only Warren thought Marsh would go much further than the British light-welterweight title and as it turned out, he was right.

Marsh became a national hero when he took the IBF title from Joe Louis Manley in March 1987 in a circus tent erected in his home town, Basildon.

The front page of the *Daily Mail* the following day was dedicated to Marsh's world title victory.

He looked to be a good hero for a certain audience, a wholesome, grounded family man who didn't appear to take himself too seriously and had to work hard for everything he got.

By his own admission, Marsh wasn't the most gifted of boxers, but he always reckoned he could dig deeper than his opponents and that belief was put to the test in his first world title defence, against Akio Kameda.

Badly cut, Marsh rallied to batter the Japanese fighter to defeat.

The expectation was, Marsh would defend next against his mandatory challenger – an American confusingly named Frankie Warren – for a career-best purse.

But he sold a story to *The Sun* newspaper that he knew would mean the end of his boxing career. 'World Champ Has Epilepsy' was the headline.

Marsh said he had suffered from blackouts and fits for the past couple of years, but had hidden the fact to prolong his boxing career.

The story shocked Warren. He had no idea it was coming, but still, he persuaded *The Sun* to hand Marsh an extra £10,000 for his story.

Warren knew that, at 29, Marsh would never box or work as a firefighter again.

Warren also successfully sued *The Sun*, his grievance being their story implied he had known Marsh had epilepsy and still backed his boxing career.

The fall-out with Warren cost Marsh his job commentating on Warren's shows for ITV and his behaviour became increasingly bizarre.

He was ejected from a venue after turning up in a Father Christmas outfit and claimed he had been underpaid throughout his boxing career.

The paperwork, supplied willingly by Warren, suggested otherwise. Even Warren's competitors, Frank Maloney and Barry Hearn, said that for a fighter with his limited box-office appeal, Marsh had earned well.

Warren had done a good job for his fighter.

Marsh later sold a story about him betting against himself when he fought Manley for the world title, but found it harder to make money out of betting shops and acting.

He reapplied for his boxing licence and was turned down, despite having the support of a doctor's letter. So confident had Marsh been that he would be allowed to box again, he had spent money on tickets and posters for his comeback fight.

Towards the end of 1989, Marsh found himself in debt and there was the promise of more trouble to come.

During an interview on ITV's *Midweek Sports Special*, Marsh implied Warren was aware of his epilepsy during his career – and Warren sued him for slander over the claim.

Marsh had motives to harm Warren, but after a two-and-a-half-week trial, he was acquitted.

Three decades on, Warren said, 'I do know who it was [who shot me]. Where I grew up was a tough area. You don't tell tales.'

Warren also said he later bumped into who he believed was his would-be assassin. 'I didn't say anything,' he said. 'He went the other way.'

'I WILL monopolise boxing,' promised Barry Hearn once. 'That is not an ambition. That's automatic. I am a benevolent dictator.'

Hearn had made money as an accountant and decided to invest it in a chain of billiard halls.

'Six months after I bought the billiard halls, the BBC started showing lots of snooker on television,' remembered Hearn. 'I was very lucky – and I've always said it's better to be born lucky than be born good looking.'

Hearn was also fortunate that the best snooker player in the world was a fellow Essex man, Steve Davis, and between them they dominated the sport.

Hearn turned to promoting boxing in 1987, alongside Terry Lawless. They co-promoted a heavyweight grudge match between Frank Bruno and Joe Bugner that Hearn convinced the public was of rather more significance than it was.

There were 40,000 fans at Tottenham Hotspur's White Hart Lane to see Bruno batter a flabby, disinterested Bugner to defeat in eight rounds and watching at ringside was an eight-year-old Eddie Hearn.

'After that, I was always around the gym,' said Hearn, who showed promise as a cricketer in his teens. 'I would get the bus to Romford after school and see people like Herbie Hide and Eamonn Loughran training.'

Eddie was also at ringside at Birmingham's National Exhibition Centre in November 1990 when his father's fighter, Chris Eubank, outlasted Nigel Benn in one of the most savage fights of modern times.

Eubank would be Hearn's biggest success story, an eccentric showman who wore a monocle, talked eloquently on many subjects and though his boxing wasn't always the most pleasing to the eye, he was fit and hard to his core.

He was a WBO middleweight and super middleweight champion and many of his 24 world title fights, a record for a British boxer, were under Hearn's Matchroom banner on ITV.

Eddie had three amateur bouts himself and won them all before deciding the boxing ring wasn't really the place for former public schoolboys.

'I left school and went to work for a sports management and marketing company in the West End,' he said.

'I was representing golfers on the US and PGA Tour. I did that for six or seven years.

'I decided to work at Matchroom and started on golf and went on to online gaming, producing online poker tournaments.

'I was at the World Series of Poker in Las Vegas and Audley Harrison was at my table.

'He asked me to get him a six-rounder, but I talked him into *Prizefighter*.'

Prizefighter was an eight-man tournament that offered fighters at opposite ends of their careers the chance to move forward with three wins over a three-round format on the same night. *Prizefighter* offered exposure to prospects on the way up and a possible way back for older fighters like Harrison, the 2000 Olympic super heavyweight champion who had fallen disappointingly short of the lofty expectations he had from himself.

'I told him if he won *Prizefighter*, then he could fight Albert Sosnowski for the European title and David Haye for the world title,' said Hearn.

Harrison got his shot at Haye's WBA belt after a dramatic last-round knockout of Michael Sprott, but the fight was a dreadful flop. Harrison barely landed a punch before being stopped by Haye in the third.

'After the Haye fight, I thought, "That's me done." I didn't have any ambitions to be a boxing promoter,' said Hearn. 'I just wanted to have fun and make a few quid.

'But a couple of weeks later, [coach] Tony Sims contacted me and said, "Do you want to look after Darren Barker?"

'Then I met Kell Brook at a *Prizefighter* in Liverpool and he said his contract with Frank Warren was coming to an end.

'We met him and signed a contract.

'A couple of weeks later, Rob McCracken rang and asked if I wanted to work with Carl Froch. It really did happen that quickly.

'In the space of a couple of months we signed up Barker, Brook and Froch and then other fighters wanted to get on board.'

This put Hearn in a strong position – and it became stronger.

WITHIN months of being shot, Warren was fighting back.

He brought 41-year-old former heavyweight champion George Foreman to London to knock over Terry Anderson in a round and in a good series of world featherweight title fights, Steve Robinson, a modern 'Cinderella Man' from Wales, beat domestic rivals Colin McMillan, Sean Murphy, Paul Hodkinson and Duke McKenzie.

Better still was the rematch between Benn and Eubank in October 1993 that Warren promoted in conjunction with Barry Hearn and Don King at Manchester United's Old Trafford stadium.

The fight ended in a draw.

There was also huge public interest in Benn's defence of his WBC super middleweight title against the ferocious-punching American Gerald McClellan in February 1995.

ITV reported an audience of 13.1 million for a brutal fight that had tragic consequences.

McClellan was left permanently disabled after Benn stopped him in the tenth round and it left Warren wondering if he had a future in boxing.

'I remember talking to the Board of Control medical officer, Adrian Whiteson, who said, "Frank, boxing's going to go on whether you're in it or not." And I thought, "I could do more good than harm."'

Two months after Benn–McClellan, Warren severed his 13-year association with ITV and took his stable of fighters to Sky Sports.

In the space of four weeks in 1995, Sky viewers saw national hero Frank Bruno win the world heavyweight championship at the fourth attempt and Prince Naseem Hamed outclass Steve Robinson to become WBO featherweight champion at 21 years old.

Warren would also twice promote Mike Tyson on the channel and take Ricky Hatton to the world championship before rejoining ITV to build the career of Amir Khan, who had thrilled the nation by winning silver at the Athens Olympics in 2004 aged just 17.

More than six million tuned in to ITV to watch Khan reverse his Olympic final defeat to Mario Kindelan in his final amateur bout, convincing the station's bosses to give Warren 20 shows for the next two years.

The contract was extended by a further year and there was a subsequent deal with subscription channel Setanta that ended messily. Once Khan had outgrown ITV, Warren took him, and the rest of his stable, back to Sky Sports.

Khan had the profile and rankings to be a pay-per-view fighter on the channel. His pay-per-view debut lasted all of 54 seconds but didn't go the way he'd hoped. He was crushed by Breidis Prescott, who had been recommended by Khan's new trainer Jorge Rubio, in September 2008.

SKY Sports screened 40 domestic boxing shows every year, dividing them between four promoters: Matchroom, Warren, Frank Maloney and Mick Hennessy.

The shows were on Friday nights and were topped by a fight for a major title – British, Commonwealth, European or world – and lasted for two hours.

Hennessy lost his contract with Sky, to be replaced by Ricky Hatton, and found work for his fighters on ITV.

Towards the end of 2010, there were changes at Sky.

Boxing chief Chris Brown left, to be replaced by commentator Adam Smith, and the channel's bosses reviewed their boxing coverage.

Sky was unhappy with its ratings and there was unrest among two of its promoters, Matchroom and Warren.

Warren reckoned ten shows every year wasn't enough to build his stable and that more should be invested in boxing. He broke away to form his own subscription channel, Box Nation, and Hearn made his move. 'I told Sky they should give us all the boxing shows, but there should be fewer shows and they should spend more money on them,' he said.

'You can't put on quality boxing every week like they were trying to, it just doesn't work.

'The deal was 20 shows plus four pay-per-views and that meant we could grow the team.'

Sky went along with the idea, putting Hearn in the strongest position of any British promoter since 'the cartel' three decades earlier.

Warren had his backers but Sky had more finances and, crucially, Hearn had a good relationship with Robert McCracken.

McCracken was head coach of the Great Britain amateur boxing squad and when one of their stars wanted to turn professional, they were steered towards Hearn, rather than Warren.

It was McCracken who convinced Anthony Joshua to sign with Hearn after he won super heavyweight gold at the London Olympics in 2012.

Warren was up against it but relished the challenge and with his judgement and some good matchmaking, he turned workmanlike fighters such as Terry Flanagan and Liam Smith into WBO world champions.

Smith, one of four boxing brothers from Liverpool, was handsomely paid when he lost his belt to Mexican superstar Saul 'Canelo' Alvarez in front of 51,240 fans in Dallas in September 2016.

Warren had learned how to get the most out of his fighters. He joked after Josh Warrington kept his IBF featherweight title against Carl Frampton in December 2018 that he had been in boxing 'around 100 years'.

It was closer to 40 years but he knew the job better than anyone.

Warren knew that boxing was all about making the right fights at the right time.

Ricky Hatton had asked for a world title shot for around a year before Warren delivered and when he got his chance, it was against a once-great champion who had fought only twice in the last three years, Kostya Tszyu. Hatton didn't leave Tszyu alone from the opening bell until he finally broke his spirit, forcing the champion to retire on his stool after the 11th round. 'He [Tszyu] wanted the torture to end, even with only three minutes to go,' wrote editor Claude Abrams in *Boxing News*.

Abrams added, 'It was a British success that will go down in sporting folklore like the 1966 win over the Germans at Wembley Stadium, Kelly Holmes winning two golds in Athens, Steven Redgrave and Matthew Pinsent's Olympic rowing feats, Virginia Wade winning Wimbledon and many more.'

Warren kept promoting the biggest shows until Sky's exclusive deal with Hearn meant there was a major shift in power in British boxing.

Warren found ways to keep producing champions on Box Nation and in 2017, he agreed a deal with BT Sport, Sky Sports' major competitor.

There would be 20 live shows every year and at the announcement of the deal, Warren unveiled his two major signings.

Daniel Dubois was a teenage heavyweight of immense promise and Nicola Adams was instantly recognisable to the public as the 2012 and 2016 Olympic champion and a role model.

Warren had also kept in touch with Fury.

As Tyson lost control of his life, Warren texted him, urging, 'Listen, you need to come back. Try to do something with yourself. Come back in another capacity in boxing – train or manage a boxer.

'The best sportsman in my lifetime, voted BBC Sports Personality of the Century, was Muhammad Ali. And that's the man who said blacks shouldn't marry whites, the white man is the devil. And they were some serious comments at the time. If he can do it, you can do it.'

FURY knew Ali's story as well as anyone and was determined not to make the same mistakes he made.

'There's no rush,' he said of his future plans after the date for his comeback fight was announced. 'Rome wasn't built in a day. I'm going to take my time. Muhammad Ali had three years out, had two warm-up fights and lost to [Joe] Frazier. Maybe if he had another two, he would have won.'

Fury's targets were Wilder and Joshua.

He described Joshua as 'a big old dosser carrying the belts for me' and said he regarded Wilder as the best heavyweight in the world.

169

The reason he gave was that Wilder was a fighter who 'only needs one punch', as he had proved a few weeks earlier by coming through moments of crisis to wipe out quality Cuban southpaw Luis Ortiz in the tenth round.

FURY was excited to be fighting again. The public and press were excited as well – until they discovered who his comeback opponent would be.

There were talks with David Price that came to nothing before gatekeeper Fred Kassi accepted the fight – and then changed his mind.

Sefer Seferi got the job instead.

He was a 39-year-old from Switzerland with a record of 23 wins from 24 fights, 21 inside the distance.

The press focused on his size. Seferi stood just 6ft 2½ins tall and for his previous two fights, routine stoppages of journeymen Marcelo Ferreira Dos Santos and Laszlo Hubert, Seferi had weighed 14st 1½lbs and 14st 6½lbs respectively.

They were decent enough credentials for a nightclub doorman, but in the boxing ring a cruiserweight who had never fought near genuine world class was surely going to be in desperate trouble against even a rusty version of Fury.

The result that gave Seferi credibility as an opponent for Fury was the sole loss on his record, a ten-round points reverse to Manuel Charr in an eliminator for the WBA title.

Seferi had shown toughness and knowhow to get through to the final bell.

Charr had gone on to become the world heavyweight champion the world didn't know, claiming the WBA Regular belt that really had no meaning.

Joshua held the WBA 'Super' belt. The only purpose the WBA's two belts served was to bring the organisation more sanctioning fees.

Based in Germany, Charr was a decent fighter, but at world level his leaky defence had let him down and he had been well beaten by Vitali Klitschko and Alexander Povetkin.

'We picked him [Seferi] because he went ten rounds with Manuel Charr,' explained Fury.

Seferi was in no mood to upset Fury in the build-up. He described him as his 'idol' and given his nickname was 'Real Deal', it was fair to assume Evander Holyfield was another inspiration.

Seferi's elder brother, Nuri, was also a professional fighter and called himself 'The Albanian Tyson' – their parents were Albanian – and growing up, the brothers must have scrapped to decide who was the best, Holyfield or Mike Tyson.

Sefer won the Swiss amateur heavyweight title in 2004 and 2006 before turning over and proving himself to be effective enough at the level – and weight – he fought at, without really getting anywhere.

THE weigh-in, held outside in the Great Northern Amphitheatre in Manchester city centre on a sunny Friday lunchtime, was bizarre.

Fury weighed in at a career-heaviest 19st 10lbs 2ozs – he had been 17st 8lbs for his win over Klitschko around 1,000 days earlier – but it was his actions that made the headlines.

He playfully picked Seferi up in his arms, a crazy gesture that brought laughter from fans, fighters and officials. Even Seferi laughed.

The heavyweight division hadn't seen anyone like Fury since playboy Max Baer won the world championship in the 1930s without apparently taking himself or boxing particularly seriously.

Fury was in playful mood again the following night. His entrance music was a nod to his past, the groovy lollop of Afroman's 'Because I Got High', and as referee Phil Edwards gave the fighters his final instructions in the moments before the opening bell, Fury leaned forward and gently kissed Seferi on the lips. Both fighters smiled.

When the fight got under way, Fury looked as good as he could have been expected to look as he used his footwork and feints to manoeuvre Seferi around the ring.

Suddenly, Seferi ran at Fury, tossing right hands at his chin. Fury grabbed, stuck his tongue out at the crowd and smiled at Seferi after they had been separated.

Seferi smiled back at him.

They exchanged Ali shuffles later in a strange, if entertaining, opening round.

The fight became even crazier in the final minute of the second when Fury, who had been looking more purposeful, turned to watch a brawl in the crowd.

Seferi was entitled to hit a distracted Fury, but either didn't want to upset him or felt it wouldn't have been in the spirit of this particular fight.

Both watched the scrapping ringsiders for a few seconds before reconnecting with their own fight.

There must have been times during the third round when Seferi wished he had tried to chin Fury while he was looking elsewhere.

It was a tough round for Seferi.

Fury banged in hard punches to his body and had him grabbing with uppercuts.

Ringsiders felt the fight may end in the fourth.

Fury was dominant again and in the dying seconds of the session, he broke Seferi's spirit.

Fury retreated into a neutral corner, inviting Seferi in to attack him. Seferi went for him – and ran on to a perfectly-timed right uppercut.

Seferi was stunned, backed off and Fury was all over him for the remaining seconds of the round.

Seferi went back to his stool feeling there was no possible way he could win – and that he was likely to get hurt.

Even when Seferi got Tyson where he wanted him – backed into a corner – he still got whacked hard on the chin.

The referee was called over to his corner and Seferi's coach told him his fighter was retiring.

No reason was given.

This wasn't the ending the crowd wanted and sections booed what one national newspaper described as 'a joke fight'.

The fight had served its purpose, giving Fury some time in the ring, and though Warren pointed out the rest of his show, including Terry Flanagan's unsuccessful bid to claim the vacant WBO super lightweight title against spindly American Maurice Hooker, had given the crowd value, he shared the crowd's frustration.

He asked the Board to consider withholding Seferi's pay – or part of it – but it was decided that Seferi had done enough in the four rounds the fight lasted to deserve his purse.

CHAPTER 16

Going for Greatness

FOR A while, it seemed the fight the world wanted to see was close to being agreed.

Between them, Anthony Joshua and Deontay Wilder held all four major heavyweight belts and their combined record was 61 wins, no defeats – with 59 wins by knockout.

It was the biggest heavyweight fight for more than a decade and in November 2017, Eddie Hearn and Shelly Finkel, Wilder's manager, had met to discuss the possibility of making it happen.

Joshua then added Joseph Parker's WBO title to his IBF and WBA 'Super' titles in March 2018 with a points win and, asked afterwards if he had a message for Wilder, Joshua said, 'Let's go.'

As ever in boxing, things weren't that straightforward. Alexander Povetkin, the former WBA champion from Russia who had somehow stayed in boxing despite failed drugs tests, was Joshua's mandatory challenger for the WBA title and two weeks after the Parker fight, Hearn was told he had 28 days to negotiate a deal for Joshua–Povetkin or the fight would go to purse bids.

A fight between Joshua and Wilder would take priority, if it could be arranged.

Hearn offered Wilder $12.5 million for the Joshua fight, by some distance the best purse of his career. The response was a shock.

Hearn and Robert McCracken, Joshua's trainer, received an email offering a staggering $50 million (£38 million) to fight Wilder in the States. Joshua's best purse to that point was the £15 million he earned for the Klitschko fight and even Hearn was surprised by the offer.

'We don't know if it's a PR stunt or if it's real,' he said. 'We haven't even seen any paperwork yet.

'Will this deal go through? Probably not, because when we get the contract, if we ever get it, there'll be all sorts in there.'

Intrigued, Hearn offered to meet Finkel, who he had taken to calling 'Shirley Winkel' in interviews, and Wilder's advisor, Al Haymon. The meeting didn't happen.

Wilder sent a tweet to Hearn offering $50 million or 50 per cent of the fight's revenue, whichever was the greater amount.

Hearn thought he knew what was going on. 'He's got $50 million for using Anthony Joshua's name, to go out and whore him out to try and attract the money,' he said.

'But that's not possible because they don't have the rights to do that. But they want the rights to do that and that's what they're trying to buy.

'But we're not really interested in people going out and using Anthony's name to try and attract $50 million for his purse.

'You've either got it or you haven't. If they wanted $50 million from Matchroom, they could have it in their account today. That's the difference.

'With all due respect to Deontay Wilder, who I like a lot, he doesn't have $50 million.

'All I have right now is an email from a guy from Alabama who is telling me he is going to give us $50 million.

'I get quite a lot of those emails. Sometimes from Saudi Arabia, sometimes from China, sometimes from Nigeria. Normally they ask me to send $50,000 first and then they'll send it back.'

HEARN had plans to add Wilder to his stable after agreeing a $1 billion (£740 million) contract with internet streaming service DAZN, which had ambitions to be the Netflix of sport.

That appealed to Hearn. 'Look at Netflix's numbers,' he said. '120 million subscribers.'

DAZN was looking to break into the American market having made inroads into Canada, Japan, Germany, Austria and Switzerland – and Hearn saw an opening.

He saw streaming, rather than television, as the future of broadcasting and reckoned his eight-year deal with DAZN could change boxing.

Hearn would stage 16 shows in the States every year on the channel and as part of the deal, DAZN would also screen the same number of shows from the United Kingdom. The deal was worth £92.5 million per year – or £5.7 million for each of his American shows.

'HBO and Showtime are the two major players over here [in America],' said Hearn, 'and that is a bigger annual budget than they have put together. It's the biggest deal in boxing history.'

Hearn promised, 'Within 12 months, we will have by far the strongest stable ever seen in world boxing.'

The DAZN deal was announced in May 2018, at a time when Hearn was also trying to make what he called 'possibly the biggest fight in the world'.

THE WBA agreed to extend its deadline for the Joshua–Povetkin negotiations while Hearn tried to thrash out a deal for the Wilder fight.

Barry Hearn met Finkel in New York on 1 June and following that, the Hearns offered Wilder $15 million for the fight.

'They accepted the deal,' said Eddie. 'So we controlled the worldwide rights, it was all agreed, no problem.'

The contract was sent to Finkel on 18 June and he replied six days later. He told ESPN he had 'a couple of notes' to add and would send them to Hearn by the end of the week.

The WBA was growing impatient. Hearn was running out of time to make the Wilder fight for the mooted date in October.

He said, 'So you've received the contract and you know the comments and you don't send them for another six days. Shelly also knew the WBA was about to pull the axe down, so whether they were just trying to run the time on this because they know this was coming from the WBA, I don't know.

'What I do know is, if you want a fight and you get a contract on the Monday, you give it straight to your lawyer and you get the comments back within 24 hours, simple as that. This would have been 12 days with no comments back.'

Hearn reckoned he knew what Finkel's comments would be.

He said, 'There are only two comments, which they said they were going to agree to anyway.

'One, they're saying was the date, they knew it was October, and then there's only one choice [for the venue]: Cardiff.

'But they know that anyway.

'But apparently the other one was talking about the rematch, which was agreed by them in terms which they were going to accept. So, if they're telling the truth, the deal's done.

'They now know the date, if that's what they think they didn't have. 13 April at Wembley.

'They're accepting that term they already agreed to, so why not sign it now? Now we want to put the pressure on and say, "You missed the boat for September. Come on, let's get it signed." I want people to put the pressure on them and say, "Get the comments back."

'Now we're saying, "Sign it or send the comments back." You've got the fight. It's there. So you can't say, "He's ducking me, he won't fight me, he'll never want to fight me." It's there. If you think we're bluffing, call our bluff. Sign it – and we'll sign it before the ink's dry.'

Hearn's reading of it all was that by delaying negotiations, Wilder's team were looking for a way to get him out of the fight.

'I believe Wilder wants the fight,' he said. 'This is either a big plan to gain exposure for Deontay Wilder, which by the way has worked unbelievably well for him, or just mismanagement. But they've got three managers as well, so every time it goes to Shelly, it's got to go to Al [Haymon] and it's got to go to Jay Deas.

'But it can't take two weeks, just to have the comments.'

Hearn's contract offer remained on the table and he had Wembley Stadium booked for Saturday, 13 April 2019, but if the fight was going to happen, Wilder said he wanted a 50/50 share.

'Joshua really wanted the fight for $50 million,' he fumed. 'Next thing we know, they're talking about fighting in his country for less money.

'We're done with that. Only thing we needed was the belt to unify. The 50 million is off the table. If they ever come back to us, it's going to be 50/50 straight down the line. I'm just glad the blindfolds are off people's eyes. Even casual fans can see what happened. For those that can't see, the ones I call "Eddie's zombies", they can be a fool behind him.'

The 50/50 split was never likely, despite the claim of Mark Breland, one of Wilder's trainers and a former Olympic and WBA welterweight champion, that the WBC belt his fighter held was worth more than the IBF, WBA Super and WBO belts Joshua owned.

The counter argument from Hearn was a simple one. Joshua was the biggest boxing attraction on the planet and Wilder was largely unknown in his own country. As a consequence, Joshua deserved a greater slice of the purse should they fight. Wilder brought a belt, Joshua brought three belts – and the audience.

To prove his point, Hearn was filmed walking around New York asking members of the public if they knew who Wilder was. Nobody did.

Hearn said of Wilder, 'Nobody knows who he is and he's the world heavyweight champion.'

It was unthinkable that Hearn could ask the same question of Joshua in any major city in Britain and get the same blank replies.

Wilder would argue that America is a much bigger country where American football and baseball were the national obsessions.

Wilder had Mike Tyson's knockout percentage – and even borrowed his 'baddest man on the planet' moniker – but to the American public, he was no Mike Tyson.

By contrast, Britain had embraced Joshua the way it had previously embraced Ricky Hatton, Frank Bruno and further back, Henry Cooper.

Joshua was similarly approachable and open. The public knew him by his changing room nicknames 'AJ' and 'Josh' and when he fought, Joshua gave them what they wanted. He took risky fights – there were those in his own camp who advised against him taking on Klitschko – had a wobble or two sometimes, but usually came through with a satisfying knockout.

The breakdown of the Wilder negotiations was damaging to Joshua.

Breland wanted to get the message across in the British media, 'We want the fight, they don't.'

Joshua replied, 'You don't get what you deserve in business, you get what you negotiate. [Wilder] doesn't deserve 50/50. But if he negotiates a good enough deal, he may get 50/50. That's what I would expect from my management team.'

Hearn made his point by saying, 'Anthony Joshua's profile is going to continue to grow and Wilder's is not.'

To the public, the back-and-forth negotiations, claims and counter claims were tedious. They just wanted to see Joshua and Wilder fight, but they would have to wait.

For the time being, Joshua had to focus on his mandatory challenger for the WBA title.

Povetkin was a proven, solid heavyweight, a former WBA champion beaten only by Wladimir Klitschko in 35 previous fights.

At 6ft 2ins, he was short but had learned how to close the gap fast and when close, his left hook had plenty of weight behind it.

The fight would go ahead at Wembley Stadium on Saturday, 22 September.

HEARN was able to make a couple of heavyweight fights for his show at London's O2 Arena in July 2018 – and they didn't disappoint.

In a clash of perennial contenders, Dereck Chisora survived a furious all-or-nothing onslaught from Carlos Takam in the early rounds to blast him out in the eighth and there was more drama in the top-of-the-bill fight between Dillian Whyte and New Zealand's Joseph Parker.

Parker was a Mormon who learned to box in the amateur ring, Whyte a hard street fighter who had stood his ground when faced with guns and knives while working on London's nightclub doors since he was 14 years old.

'I had a kid [Whyte became a father at 13] and I needed money,' he said.

Both Whyte and Parker had lost to Joshua and those fights gave some guide as to what would happen when they met.

Whyte still wanted to carry on fighting even after Joshua had punched him into semi-consciousness, while Parker gave rather less of himself when he lost his WBO belt to Joshua, allowing the fight, and his world title, to drift away from him.

There had been more caution from Parker since he reached world level after a violent rise up the rankings, while Whyte had the chin and heart that would keep him in fights for 12 rounds and under coach Mark Tibbs, he had improved.

The novice Whyte was forever looking to set up a right hand with a stiff jab to the body, but under Tibbs, he had shown a fast left hook counter, a long, spearing jab, a good engine and that unbreakable will to win. He used them all against Parker, clinging on to win on points after being dropped heavily in the final 40 seconds having earlier scored two knockdowns.

That preserved Whyte's number one position in the WBC rankings and though champion Wilder had a mandatory defence against Dominic Breazeale due, Hearn was willing to splash out to make Wilder–Whyte happen.

'I'd probably go up to $7 million or $8 million for Whyte to fight Wilder now,' he said. 'Wilder seems worried about coming to the UK, so we'll do it in Brooklyn. It will make fortunes for all of them.'

Hearn's proposed offer to Wilder got the headlines in Monday morning's newspapers, but by lunchtime, all the talk was about Fury.

THE Monday morning after Whyte had beaten Parker, Frank Warren was a guest on *Alan Brazil Sports Breakfast* on radio station TalkSport and made a startling revelation.

He said he was close to agreeing a deal for Tyson Fury to challenge Wilder for the WBC heavyweight championship in America by the end of the year.

Warren said a match-up with Whyte was also a possibility, but the likeliest outcome was that should Fury look and feel good enough during his forthcoming fight at Belfast's Windsor Park, he would then meet Wilder.

'I'm pretty confident we can make it happen,' Warren told Brazil. 'It takes two to make a deal and if you really want to make a deal, you will make it happen.'

Fury wrote on social media, 'I can confirm that me and Deontay Wilder are in negotiations – very close to being done.'

He knew that should the fight happen, he would score a victory over both Joshua and Hearn. Tyson said, addressing Wilder and his representatives, 'You've been dealing with shithouses in the past – Eddie Hearn and Joshua. But I am a man of my word and if I say I'll fight, I'll fight ya – end of.'

This news really did come out of nowhere.

Fury himself had said he was in no rush to face Wilder or Joshua and now, after a meaningless four-round workout against a cruiserweight, he was on the brink of securing a fight with the most feared puncher in the world.

There were those, Hearn among them, who doubted the Fury–Wilder fight would happen and even those who thought the fight would go ahead questioned Fury's thinking.

This looked to be a huge, and unnecessary, gamble after so long out of the ring, but as Davison said of Fury, he does things to show that he's different. No other heavyweight in the world – or even the division's history – would surely contemplate doing what Fury was contemplating.

There were more revelations to come later that day when Warren and Tony Bellew, a fighter he formerly promoted and who had a long-standing feud with Fury, were both invited into TalkSport's studios.

Warren made another astonishing claim.

WARREN said, 'All I know is that Anthony Joshua turned down a guaranteed $80 million (£60.95 million) – that's $50 million (£38m) for a purse and $30 million (£23m) guaranteed for a rematch [against Wilder]. That wasn't the purse, that was the guarantee. It could have been much more than that.'

Bellew, the former WBC cruiserweight champion, said no such contract existed. 'There was a contract sent,' answered Warren. 'I've seen it so I know exactly what went down.'

Bellew insisted, 'I know for a fact that if a contract was sent for £50 million, he'd have taken it.' Warren said, '100 per cent the offer was sent through.'

NO wonder Fury was in a particularly perky mood the following day when he met the press at Hatton's gym.

He swept out of the changing rooms wearing a pair of tight-fitting shorts and into the ring to pepper Davison's pads with fast combinations.

Fury looked impressive and then filled every newspaper reporter's notebook with soundbites.

He took delight in saying Hearn and Joshua had made British boxing 'a laughing stock'. If you really want to fight, you fight, was Fury's message.

He would fight Wilder for less money than Joshua was offered, away from home and without proper preparation.

The public wants their boxers to be fearless fighting men, not businessmen. Fury was a fearless fighting man.

Fury, and Warren, had scored a victory over Joshua and Hearn and what's more, so had Wilder.

Fury and Wilder didn't need Joshua to capture the world's attention – and make millions of dollars.

Fury went as far as to say he would never fight Joshua – unless he was given a fair deal. In his view, he deserved 60 per cent of any deal. Fury was, he believed, still the true heavyweight champion of the world, Joshua someone who had merely capitalised on the circumstances.

Talk of Fury–Wilder dominated the press conference, but if it was going to happen, Fury still had a fight to win.

FOLLOWING victory over Seferi, Fury told the press he needed to fight 'big, big guys to prepare me for AJ and Wilder', and matchmaker Mervyn Turner came up with Francesco Pianeta.

The 33-year-old southpaw from Italy, who was based in Germany, had the requisite size. He stood 6ft 5ins tall and weighed around 17½ stones, and had credibility having twice challenged for world honours, losing in six to Wladimir Klitschko and a round to Ruslan Chagaev.

Boxing News was underwhelmed by the news Fury would be fighting Pianeta, pointing out he had lost two of his previous three fights and was a fighter defined by his losses to Klitschko, Chagaev, Kevin Johnson and Petar Milas.

Fury himself seemed a shade apologetic when asked about Pianeta. 'There aren't too many big guys out there who are available at the moment,' he said.

Still, Pianeta was several levels above Seferi, a fighter Davison said 'didn't have the size to get Tyson's respect' and never seemed to believe he had any chance of winning.

Pianeta was different. In fact, he looked the perfect opponent for Fury.

He was plodding, but willing, the sort of fighter who would make Fury work, but surely lose, as he always did when he fought in world class.

The priority for Fury appeared to be getting time in the ring. 'I need rounds,' he said honestly.

There was a sizeable gap in class between Pianeta and Wilder, but the feeling in Fury's camp was that all he needed was time in the ring and to be mentally right to compete with the best again.

Fury regarded Wilder as the world's second best heavyweight, behind himself, of course.

FURY rang his taxi driver to tell him he was fed up. 'I only got a silver medal today,' Fury told him.

'What do you mean, Tyson ?'

'I had 20 wanks, but someone else had 30. I'm going for gold tomorrow.'

The taxi driver laughed as he told the story. He had driven other celebrities around Belfast, but never anyone like Fury.

'Crackers,' he said.

The taxi driver had a ticket for the show at Windsor Park on 18 August 2018, topped by Carl Frampton defending his interim WBO featherweight title against Luke Jackson, and hoped Fury's opponent would give rather better value than Seferi.

'We won't put up with that here,' he warned.

'All business in Belfast,' was the promise from Fury, pleased with his use of alliteration.

Belfast, torn apart for decades by the Troubles, was a boxing city and they wanted to see a fight, not a pantomime.

Paddy Gallagher, Commonwealth Games gold medallist in 2010, said, 'Everyone loves boxing in West Belfast. Every single person has tried boxing. Some stuck at it, some said, "Fuck it, this is too tough" after their first spar.

Fury wasn't the only heavyweight getting attention in Belfast that weekend.

Wilder flew in for the fight and from the moment he stepped off the aeroplane, he was in demand. Every interviewer and fan found him to be softly spoken and charming.

Wilder loved Belfast, thanked its people for their hospitality and spoke of his admiration for Fury for agreeing to fight him.

He also gave his version of the failed Joshua negotiations. 'No matter what you think of me, $15 million and no percentage?' he said.

'When you give a guy lower than me that has done nothing for the sport a percentage, but you want to give me, the baddest man on the planet, no percentage? It don't get no clearer than that. They don't want the fight.'

The message from Wilder and Fury was that they were willing to take risks – and Joshua wasn't.

Wilder said that once he had dealt with Fury, he wanted the British public to put pressure on Joshua to agree to fight him.

THE weigh-in for the show was staged in a function room at the historic Europa Hotel in the city centre and was predictably chaotic.

As Fury stepped on to the scales, Wilder made his way, almost unnoticed, to the side of the stage. Fury spotted him out of the corner of his eye as he stepped off the scales, weighing 18lbs lighter than the Seferi fight at 18st 6lbs, and looked away.

Wilder decided it was time to make himself known. He leaned back, cupped his hands to his mouth and bellowed his trademark, 'Bomb squad!'

John Fury snapped back in a light-hearted way, 'Shut up.'

Wilder and Fury repeated themselves a couple of times – and then the mood of the exchanges darkened.

Fury's eyes were ablaze and he sneered at Wilder, 'You can't beat me.'

'Bomb squad!' came the reply.

'You can't beat me.'

Davison and a couple of security guards sensed the situation could turn ugly. Fury wasn't playing to the crowd, wasn't trying to sell a fight. He was deadly serious.

It took Davison and a couple of burly security guards to usher Fury away from Wilder.

THE following night, Wilder found his way to ringside and from there, he shouted instructions and encouragement to Fury.

'I want him to win,' he explained. 'I want the fight to happen.'

The talk was the fight would happen somewhere in America on either 10 November or 17 November, unless Pianeta could somehow pull off a shock.

The Pianeta game plan was simple enough. He would get his hands up, look to push Fury back into the corners and unload.

In the final minute of the opening round, Fury let Pianeta put him exactly where he wanted him and gave him every chance to hit him.

Fury stood in a corner with his hands by his sides and for a few jaw-dropping seconds, he slipped and swerved every punch Pianeta aimed at him before sliding away to the centre of the ring and peppering Pianeta with rat-a-tat combinations.

The Fury reflexes, anticipation and judgement of distance all looked good and what's more, Pianeta's confidence was surely dented.

There was another moment of quality from Fury in the dying moments of the second. He fired off a long left-right and then dropped his shoulder to let Pianeta's attempted counter punch sail wide of its target.

He kept making Pianeta miss and kept walking him into traps.

In the fourth, Fury shaped to throw a right hand and Pianeta moved away from it – and into the path of a left hook.

Fury showed no urgency to follow up this success. He just kept pecking away with jabs and combinations. There was a fluency and rhythm to his work.

There was more aggression for Fury in the sixth. He came down off his toes, forced Pianeta back to the ropes and picked up a telling-off from referee Steve Gray for rubbing his forehead into Pianeta's face.

Pianeta got another welcome break in the seventh after Fury landed a low blow. The fight resumed after a few seconds and Tyson continued to do as he pleased.

There was applause from Fury's corner early in the eighth after he shaped to throw a right uppercut and instead whipped a left hook around Pianeta's guard, but despite the quality of Tyson's boxing, sections of the crowd became restless.

The knockout they wanted looked unlikely to happen. Fury seemed happy enough with how the fight was going and Pianeta had accepted there was no way he could win the fight and the best thing he could do was stay tucked up and not leave too many gaps.

Pianeta was beaten, Fury still fresh and full of ideas.

Early in the ninth, Fury pushed him to the ropes and repeatedly feinted, trying to get Pianeta to launch a punch for him to counter.

Pianeta refused to take any chances and Fury got back on his toes and boxed his way to the final bell.

Fury seemed pleased enough with his night's work afterwards, describing it as 'a calculated boxing performance' and adding, 'I came here to get the rounds. I was slipping and sliding, jabbing.

'I thought it was a step up and a better boxing display. I did the ten rounds and had plenty left in the tank.'

WILDER made his way into the ring and on Warren's insistence, it was the WBC champion who announced his next title defence.

'We're ready now,' he hollered to cheers. 'This fight is on, baby.

'The best fighting the best.'

Warren said, in a tone of triumph and relief, 'The fight is on.'

Fury didn't miss his chance to score a victory over Joshua. 'This man [Wilder] has been trying to make a big fight with the other chump, the biggest shithouse in boxing,' he said. 'They called, I answered and now he gets his chance to fight the lineal champion of the world.'

Fury turned to address Wilder and his mood changed. 'I'm knocking you the fuck out,' he promised.

Wilder made the same promise and Fury told him, 'You can't knock out what you can't hit.'

Pianeta had managed to hit Fury only 37 times over the course of the ten rounds.

Fury went on to charm his audience. 'Belfast, you are beautiful,' he told them, adding that once he had beaten Wilder, he would come back to the city to defend the world championship.

Wilder's response was to be similarly complimentary about Belfast and its inhabitants, but his words were drowned out by boos.

Fury was their man.

Once the microphone was taken away, Fury and Wilder appeared to be on better terms. They shared a firm handshake. Fury appeared to appreciate the opportunity, Wilder respected Tyson for stepping up to face him.

Five weeks later, Joshua kept his WBA Super, WBO and IBF belts, surviving a brief wobble or two to stop Povetkin in seven rounds, a result that was more satisfying to himself and his audience than his previous two fights, the late stoppage of Carlos Takam and the points win over Parker.

CHAPTER 17

People's Champion

'BEING HEAVYWEIGHT champion of the world wasn't good enough for me,' said Fury.

'Even if I had continued after the Klitschko fight and beaten Wilder and Joshua, that would not be good enough for me.

'I had to be the controversial, outspoken, idiot of a champion who gets interest from people who aren't interested in sports.

'The comeback and the story behind it is a movie. Beating Wilder is a fairytale ending.

'A man goes from rags to riches, loses it all in a year and then wins it back within a year of his comeback. How great a story is that?'

Even Fury had to accept there was a chance this story would not end well for him.

He knew fighting Wilder after those two straightforward, undemanding wins 'isn't a wise man's move.

'But a great man once said, "He who is not courageous enough to take risks will accomplish nothing." Muhammad Ali said that.

'This is a dare-to-be-great move. Beating Wilder cements my legacy as a great heavyweight of my time.'

There was speculation the fight wouldn't happen.

Warren had said it would be announced days after Fury had beaten Pianeta and when there was no press conference, there were various whispers.

Respected writer Dan Rafael reported there were doubts in the Fury camp, a story denied by the fighter. Eddie Hearn was convinced there would be no fight and Sky Sports claimed Fury didn't have a licence to box in the States.

The truth of the matter was the promoters were struggling to pin down a venue.

The Staples Center in Los Angeles was available on Saturday, 1 December and that's where the fight would take place – provided Fury was allowed into the country.

He said that on his way into the States he was strip-searched because 'they said I looked like a shady character.

'I was held up at the airport for about four and a half hours and it took me nearly two and a half years to get a visa because they said I could have instigated a riot when I attended the Wilder fight [against Artur Szpilka in January 2016].

'I had to have loads of meetings and eventually I was allowed in.'

ONCE he was in the States, Fury headed to the Big Bear mountains east of Los Angeles, where he found Abel Sanchez's gym.

The Summit Gym, built in what had been the garage of one of Sanchez's properties, stood around 7,000 feet above sea level and was where Sanchez had turned Gennady Golovkin into the most destructive middleweight of his generation.

In London heavyweight Joe Joyce, he had another fighter with what he described as 'a seek-and-destroy' mentality.

Joyce, robbed of super heavyweight gold at the 2016 Rio Olympics by controversial scoring, had left London to train with Sanchez and made quite an impression in their first fight together, bashing Iago Kiladze in five rounds.

Purists didn't always enjoy watching Joyce hunt down his opponents and clobber them, but he was hugely effective; a 6ft 6ins tall, 18-stone, granite-chinned fighter who appeared to get stronger as fights went on.

His style was to grind opponents down, but in three weeks' sparring Fury, he struggled to land a punch.

'I found it hard to pin him down,' admitted Joyce. 'I thought I had him in the corners and he would escape and get to the centre of the ring.

'You have to be quick to catch him.

'Even when he's on the ropes, he's still really hard to hit.

'He's a big guy with long arms who moves his upper body well and his footwork is really good as well.'

Fury, who spent his spare time reading *The Art of War*, a 2,500-year-old book written by military strategist and philosopher Sun Tzu, relocated to the Wild Card gym in Los Angeles and according to Wilder that was because 'he could not handle the heat and the altitude [in Big Bear] – he was so high up over there that he could not breathe.

'Just being up there for two weeks isn't going to be enough time to prepare for me. Either you have stamina or you don't.'

At the Wild Card gym, Fury added the hugely knowledgeable Freddie Roach to his team.

To Manny Pacquiao, a world champion at eight weights from flyweight to super welterweight and one of the finest fighters of his generation, Roach was his 'master'.

Others who benefited from his wisdom included Puerto Rican idol Miguel Cotto and Amir Khan.

As a fighter himself, Roach, known as 'The Choir Boy', had been unable to break into world class and towards the end of his 53-fight career, he started to develop Parkinson's disease, a consequence of the punches he had taken in numerous hard battles.

Despite that, Roach became one of the most highly regarded boxing coaches in the world. As his coaching record proved, nobody knew boxers and boxers like Roach and he liked what he saw of Fury.

'He's got good legs, he feints well,' he said. 'Tyson's best asset is his sight. He sees what's happening in there, he's not going to get hit with a right out of left field.'

The way Wilder threw his punches, particularly his right hand, had been much discussed throughout his career and even coach Mark Breland admitted he wanted his fighter to shorten the punch.

The gangly Breland stood a lofty 6ft 2ins and knew the benefits of a straight one-two. They were the punches that had taken him to Olympic gold in 1984 and the WBA welterweight championship twice as a professional.

Breland admitted he had struggled to get his message through to Wilder and told me he feared the biggest heavyweight fight for years would end up as an embarrassing spectacle.

'We know Tyson is going to jump around, do crazy stuff and try to frustrate Deontay,' said Breland.

'Both are very awkward fighters, but if Deontay just boxes him and doesn't go crazy, he can make it easier for himself. I don't want to see them swinging like two girls. I don't mind if one of them does, but not both of them.

'I've told Deontay, "Be patient and eventually you will catch him." Fury can't jump around all night and once Fury feels his power, he will either get stopped or stay away. I can see Fury losing on points and saying, "He couldn't knock me out," but so what? It's better to win an ugly fight than lose a pretty fight.'

That was a prediction that reckoned without Fury's pride. He would surely rather be knocked out than tamely accept Wilder was the better man and settle for losing on points.

The subject turned to Joshua.

Hearn had promised that should he beat Fury and attract one million pay-per-view buys, Wilder could have a 50/50 split for a fight with Joshua, at Wembley Stadium on Saturday, 13 April.

Hearn knew it was highly unlikely that figure would be reached but Breland said that regardless of pay-per-view sales, the fight with Joshua needed to happen.

'Joshua is saying Deontay doesn't want the fight,' he said, 'but Deontay is chasing him.

'*They* don't want the fight and it bothers Deontay, but I just say to him, "It will either happen or it won't happen." Everyone knows Deontay wants the fight and Joshua doesn't. Eddie Hearn says Deontay doesn't want the fight, but he's just doing his job as Joshua's promoter.

'I thought boxing was about boxing each other to see who's best and pleasing the fans, but it turns out, it's about who can make the most money.

'People want to see Joshua fight someone of substance.

'Why not fight Luis Ortiz? Because Deontay just beat him, but can Joshua beat him?

'Ortiz would stop Joshua.'

Ortiz had been just one clean punch away from beating Wilder earlier that year.

A product of the La Finca Gym in Cuba, Ortiz had to escape kidnappers on his way to Miami after deciding to defect to turn professional.

Opponents would regard him as a solid and slick southpaw.

For a while, Ortiz was regarded by many as possibly the best heavyweight in the world, even though he didn't hold a belt. That opinion was revised after he rather laboured against both Malik Scott and Dave Allen when Hearn promoted him, but as it turned out, Ortiz was a fighter who fought to the level of his opposition and when he faced Wilder, he boxed superbly.

He was able to outjab the taller champion and use his feet to manoeuvre him around the ring. The thing with Wilder was, he had the punch to turn any fight around and in the fifth, he found it. All of a sudden, Ortiz, who had appeared in control and comfortable, was on the floor.

The bell came to Ortiz's rescue but by the end of the sixth, he looked to have resumed control again.

There was drama late in the seventh.

Wilder went looking for Ortiz after connecting with a trademark right-hand thunderbolt and ran on to a beautifully timed short right hook. Wilder's body slumped dramatically. He groped and fumbled his way through the next few seconds, but once Ortiz had shrugged him off, Wilder found himself on the ropes, only one clean punch from defeat.

Ortiz couldn't land it and Wilder made the most of his reprieve. Wilder landed a right hand in the tenth that convinced him to launch an all-out attack. He continued throwing punches until Ortiz hit the floor. Ortiz got up but was dropped again by a thunderous right uppercut. The referee didn't bother to count. The fight was over.

Fury said: 'I got up at 5am and watched it and hoped he [Wilder] would win so that he could fight me.

'All the way up to the seventh round, I was saying, "You'd better pull a punch out" because I had Ortiz ahead.

'If Ortiz had been fitter, he probably would have beaten him.

'Ortiz is 147 years old, though. I'm 30 and in my prime. I could do 15 rounds on my toes, like Muhammad Ali.'

THE size of the task facing Fury was spelled out in a simple statistic.

In his 40-fight professional career, Wilder had stopped or knocked out every opponent he had faced.

Only Bermane Stiverne had heard the final bell, possibly because Wilder hurt his right hand in the fourth round when he took the WBC title off him in January 2015. When they fought again, Wilder polished Stiverne off inside a round.

Stiverne went into the rematch rusty having not boxed for a couple of years and flabby – and Wilder dealt with him with contempt.

Wilder caused outrage when he said ahead of that fight, 'This is the funeral, there's just no casket yet. He's gonna be the body.'

On another occasion, he said, 'I want a body on my record' and in the days leading up to the Fury fight, Wilder talked about how he was undergoing a metamorphosis from Deontay Wilder into 'The Bronze Bomber', his alter ego.

'When my mind transforms, it is a scary feeling because it is a source of power that takes over and allows me to feel like I know I can kill a man,' he said.

'The week of the fight is when I start to transform. It just takes hold, especially the day of the fight. I'm no longer myself. Nothing is funny, everything is serious.'

He screamed in the face of one British reporter that Fury 'should fear for his life. I want you to look into my eyes. I mean it: fear for his life.'

Richard Towers added to the Wilder myth.

'I've sparred with every single heavyweight you could think of, apart from Joseph Parker, and when it comes to power, Deontay Wilder is in a league of his own,' said the former professional from Sheffield.

'He hits four times harder than Vitali Klitschko, he hits five times harder than Wladimir Klitschko, he hits six times harder than Anthony Joshua and he hits eight times harder than Tyson Fury.'

Others who had shared a ring with Wilder spoke similarly of him. 'Hard as nails,' said Audley Harrison, smashed into retirement in just 70 seconds by Wilder, and Malik Scott, another crushed inside a round, described Wilder as 'the fastest heavyweight on the planet – and really mean'.

Fury seemed unconcerned. He said that because Wilder often weighed only around 15st 7lbs, he would punch like a cruiserweight, but the truth was, not even someone with Fury's confidence in their chin wanted to take a clean shot from Wilder.

AHEAD of the fight, the most commonly held view appeared to be that if the Fury who had bamboozled Klitschko made a reappearance, the title would change hands.

That seemed unlikely, given everything Fury had been through since that fight.

Warren asked the questions everyone was asking at a press conference in the week of the fight.

'The big question is, "How has his time out of the ring affected him?" he said.

'He's had two easy comeback fights, where he trained to make the weight rather than training for the fight.

'He's lost ten stones, so what has he got left? But I think if he's 80 per cent of what he was, he beats Wilder.'

Those closest to Fury had their doubts.

His father, John, wasn't happy with Tyson's decision to fight Wilder so soon into his comeback.

John wouldn't be there to see the fight. He knew that because of his criminal convictions, he wouldn't get a visa.

Wilder felt the absence of Peter Fury might be crucial.

Towards the end of the first press conference to promote the fight, at broadcaster BT Sport's headquarters in Stratford, east London, Wilder told Fury, 'Better go ring up Peter. You're going to need him.

'You better go get Peteeeerrrrr!'

For a few seconds, Fury appeared lost for words. The only response he could muster was a slow, mocking nod of his head.

Wilder wasn't the only one wondering if Davison had the knowledge and experience to get Fury through the fight.

Fury himself seemed to be happy enough. He had a fight to look forward to – and an audience to entertain.

He puzzled Wilder, and the American public, by calling the champion 'a dosser'. Asked to explain what he meant, Fury said Wilder was 'dossing around with the belt', hinting that he was an unworthy champion.

Wilder admitted he went to the trouble of discovering what 'dosser' meant.

In another interview, Fury took the pressure off himself with a reminder of how far he had come just to be in a position to challenge for the world championship again.

'The only reason people are talking about this fight being competitive is because I have had two and a half years out of the ring and ballooned up to 28 stones,' he said.

'If I didn't do that, this fight would not be seen as competitive.

'It's been a helluva ride and no matter what happens in the Wilder fight, I've already won.

'Just to be healthy and in shape is worth all the wins in the world.

'I wouldn't be alive if I didn't change my act back then. I would have been spiralling out of control and ended up in a padded room somewhere.'

As it was, Fury had become the 'people's champion' he had hoped to be.

'I'm outshining him,' he said of Wilder.

'People in America don't know who Deontay Wilder is, but they know who I am.

'I don't know why.

'He has everything that would attract a boxing fan. He's got the looks, he's got the power, he can talk, he's heavyweight champion of the world.

'But they don't take to him.

'I get the crowd screaming, "There's only one Tyson Fury" everywhere I go. 'Deontay Wilder must be thinking, "Everywhere he goes, he takes over."'

Wilder seemed to accept that even though he had made seven defences of the WBC title, he was still fighting for recognition.

'This is the one that solidifies my name, especially in America,' he said.

No question, Fury had the neutral support.

He connected with a wider audience because he was vulnerable, daft, honest – and disappointed with life.

He became the heavyweight champion of the world, a title he had chased since he was a boy, but it didn't bring him acceptance – or happiness.

'Everybody has the same struggles, no matter who you are and what you have achieved,' he said.

'Don't forget, I'm a multi-millionaire, a very high-achieving sportsman, very good looking and I can say all that material stuff will not make one happy.

'I've got 15 belts at home and not one of them ever brings me any happiness.'

Fury appeared to find contentment and purpose by spreading awareness of mental health.

'I stand as more than a champion, an ambassador for mental health,' he said. 'I am the people's champion.

'I am not just fighting for me. I have millions of people that look up to me.'

He was guaranteed £3 million for the Wilder fight – the champion would receive £4 million – and vowed to use it to help build shelters for the homeless.

'They think I've just come over to pick up a few quid,' said Fury, 'but I couldn't care less about the money. I don't have much use for it.

'I'm planning to give it all away to the poor and for building houses for the homeless. I will probably end up like all the other boxers down the years, skint.'

Fury was genuine. Away from the media glare, he went around the poorest areas of Los Angeles feeding the homeless.

On one occasion, Tyson found a man around his size who was without shoes. Fury gave him his shoes and walked back to his hotel in his socks, an unpublicised and spontaneous moment of generosity.

FURY reckoned he had laid a trap for Wilder.

'I asked Frank [Warren] to tell them I was coming back just for the money,' he said. 'That's how he got the fight made. I tricked them into it. They think they're fighting some fat English idiot. They don't know what they've let themselves in for. He's made the biggest mistake of his life letting me talk them into this fight.'

On another occasion, Fury said, 'People underestimate me because they look at my body shape and think I'm tall, gangly, slow and fat.

'But one thing that's excellent is my range.'

Interesting that Fury didn't deny the impression that he was 'tall, gangly, slow and fat', but at the same time, when a fighter stands 6ft 8¾ins tall, has a reach of 85 inches and can control the range, he will win most fights.

Fury had the size to keep opponents where he could hit them and they couldn't hit him.

But what happened when, as he was sure to do at some point, Wilder hit him?

Neven Pajkic and Steve Cunningham – the latter only a cruiserweight – had both dropped Fury with right hands.

That was known to be Wilder's knockout punch and to take it out of the fight, Roach hinted Fury would box him as a southpaw.

THE Wednesday of fight week was the third anniversary of Fury's victory over Wladimir Klitschko and at a press conference at the Westin

Bonaventure Hotel, Fury, looking like crazed murderer Charles Manson according to *Boxing News* editor Matt Christie with his lengthy beard, was happy to relive how he had beaten the second-longest-reigning heavyweight champion in history.

'I did maybe ten per cent of what we did in the gym,' he claimed. 'I didn't practise all the herky-jerky and feinting, or putting my arm back and brushing my hair with it. I watched it and wondered, "Whatever was I doing?" I practised for ten weeks switching between combinations and never did it once.'

Fury had relied on his instincts to manipulate, manoeuvre and confuse Klitschko and fancied he could do the same to Wilder.

He said, 'Wilder has everything a heavyweight champion of the world should have – and I'm going to overcome it with brain power.'

At that press conference, Fury was in turn amusing and proud, while Wilder came across as a sort of unhinged preacher.

One moment he was passionate and sincere, the next loud and aggressive, and then he would sit quietly, chuckling to himself, 'I can't wait.'

Fury said Wilder 'repeats himself, talks nonsense' and he was by far the quicker-witted of the two. 'We come from two different places,' said Wilder, to which Fury responded, 'I can see that by the way you dress, son.'

Fury took up the theme. He was only ever going to be a fighter, while Wilder had previously played basketball and American football.

'He came to this as a third option,' said Tyson. 'I was born to do this. I was asked if I wanted a basketball scholarship and I said, "No. I'm going to be heavyweight champion of the world."'

Wilder was, in Fury's opinion, 'a snide and a fraud, a pretender'.

Wilder said his reading of Fury's greatest night was 'Klitschko beat himself' and as they both started to shout to be heard, it became clear that when they stood nose to nose for the cameras there would be chaos.

Wilder was the instigator. 'I'm going to knock you the fuck out,' he screamed. 'I promise.'

Fury replied calmly, 'I hope you do.'

Tyson reckoned he had spent years trying to find someone who could keep him on the floor and that so far, nobody had been up to the challenge.

Warren was told by a member of Wilder's entourage, 'Don't push' as he sought to help keep control and though that disagreement ended there, trouble wasn't far away.

Wilder continued to rant aggressively and rather than try to shout over him, Fury suddenly ducked his head towards him and over first one shoulder, then the other.

Wilder barely blinked. He carried on maniacally screaming in Fury's face. Tyson appeared bored and decided to run his fingers along Wilder's shoulder.

Mayhem followed.

The fighters were swiftly pulled apart and the job of the security guards became to separate their teams. The moment Wilder reacted to Fury touching him, Shane Fury had waded in and Wilder's backers stood their ground.

Somehow, nobody was hurt amidst the chaos and Fury appeared to have the final word.

Tyson ripped off his shirt and stabbed a finger at Wilder before being calmed down and ushered off stage.

Fury regarded the events at the press conference as a victory. 'I took my shirt off to get involved and frightened them away,' he said. 'Everyone thinks the rivalry is fake. But they can guess again as it nearly went off again.

'Wilder thought he needed to spit in my face, or whatever he was doing, shouting. He feels pressured. You can see the pressure he is under out there.'

Fury made the rather more outlandish claim that Wilder had been hoping to spark a riot, so the fight would be called off.

The following day, the fighters had more press commitments and Fury was becoming bored with all the interviews, answering one question with, 'Yes, I'm going to win.'

One talking point was Fury's beard. Or rather, what had happened to it.

The feral-looking Fury of the chaotic press conference was now clean shaven.

Fury revealed he had been involved in a competition with Davison and Isaac Lowe to see who could grow the longest beard.

'I think I look 15 years younger without the beard [making him 15],' he said, 'and my wife says she fancies me more without it.

'I cut it off myself. I buzzed it all off. It took me six months to grow and two seconds to get it off. Isaac won the bet and he gets £1,000 to the charity of his choice.

'I could have continued with the beard, but after watching all the animalistic stuff that was going on, I thought to myself, "You know what, I'm just going to be a clean-shaven and happy-go-lucky kind of guy."'

Fury didn't come across as happy-go-lucky in another interview.

'I'm not interested in boxing, really,' he said. 'I have no interest at all.

'Tyson Fury achieved his dreams in Dusseldorf three years ago. He became a world heavyweight champion, he beat a legendary fighter – that is dream stuff.

'Now I'm here to inspire and give people hope because I don't believe there are many people doing that around the world at the moment.

'I'm their guy. I'm not going in there to make me and my family proud and get a pat on the back. I'm going in there because people need me, people are suffering quietly.

'I suffered for years with depression and anxiety because I didn't know what it was and I had no education on the matter.

'Every day was a grey day, but every day shouldn't be a grey day because every day is a blessing. Now I understand every day is a rose-coloured, sunshine day and I appreciate every second, every hour, because I know it could be taken away at any minute.'

THE weigh-in was held outside the Los Angeles Convention Center in sweltering temperatures.

Fury made quite an entrance, standing through the sunroof of a chunky sport utility vehicle, and walked on stage shirtless. Everyone there seemed to be supporting him and, as ever, he liked the limelight, dancing to the music that accompanied Wilder's entrance.

Wilder was dressed in black with a black mask, resembling a gas mask, covering his face.

Fury scaled 256½lbs – or 18st 4½lbs – with Wilder a career-lightest 212½lbs (15st 2½lbs).

As Wilder stood on the scales, Fury faced the crowd, jabbing a thumb at him and saying, 'Dosser.'

He then started shadow boxing while the crowd chanted, 'There's only one Tyson Fury.'

The California State Athletic Commission had warned both fighters that if there was a repeat of the unrest seen at the press conference, they could lose their purses, so rather than go nose to nose for the photographers at the weigh-in, they were kept around six feet apart.

This time, it was Fury who erupted into a screaming, finger-pointing frenzy.

Wilder stared back at him blankly until Fury was steered off stage, where his mood lightened instantly.

EXPERTS found more reason to pick Wilder over Fury.

Eighteen of the 30 quizzed by the British trade magazine *Boxing Monthly* went for Wilder on the grounds of his activity, punch and home advantage.

Joshua said he was hoping for a Wilder win, angering some British fans.

Joshua presumably felt a fight with Wilder was bigger at that stage – and may well have been enraged by a story Fury told American audiences in the build-up to the fight.

'He [Joshua] seems pretty spirited, doesn't he?' said Tyson. 'But when I stood face to face with him and said, "Do you want to get outside?" his arse started flapping. He shit himself.

'It doesn't matter what weight I was at the time. I wasn't in shape, but I'd have took him outside and kicked his arse right in for him.'

To the delight of Fury and Warren, Joshua and Hearn were not having things all their own way any more.

Hearn reacted to the news of Fury–Wilder being made by saying the fight would 'stink the place out'.

THE mood in Fury's dressing room at the Staples Center was tense, but relaxed.

Warren found Fury to be 'as unconcerned as someone going out to buy a paper'.

Hatton appeared more anxious. He paced up and down, chewing gum. 'We are going to do this tonight,' said Warren. Davison promised, 'This is going to be a movie.'

The soundtrack to this part of the movie was country music. 'This is strange music to have before a fight, innit?' said Fury, but more upbeat tunes were to follow by Tom Jones, The Kaiser Chiefs and AC/DC.

With the fight minutes away, the group huddled together in the centre of the room and prayed, the first read out by Tyson and the second by his friend and cornerman, Asgar Tair.

As is the way in boxing, the challenger made his entrance first and Fury soaked up every single moment of his walk to the ring, pumping his fists to the beat of his music and acknowledging as many fans as possible.

Tyson estimated thousands of Travellers and British fans had made the journey to support him and he danced for them on the ring apron before heaving his right leg over the top rope and easing himself into the ring.

Wilder's entrance was altogether more serious – or rather, as serious as it's possible to be for someone who's wearing a fake gold mask and crown. He was joined by a rapper whose finger-stabbing and aggressive barking made it clear that trouble was on its way. Fury paid him no attention. He hit the pads with Davison.

Once Wilder was in the ring, Fury fixed him with a maniacal glare from across the ring and started talking to him and licking his lips. Wilder turned his back.

There was a break from boxing tradition during MC Jimmy Lennon Jr's introductions. The champion is always introduced second but on this occasion, it was Fury, the challenger for the title, who had top billing. Fury was stubborn in his claim to be the true heavyweight champion of the world, the lineal champion.

Of the two fighters, Fury got the better reception and at the bell he raced to the centre of the ring – but didn't throw any punches.

Boxing out of the orthodox stance, a surprise to many, Fury jerked his upper body this way and that, his eyebrows dancing up and down as he feinted with his fists, promising to punch and then not always doing so. Wilder was too busy trying to figure out what Fury was up to – what trap he was being lined up for – to throw many punches and when the champion did sense the time was right to attack, Fury blocked everything.

Fury responded with jabs that came out fast and in twos and threes. Not everything Tyson threw landed, but some got through and he surely made certain of winning the round with a combination in the dying seconds.

This was a hugely encouraging start for Fury. His reflexes looked sharp, his legs strong.

Wilder looked to impose himself more at the start of the second but Fury slipped his jabs and when Fury jabbed in reply, he landed. The jab was crucial to both fighters – it was the shot that set up Wilder's right hand – but it was Tyson who was winning the battle of the lead hands. He knew it, raising his arms in triumph.

Fury decided to try something different. He turned southpaw. It didn't work. He shipped a left hook that convinced him he was better off boxing orthodox.

In the dying seconds of the round, Fury took a right-hand blast in the face – and didn't budge. 'Dosser!' Fury screamed at Wilder at the bell.

Not an awful lot landed in either of the opening two rounds, but if either fighter won them, it was surely Fury.

He started the third with a hard left to Wilder's stomach after distracting him with feints to the head. Wilder responded with a jab to Fury's face, his best punch so far, to bring murmurs from the crowd.

That punch landing looked like a possible turning point. Once Wilder found the range with his jab, the right hand followed and when the right hand landed, his opponents usually hit the floor.

Fury seized back control instantly. He slotted home jabs, then slammed a double jab-right hand combination off Wilder's jaw. The crowd roared but rather than follow up, Fury took a step or two back, smiling to himself, and went back to jabbing and feinting, to the delight of his corner. 'Don't get greedy,' Davison told him, meaning that landing one or two punches was enough. He didn't want to give Wilder the chance to swing back. Davison knew there was danger if Fury punched with Wilder. He wanted him to land his punches and move – and the tactic was working.

There were signs of bruising around Wilder's face by the end of the third and most ringsiders had the challenger three rounds up.

Early in the fourth, Fury and Wilder landed jabs simultaneously – and it was Wilder who was rocked back on to his heels.

For the remainder of the round, only a handful of scoring punches landed. Fury stood in front of Wilder, an inch or two out of range, feinting and swerving his upper body one way, then the other. It stopped the champion letting his hands go, until the closing 30 seconds. Wilder slung a big right hand – and it missed by inches.

At the end of the fourth, Fury boasted, 'I'm boxing well, aren't I?' Davison replied, 'You're boxing beautifully.'

At that point, there hadn't been much drama, but there was always the promise of some and the millions rooting for a fairytale had to be pleased with what they had seen so far.

Fury was surely ahead on the scorecards.

Not much happened at the start of the fifth. Fury edged Wilder back with his feet and landed a looping left hand before Wilder came back with jabs.

The best action came in the last 30 seconds of the round. Fury made Wilder miss again and punished him with a flurry of counter punches, a sequence that was enough to win the round for Tyson on all three judges' scorecards.

The sixth followed a similar pattern. Wilder thought about throwing punches and when he eventually did, he missed. Fury feinted and jabbed. It looked to be another Fury round. The crowd thought so. By the closing moments of the session, they were chanting, 'There's only one Tyson Fury.'

At the halfway point, British and American television commentators both had Fury ahead and the seventh was another good round for the challenger.

Early in the round, he found Wilder's chin with a right hand and when Wilder looked to throw back, Fury wasn't there.

This was a fight of few clean scoring punches and that Fury punch meant Wilder had to start landing – or the round would be lost.

Wilder saw an opportunity in the dying moments of the round and put everything into a left-right-left. Each punch missed and Fury went back to his stool nodding, confident he was in control. Not only that, Wilder looked short of ideas.

When he came forward and let his hands go, he missed and if he stood off and tried to walk Fury on to a right hand, Tyson didn't take the bait.

Wilder's most effective punch was his jab, but still, more often than not, he couldn't land it. Sections of the crowd chanted 'You big dosser' at the champion during the eighth and with around 30 seconds left in the round, Fury crashed a right hand off his jaw.

For a split second, Wilder's legs appeared to stiffen, but Fury didn't rush in and just before the bell, it was Wilder's turn to land a right hand. Fury drummed his gloves on his chin to show he was untroubled and at the bell, Finkel, Wilder's manager, was spotted shaking his head.

The title appeared to be slipping away from Wilder.

The message got through to him and at the start of the ninth, he quickened his feet in a bid to get closer to Fury.

Wilder got into range and started firing right-left hook combinations – and one of them landed with enough force to leave Fury on the seat of his trunks. The blows only appeared to be glancing and Fury was clear-eyed as referee Jack Reiss counted and when he reached 'nine', Fury got to his feet.

Amazingly, the rest of the round belonged to Fury.

He made Wilder miss when he went for the finish and then pushed him back with a burst. The crowd cheered and they cheered louder at the sight of Fury, on the floor a minute earlier, putting his hands behind his back and sticking his tongue out.

Wilder had missed his chance and needed to take a breather, while Fury looked into the crowd and said, 'Come on.' For eight rounds, Fury had boxed beautifully and the knockdown had stirred his fighting passions.

As it turned out, Wilder did punch hard enough to put Fury on the floor, but he couldn't keep him there.

Even though he finished the ninth well, the knockdown meant it was sure to be scored against Fury. He knew that and started the tenth positively, firing out left-rights.

Wilder needed a big finish to the round and launched six or seven huge swings at Fury. Tyson dodged them all and stuck his tongue out at him at the bell.

The mood in Fury's corner after the tenth was understandably upbeat.

'Two rounds, buddy, and it's going to be the greatest comeback in boxing history,' Davison told him. 'If you're feeling tired, you've got to dig more than you have ever digged [sic] in your life.'

The 11th was quieter. Perhaps they were saving themselves for the final three minutes.

The advice to Wilder ahead of the last round was 'Let's do this' and while there was less urgency in Fury's corner, still, the challenger was told to finish positively. Sure enough, it was Tyson who landed the first punches of the 12th, a left-right after around 30 seconds.

Wilder found an instant response. He spotted the opening he had been looking for all night and launched a right hand. It detonated on Fury's jaw, sending him falling backwards.

As he fell, Wilder smacked him on the cheek with a left hook. Fury landed flat on his back and for a few moments, he didn't move. He looked to be unconscious. Wilder seemed to think so. He started blowing kisses into the crowd, confident the fight was over. 'I seen this man's eyes roll in the back of his head,' he said later. 'When I seen [referee] Jack Reiss on the ground with him checking him, I'm like, "It's over".'

That was how it looked to everyone watching, but as the count reached 'six', Fury started to stir and by 'nine' he was on his feet.

'I was quite conscious,' said Fury later, 'but couldn't feel my legs. I didn't want to get up because my legs would have been so unsteady they would have stopped the fight.'

Reiss asked him, 'You all right?'

Fury replied, 'Yes.'

Tyson remembered later, 'He said, "Go to the left." I went to the left. He said, "Go to the right." I went to the right.'

Reiss said to him, 'Well, if you ain't capable, most experienced referees in America will stop the fight. But if you can continue...'

Fury had convinced Reiss he was able to continue, but still, he had to survive two minutes and three seconds – and given Wilder's punch, that seemed unlikely.

Fury blocked the next punch Wilder hurled at him – a right hand – but the follow-up left hook glanced off his chin. 'Hold him!' screamed Davison and though Fury did as he was told for a few seconds, once Reiss parted the fighters, Tyson came under fire again.

Mostly, he blocked Wilder's swings and once he was convinced the danger had passed, Fury put his hands behind his back.

Wilder was too tired to take advantage and Fury belted him with a left-right-left that forced him to give ground and hold.

The crowd screamed in disbelief.

On the brink of victory seconds earlier, Wilder was suddenly on the brink of defeat. Fury was tired himself and for a few seconds no punches were thrown as both got their breath back.

With around a minute left, Fury started jabbing again and an exhausted Wilder back-pedalled.

Wilder dragged another couple of big punches out of himself in the dying seconds, a right and left. Both missed.

The bell went and Fury raised his arms, while Wilder stood on shaky legs, his mouth hanging open, his arms by his sides.

Fury raced to a corner and jumped on the ropes in celebration. The crowd rose to him. They believed what Fury believed, that the WBC heavyweight championship was about to change hands.

Wilder celebrated with rather less conviction and once passions had cooled, the fighters embraced. 'Great fight,' Fury whispered in Wilder's ear. 'Love you. Thank you for the opportunity.'

BT Sport and Showtime both had Fury ahead by four points and Lennon's announcement that it was a split decision brought howls from the crowd.

The first score he read out really was puzzling. Alejandro Rochin somehow had Wilder ahead 115-111. The crowd booed. Robert Tapper had Fury winning 114-111, a more popular reading of the fight, but Phil Edwards came up with a score of 113-113.

The fight was a draw.

Fury shook his head sadly and slowly. On the advice of his family, Tyson hid his rage. He explained later, 'There were about 10,000 Travellers and Brits came from around the world. They probably would have smashed up the ring if I'd initiated it.'

He added, 'For all the people out there with mental health issues, I did it for you.'

Fury let his true feelings be known at the post-fight press conference. 'This man [Rochin] should be banned for life,' he said.

'Even if I hadn't been knocked down twice, he would still have had me losing. Disgrace.

'I've never seen a worse decision in my life. These controversies give boxing a bad name.'

Closer inspection of Rochin's scorecard showed he gave Wilder the first four rounds. To most ringsiders, Wilder had struggled to land a clean punch on Fury in those opening sessions.

Wilder admitted afterwards, 'It felt like he had baby oil on him. He was slippery.'

As he had to, Wilder said he thought he had won the fight, but he was in the minority.

CHAPTER 18

The Aftermath

'I HAD four pints of beer before the Wilder fight,' revealed Fury. 'The night before. Didn't do me any harm, did it?

'Fighters from the past used to drink a bottle of whiskey before going in the ring. It didn't hurt them, did it?

'Years ago, people used to have a shot of whiskey in the corner. The thing is, if you can fight, there is no set way in what you should do.'

Frank Warren had every reason to sound pleased with himself upon his arrival back in London after the fight.

'They said it wouldn't go ahead – well, it did go ahead, didn't it?' he beamed.

'They said it was going to be a boring fight. It was one of the most exciting fights – certainly the most exciting I've seen at heavyweight since Lennox Lewis–Vitali Klitschko [in 2003].

'I've worked with Mike Tyson, Frank Bruno, all of those. Now Fury's the people's champion.'

If anything, the poor decision of the judges deepened Fury's connection with his public. Fury didn't always get what he deserved, either.

This was a fight that had a message bigger than boxing.

Fury told his public, 'If I can get up, so can you!'

That was a comment made with regard to his struggles away from boxing – and that astonishing last round.

The Ring magazine rated the 12th round as the best seen in 2018, explaining it 'is what fans for decades will ask about when they ask the two for autographs'.

Fury, who took the magazine's prestigious Fighter of the Year award following his victory over Klitschko three years previously, also took the Comeback of the Year award, by some distance you would imagine.

'The result has become almost redundant,' wrote *The Ring*.

'Fury has become the object of ridicule for a period of years, but turned all of that around, winning over some of his harshest critics with an amazing performance.

'His greatest victory, however, has been raising awareness for mental health conditions. Despite the obvious disappointment of not regaining the heavyweight title and the controversy surrounding the result, Fury displayed true sportsmanship by accepting the decision with grace.'

The public really warmed to Fury.

He was flooded with messages on social media telling him he was an inspiration and former fighters were full of praise for him, including George Foreman.

Foreman had a brief and violent reign as heavyweight champion in the 1970s before running into Muhammad Ali. After a decade away spent preaching in church and eating cheeseburgers, he returned to clobber his way to the heavyweight championship again, laying out Michael Moorer in 1994, a couple of months before his 46th birthday.

Even that story, Foreman conceded, couldn't compare with Fury's.

'Fury getting a draw was the best comeback ever,' said Foreman. 'For Tyson Fury to take off over two years and fight one of the best fighters in the world, I think that was probably the most heroic thing in the world.

'It proved he is the most courageous fighter out there.

'Tyson Fury is the people's choice. We need to get him a robe like Muhammad Ali had and write on the back of it, "The people's choice."

Kevin Mitchell wrote in *The Guardian*, 'Fury is no Muhammad Ali, but he revives memories of that era when charisma had a believable link to its classical roots, "a divinely conferred power or talent", as the Oxford English Dictionary puts it.

'Like Ali, he [Fury] backs himself to do things that are extraordinary.'

There were other similarities between Ali and Fury.

Both were considered unbalanced before their unlikely world title wins and after shaking up the world by dethroning Sonny Liston, Ali, known then as Cassius Clay, alienated much of it with his political views, much the way Fury would do half a century later.

Like Ali, Fury won over his public with his fighting heart and the generosity of his spirit.

There was a further public vote for Fury three weeks after the Wilder fight.

In a battle apparently to decide Anthony Joshua's next challenger, Dillian Whyte laid out Dereck Chisora in the 11th round with a thunderous short left hook.

Afterwards, Joshua made his way into the ring and for possibly the first time, he heard boos after his name was introduced.

The British public had a new boxing hero.

Fury had done what Joshua hadn't done. He had gone to America to face Wilder and what's more, everyone who saw the fight appeared to believe he had done enough to win.

Tyson kept his pre-fight promise to donate his purse to charity.

Pay-per-view sales of the fight swelled his earnings to £7 million – and Fury gave it all away. 'I don't do charity work for a pat on the back,' he said. 'I do it to help people, but I do not want praise for it. I don't want to be called "a do gooder".'

CHAPTER 19

Conquering America

FIGHT FANS groaned when it was announced that Tyson Fury had signed an £80 million, five-fight deal with Top Rank and ESPN.

The hope – and expectation – of every fan was that Fury would meet Wilder in a rematch.

'We were very close to a rematch,' said Fury.

'We had contracts, they had contracts. We were trying to agree terms.

'All of a sudden, I had a massive deal from ESPN. They made me an offer I couldn't refuse. Apparently Deontay Wilder signed a three-fight deal before I signed the ESPN deal.'

The ESPN deal meant the world's three leading heavyweights were all with different television channels and promoters.

Joshua was with Eddie Hearn and DAZN, Wilder fought on Al Haymon shows on Showtime – and Fury was with ESPN.

The fights the public wanted to see would therefore be harder to make.

Frank Warren explained the thinking – apart from the £80 million – behind the move to ESPN.

'We need to get Tyson the exposure he needs so that when we try to make these fights with these people [Wilder and Anthony Joshua], he has an equal seat at the table,' he explained.

ESPN, Warren said, was screened into 75 per cent of American homes, giving Fury the chance to reach a massive audience.

He was sure to put on a show when he fought unbeaten German Tom Schwarz at the MGM Grand in Las Vegas on 15 June 2019.

Fury went into the fight as the number one heavyweight in the world, according to *The Ring* magazine.

He had replaced Joshua at the top after Joshua was humiliated in seven rounds by huge underdog Andy Ruiz Jr on his American debut at Madison Square Garden.

It was, in the opinion of Thomas Hauser, Muhammad Ali's biographer, an upset comparable to Ali's taming of Sonny Liston in February 1964.

Ruiz didn't look much like a heavyweight contender – or any sort of athlete.

He stood 6ft 2ins tall – four inches shorter than Joshua – and weighed a salad-dodging 19 stones.

Ruiz was fat.

He said his diet consisted of steak and chocolate bars – and that was how it looked.

Ruiz was rather better thought of in the trade than he was by the public, who couldn't see past his rolls of fat.

He had quick hands and in 33 previous fights, only Joseph Parker had beaten him, on a majority vote for the vacant WBO heavyweight championship.

Had Ruiz won the last round on the judges' scorecards, the fight would have been a draw.

Ruiz came back with three wins, putting him in a position to step in to face Joshua after Jarrell 'Big Baby' Miller failed a drugs test.

The expectation was that Joshua would steamroller him.

Ruiz was dropped in the third but picked himself up like 'a lardy Lazarus', in the words of *The Times*, and by the end of a sensational round, it was Joshua who was on the brink after being floored twice.

Joshua, who had looked tentative from the outset and gave Ruiz too much ground, was down twice more in the seventh. After the fourth knockdown, referee Mike Griffin looked into his eyes for a few seconds before deciding he couldn't continue.

Wilder was brutal in his assessment of Joshua, saying, 'The worst thing you can do in life is fucking quit.'

Ruiz said, 'He could have still kept going, but I would have put him away. The referee did his job.'

Fury took to Twitter to give his opinion. 'We have our back and forth's [sic],' he wrote, 'but Anthony Joshua changed his stars through life. Heavyweight boxing, these things happen, rest up, recover, regroup and come again.'

Days later, Fury was harder on Joshua when interviewed.

'Can you imagine? You're built like an Adonis, you're 6ft 6ins, you're ripped, carved in stone, and a little fat man who has eaten every Snickers and Mars bar in California comes in there and bladders you all over?' he said.

'What a disgrace.

'If that was me, I would never show my face in public ever again.'

Two weeks after Joshua's humiliation, it was over to Fury.

THE British press were critical of Fury's choice of opponent.

Ben Davison explained Fury's handlers were looking for 'somebody big' and ranked in the top five in preparation for Joshua and Wilder, but most of the fighters who fitted that criteria were tied up, including Dominic Breazeale and Whyte.

Schwarz was 25 years old, stood 6ft 5½ ins tall, had won all his 24 fights – 16 inside the distance – and was ranked number two by the WBO and number eight by the IBF.

The above made him a credible opponent.

'I'm a fast heavyweight,' Schwarz told *Boxing Monthly*. 'I'm quick on my feet. I have a good right hand and I'm the right size for a heavyweight. I have good skills and throw good combinations, good straight punches and uppercuts. But I need to work on my defence more.'

Schwarz said he started boxing at '11 or 12', explaining, 'I was mocked in school for being a fat little boy. I was brought up by my mother and grandmother and I had a hard time growing up and at school.'

As an amateur, he didn't make an impact beyond regional level before making his professional debut at 19.

Schwarz did have impressive statistics. He had handed six fighters their first loss and his previous six opponents had a combined record of 84 wins, five losses and one draw.

He was dangerous early – at the level he had been boxing at – with eight first-round wins.

Still, Fury looked way too good for him.

If Tyson boxed the way he could and Schwarz boxed the way he had been, there was only one winner. If Schwarz was going to get his hands up, walk forward in straight lines and look to land the right hand, he was quickly going to walk into trouble. The word from the gyms in Manchester and the States was that Fury was setting about his sparring partners and hurting them rather than standing off and bamboozling them.

Fury was planning to put on a show.

THE fight with Schwarz was billed as for the 'lineal heavyweight championship' and in the build-up, Fury gave the public a reminder of his place in boxing history.

He went to a press conference dressed in a suit that was decorated with replica cigarette cards of former heavyweight champions.

The American boxing public warmed to Fury, snapping up all 9,012 tickets for the show, and as he approached the venue on the night of the fight, Fury said to Paris, 'I think we made it, Paris.'

She asked, 'Why?'

'Because we are headlining in Vegas. This is it.'

To mark the occasion, Fury, who looked well on the scales at 18st 11½lbs, made an outrageous ring entrance.

He appeared dressed as Uncle Sam, complete with a stars and stripes top hat, in a nod to Apollo Creed from the *Rocky* movies.

MC Jimmy Lennon Jr announced Fury was making his 'fourth defence of the lineal heavyweight championship' he had taken off Wladimir Klitschko and by the end of the opening round, it seemed certain Tyson would hold on to his cherished crown.

Schwarz spent those opening three minutes walking on to punches – and barely landing anything in reply.

Fury came out for the second boxing as a southpaw – and putting more weight into his punches.

After landing blows, Tyson pulled faces and looked into the crowd. He was toying with Schwarz, whose nose leaked blood.

Schwarz wasn't beaten yet and when Fury lingered on the ropes in front of him, he saw an opening.

He unloaded eight punches – and every one of them missed.

Fury twisted his body this way and that and once Schwarz had stopped throwing, a maniacal grin crept across Tyson's face.

Now it was his turn and he launched a counter attack that left Schwarz on one knee, looking bewildered. He dragged himself up and for the next few seconds, Fury let his hands go, some punches hitting arms and gloves, others finding their way through, until the referee decided he had seen enough.

'I felt this was my coming-out party,' said Fury. 'I hope it went down well in America. I hope they enjoyed the performance. I came here to have fun and enjoy myself. I don't take myself too seriously.'

CHAPTER 20

'I Live for this Shit'

TYSON FURY described the 30th opponent of his professional boxing career as 'just my type'.

He went on to explain: 'He's tall, blonde, with blue eyes and he's sexy.'

Otto Wallin was also Swedish, a southpaw, unbeaten in 21 fights (one no contest) and ranked No 4 by the WBA.

The problem for the public was, he wasn't Deontay Wilder. The rematch, the Fury camp claimed, had been signed and agreed for 22 February 2020, but first, Wilder had to get past Luis Ortiz in a rematch and Fury faced Wallin.

'There are so many different promoters and TV stations it's very hard work to secure the big names in the division,' Fury answered when asked why he was fighting Wallin.

'Ideally, I wanted an American, but we couldn't get him.'

The consensus was, Wallin was a step up from Tom Schwarz.

Unlike Schwarz, Wallin had boxed internationally as an amateur, winning 34 of 46 bouts.

Two of his losses were inflicted by Anthony Joshua and he put himself forward to challenge Joshua for his world titles after Jarrell Miller failed a drugs test.

Andy Ruiz got the job, pulled off a huge upset and Wallin faced similar odds when he got a shot at Fury's lineal heavyweight championship he had claimed with victory over Klitschko.

The bookmakers made Wallin a 25/1 outsider to win the fight at the T-Mobile Arena in Las Vegas on Mexican Independence Day.

Fury made every effort to win over the Mexican fans. He took to calling himself El Rey Gitanos and wore a Lucha Libre Mexican wrestling mask at press conferences.

The opening two rounds went as expected, with Fury, at 18st 2½lbs the lightest he had been since beating Klistchko, outboxing Wallin.

But in the third, Wallin opened a deep, inch-long gash on Fury's right eyebrow with a left hand.

It was a dreadful wound and if referee Tony Weeks and the ringside doctor thought it too bad for the fight to continue, Fury would lose.

In Fury's corner, Jorge Capetillo went to work on the cut and Tyson shouted at ringsiders: 'I live for this shit.'

He was angry with Wallin and went for him. The Swede shipped some heavy punches, stayed upright and worse was to follow for Fury when a second cut appeared on his right eyelid.

The referee and ringside doctor let the fight continue and Fury dominated, outpunching Wallin 119-51 between the seventh and 11th rounds.

There was late drama. Around 40 seconds into the last, Wallin detonated a left hand on Fury's chin that dazed him. He stumbled and grabbed Wallin. His head cleared and he made it through to the final bell, winning unanimously by scores of 118-110, 117-111 and 116-112.

'I went to the hospital, had a few stitches, went home and had an early night,' said Fury, who had 47 stitches inserted in his two wounds.

'Then I've got up, gone to the casino, won five grand and had a few beers.'

Tyson Fury Professional Record

2008
Dec 6 Bela Gyongyosi w rsc 1 Nottingham 18st 9lbs

2009
Jan 17 Marcel Zeller w rsc 3 Wigan 18st 1lb
Feb 28 Daniel Peret w ret 2 Norwich 17st 10lbs
Mar 14 Lee Swaby w ret 4 Birmingham 17st 12lbs 6ozs
Apr 11 Mathew Ellis w ko 1 Bethnal Green 18st 1lb 8ozs
May 23 Scott Belshaw w rsc 2 Watford 18st 4lbs 8ozs
July 18 Aleksandrs Selezens w rsc 3 Bethnal Green 18st 8lbs
Sep 11 John McDermott w pts 10 Brentwood 17st 9lbs
Sep 26 Tomas Mrazek w pts 6 Dublin 18st 9lbs

2010
Mar 5 Hans-Joerg Blasko w rsc 1 Huddersfield 18st 12ozs
Jun 25 John McDermott w rsc 9 Brentwood 19st 4lbs
(Vacant English heavyweight title, British heavyweight title eliminator)
Sep 10 Rich Power w pts 8 Bethnal Green 18st 11lbs
Dec 18 Zack Page w pts 8 Quebec City, Canada 19st 2lbs 4ozs

2011
Mar 19 Marcelo Luiz Nascimento w ko 5 Wembley 18st 9lbs
Jul 23 Dereck Chisora w pts 12 Wembley 18st 3lbs 8ozs
(British and Commonwealth heavyweight title challenge)
Sep 17 Nicolai Firtha w rsc 5 Belfast 18st 1lb
Nov 12 Neven Pajkic w rsc 3 Manchester 18st 5lbs
(Commonwealth heavyweight title)

2012

Apr 14 Martin Rogan w rsc 5 Belfast 17st 7lbs 12ozs
(Vacant Irish heavyweight title)
Jul 7 Vinny Maddalone w rsc 5 Clevedon 17st 7lbs 8ozs
(Vacant WBO Intercontinental heavyweight title)
Dec 1 Kevin Johnson w pts 12 Belfast 17st 10lbs
(WBC heavyweight title eliminator)

2013

Apr 20 Steve Cunningham w ko 7 New York 18st 2lbs
(Eliminator for IBF No 2 ranking)

2014

Feb 15 Joey Abell w rsc 4 Hackney Wick 19st 8lbs
Nov 29 Dereck Chisora w ret 10 Docklands 17st 12lbs
(European heavyweight title, vacant British heavyweight title, WBO International heavyweight title)

2015

Feb 28 Christian Hammer w ret 8 Greenwich 18st 8lbs
(WBO International heavyweight title)
Nov 28 Wladimir Klitschko w pts 12 Dusseldorf, Germany 17st 8lbs
(WBA Super heavyweight title, IBF heavyweight title, WBO heavyweight title, IBO heavyweight title)

2016 & 2017

Inactive

2018

Jun 9 Sefer Seferi w ret 4 Manchester 19st 10lbs 2ozs
Aug 18 Francesco Pianeta w pts 10 Belfast 18st 6lbs
Dec 1 Deontay Wilder drew 12 Los Angeles 18st 4lbs 8ozs

2019

Jun 15 Tom Schwarz w rsc 2 Las Vegas 18st 11lbs 8ozs
Sep 14 Otto Wallin w pts 12 Las Vegas 18st 2½ lbs

Fights 30 Wins 29 KOs 20 Losses 0 Draws 1

Bibliography

Boxing News, Boxing Monthly, The Ring magazine, The Sun, The Times, The Sunday Times, The Guardian, The Sunday Mirror, The Daily Mail

King of the Gypsies, by Bartley Gorman and Peter Walsh (2003, Milo Books)

On The Cobbles: The Life of a Bareknuckle Gypsy, by Martin King, Jimmy Stockin, Martin Knight (Mainstream, 2001)

Crown of Thorns: Bitter History of a Century's Heavyweight Championship Boxing, by Norman Giller and Neil Duncanson (Pan Macmillan, 1996)

Lords of the Ring, by Harry Lansdown & Alex Spilius (Heinemann, 1991)

That Night In The Garden, by Jim McNeill (Robson Books, 2003)

The Heavyweights, The Definitive History of the Heavyweight Fighters, by Bob Mee (The History Press, 2006)

Acknowledgements

THANKS TO Tyson Fury, the late Hughie Fury, Jerry Gorman, Dave Farrar, Glynn Evans, Mervyn Turner, Clifton Mitchell, Matt Legg, Ashley Lane, Kieran Pitman, Kyle Haywood, Paul Butlin, Nick Griffin, Sam Bowen and Ray Revell.

Index

Also available at all good book stores

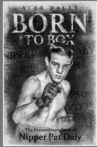
9781785313684

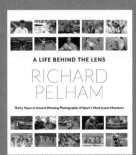
9781785315466

9781909626522

9781785313196

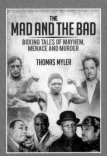
9781785313950

9781785314438

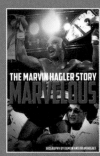
9781909178854

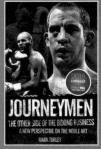
9781909626539

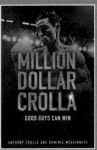
9781785312984

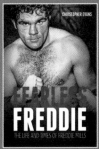
9781785312823

9781785311796

amazon.co.uk W Waterstones WHSmith

STAPLES
Center
WILDER vs FURY
SAT DEC 1
LIVE ON PPV
PPV
Corona